JC

SCHOOLING FOR WHAT?

BY DON H. PARKER

Schooling for Individual Excellence

Schooling for What?

SCHOOLING FOR WHAT?

BY DON H. PARKER

McGRAW-HILL BOOK COMPANY

New York   Toronto   London   Sydney   San Francisco
St. Louis   Mexico   Panama

To

E. M. P.

A. L. P.

R. C. P.

E. C. P.

CONTENTS

PREFACE

On a fine April morning in 1968—insulated from the shock waves of revolt spreading across the country in the wake of the assassination of Martin Luther King and the Columbia University uprising—I sat musing at a conference on "improving education," one of dozens I had attended over the previous eighteen years. "To what avail?" I asked myself. "What are the young trying to tell us out there?" Suddenly my thoughts coalesced around one burning question: *Schooling for what?* Later that day I put this question to top educators in corridors, over cocktails, at meals; I even scrawled it on a note pad and passed it, schoolboy fashion, to others during the sessions of the conference. Reactions ranged from jaw-dropping and head-scratching to cop-out answers such as, "Well, I guess to pass on the culture." One of the sharpest educators I know simply said, "I'm afraid I don't really know." If the educators didn't know, who did?

The question set me on a 33,000-mile trek across the nation, to thirty states and the District of Columbia, at my own expense. I ended up with personal, private tape-recorded interviews with 1,000 people of all ages, from every walk of life, representing as accurately as possible 200 million Americans in our various ethnic groups and life styles—all zeroing in on the question, *Schooling for what?*

It was not always easy to get the interviews that lasted from fifteen minutes to an hour and a half and covered the spectrum of American life from a sidewalk academy in Oakland to a squalid Appalachian cabin, from behind the walls of a penitentiary to glass and chrome offices on Madison Avenue. Friends across the nation opened doors I could never have cracked by formal request. Even so, there were times when it was easier than I expected; more than once a busy top executive would usher me politely but grimly into his office, saying, "Yes, I'll give you fifteen minutes," then end up giving me an hour on tape, only to ask, "Say, would you like to talk to some of my employees?" Such opportunities enabled me to get to every level of white and blue-collar worker in several industries, and on company time. I buttonholed, too, in streets, campuses, parks, airplanes—wherever there were people.

No one was paid for an interview. Schooling and its relationship to society were covered in ten standardized, free-response questions ranging from "Why should we have schools?" to matters of sex, war, money, and "Why is it all happening?" I have come away from this experience convinced that if our schools and many of our life styles and institutions don't change radically, and fast, we are in for trouble. In this book 1,000 people are telling it like it is, how it ought to be, and how it's got to be if we are to survive.

Although at times I may seem to address myself principally to the older generation, my own, this book is intended as a mind expander for both the "over thirty" and the "under thirty." It is a curtain raiser for questions rather than a compendium of answers. I have often counterpointed interviews of the young with those of the older, black with white, minority with majority. You, the reader, will be following the thought patterns of the many age and ethnic groups now crying out to be heard; you will be finding your own clues to what they are really saying, and, hopefully, you will be involved in formulating hypotheses for new horizons, new life styles. In any event, by comparing yourself with others here, I hope you will be encouraged, even emboldened, to get into active dialogue with others, particularly people in a different age bracket from yours, whether you are under thirty or over thirty or have a foot in each camp. If you do, and we reduce our race toward anarchy to mere revolution, this book will have served its purpose.

ACKNOWLEDGMENTS

It is a little awkward for me to claim authorship of this book, since a great many of the words are those of other people. Because of the intense personal significance of the questions to most of the people interviewed and the emotional depth of their responses I have come to feel like a walking confessional booth. While each interviewee began as a numbered key-sort data card, each immediately became a person, and many became my friends. One of these 1,000 may live next door to you, may be a commuter in the next seat, or a face you saw on TV last night. If you are one of the 1,000, I hope I have heard and felt what you said and have communicated your meanings. May I say again, "Thank you."

There are those, however, who have provided a rich tapestry as background for "where it's at"—the "it" being myself, the one who set forth on the *Schooling for What?* adventure. For twenty years, from my first contact with her writings, and particularly over the last fifteen years as I have had the experience of living with her thought, many times in person, there has been Ruth Strang, professor emeritus at Columbia University. She has contributed both warp and woof—and her ideas are timeless. Phil Lange, of my own generation and also of Columbia University, has added vibrant colorings. Over a period of twelve years Donald W. Stotler, supervisor of science for the Portland Public Schools and my coauthor in science learnings materials for children, has shown me the cosmic design of the universe. My everyday working colleague, William H. Fryback, has extended for me the human dimension. Edmund Ware Sinnott, scientist, whom I hope one day to meet, has written "The two roads to truth—the way of science, confident in reason, and the way of faith, depending on the insights of the spirit—do not follow the same course." Yet man should not "regret these differences but rather rejoice in them. They are the two halves that make men whole; from tension between them, character is born."

John Gardner, former secretary of Health, Education and Welfare, in his book *Excellence,* reinforced much of my thinking when in 1961 I wrote *Schooling for Individual Excellence.* His later books, speeches, and articles have further strengthened the fabric. Perhaps we will meet one day.

Arthur Chapman, attorney, has shown me how even "the law" can be compassionate.

Bob Locke, executive vice president of McGraw-Hill Book Company, "discovered" *Schooling for What?* Introducing me to Frank Taylor, he opened the door to its publication. Frank selected Tim Yohn as my working editor. How lucky can I get!

There is a woman called Bonnie. Bonnie Gartshore, "only" my secretary and research assistant, lived *Schooling for What?* with me for nearly two years. I never knew her as man knows a woman, but with her I have daily touched a kindred spirit as I have with few people. Her "here and now" awareness has imbued the tapestry with new sparkle.

At unexpected points LuVerne C. Walker, curriculum director in a large Eastern city school system, has embellished the whole with threads of gold.

There is one more person about whom you should know,

now that the manuscript is finished—Shelby Wegner—because at a recent luncheon in San Francisco she said, "Today is the first day of the rest of your life."

Don H. Parker
EMLIMAR
April, 1970

CHAPTER 1

1,000 TALKED

Schooling for what? How would you answer that question? How would the man in the street answer the question? The black man—the white man? What about the farmer, the small-town shopkeeper, the head of a giant corporation? What do housewives and career women say? What is schooling for— to first-graders, high school youth, college students, and university presidents? *Schooling for what?* In suburbia, in the ghetto? One thousand people throughout the United States have considered ten questions, based on this central question —in individual, private, tape-recorded interviews ranging from fifteen minutes to an hour and a half. The first questions ask about schooling as it is viewed today, as it might be, and as it *must* be. The next probe such fundamental concerns of life and living as the new work ethic, the meaning of leisure, pressures on individualism, and the sexual revolution. The last explore causes for the massive unrest now gripping the United States.

Ages of the respondents ranged from six to eighty-two, with a preponderance of the generation coming into power, the fifteen to twenty-four-year-olds reflecting their ratio to the general population. Blacks and whites were likewise represented

1

in a proportion roughly equivalent to their populations. Protestants, Catholics, Jewish, and those of other faiths talked, as did migrant workers, millionaires, and every economic group in between.

Because the tape recording equipment was battery operated and completely portable, I was able to interview almost anywhere. Sometimes it was 39,000 feet in the air on transcontinental jets, other times in steaming cubbyholes of big-city ghettos; at times in the air-conditioned, walnut-paneled offices of the high and mighty, or in dimly-lit dens of bearded revolutionaries, or on a woodpile surrounded by pigs and chickens in Appalachia. This is the way it worked. Imagine the two of us sitting in front of a diplomat case fitted with twin tape recorders. We might be anywhere—in your office, in your living room, on a park bench, or in the corner of some college student center. Wherever, we'd be alone. All interviews are private. First, I'd note the following on a 5×8 key sort card—name, address, kind of work, special interests or college major, and a few other background items important to the interview sampling. Then, after showing you how to push the buttons of the tape recorders, I'd try to be as inconspicuous as possible, as I have done, not always successfully, more than 700 exciting times. Now, if you will just push that blue question button and listen a moment, my voice on the tape will take it from there:

> Why did I go to school? Why should we have schools and colleges? Have you ever asked yourself these questions? I'll bet you have. Today *I'd* like to ask you a few questions. Just think of me as a voice on a tape recorder. I'm interested in what boys and girls and men and women are thinking about these days, especially what they are thinking about schooling—the things that go on in school. I go to many

schools, colleges, and places of business and industry throughout the United States and ask questions, and today I'd like to ask *you* some questions. I'd like to know what *you* think about them. Here's how it works. In a moment you will hear a question; then you will hear a bell tone like this. (Bell.) When you hear the bell tone, reach for my stop button and turn me off. Then think about the question and what you want to say about it. When you are ready, pull the mike answer button down and talk your answer into the mike. When you are through answering, push the mike stop button up. Then go back to me and push my question button and I'll give you another question. Ready? What's your name? (Bell.) There, it *was* easy, wasn't it? Now here's the first question, and I'd like to know what you really think about it:

1. Why should we have schools? (Bell.)
2. Can you think of ways to make schooling better? (Bell.)
3. What do you like most about schooling now? (Bell.)
4. What do you like least about schooling now? (Bell.)
5. Why should people work? (Bell.)
6. What else should people do besides work? (Bell.)
7. Do you think schooling helps you learn about these other things? (Bell.)
8. Now what about the individual? In these days we hear a lot about trying to be an individual. The idea of trying to be an individual is probably not very new, but "being an individual" seems harder than ever in these times. Why do you think this is so? (Bell.)
9. If you believe we should have sex education in the public schools, what kinds of things should be learned? (Bell.)
10. Now, in conclusion, can we consider this. It is being said that we are living in an "age of contention," an "age of controversy," between the younger and the older, between race groups, and between various other kinds of groups. Why this sudden outburst—the demon-

strations, the riots, the marches, the sit-ins, even the long hair and the funny clothes? Why do you think this is happening? (Bell.) *

Our formal interview concluded, I might then ask you an off-the-cuff question to clarify or illuminate one of your responses, or to tap what I sensed might be a wellspring— something you wanted to say from deep down inside. When the latter happened, when feelings really gushed out, I felt like a nerve through which coursed the electric currents of humanity crying out to understand—and be understood.

Being fifty-seven years old, having worked thirteen years in one of the biggest of the big business establishments, quitting at the age of thirty-six to work my way, beginning as a freshman, through a bachelor's degree to doctorate degrees in clinical and educational psychology, and having served for nearly twenty years throughout the education establishment from country school to major university to big publishing, I have had to "work for what I got." When I began interviewing in mid-1968 I deliberately sought out campus radicals—having mentally catalogued them as spoiled brats who didn't appreciate what was handed to them on a silver platter. But after hearing many of their ideas and ideals echoed by a huge cross section of students on campus after campus, my own intellectual attitude turned to a gut reaction. It was a gut-tearing experience to be caught in the cross-fire between the young and the Establishment.

Typical was my encounter with a group of campus radicals, followed by interviews with administration officials, at Columbia University. The students were mainly at the graduate level, working for advanced degrees in such areas as political science and psychology. After a brief talk with the group to

* Questions 1 to 6 were asked of all interviewees. Questions 7 to 10 were asked of all teenagers and older.

explain my mission, I interviewed several volunteers privately in a small closet off the student headquarters. Question 4— "What do you like least about schooling now?"—unleashed a torrent of criticisms of the *status quo*. The general feeling was perhaps epitomized by the response of a twenty-four-year-old doctoral candidate in English literature:

> The fact that students are—that the ideas, opinions, thinking of students is not taken seriously by many, many professors, and that their integrity as human beings, their capacity to be responsible for themselves, is not taken seriously by many people in the institution at many different levels. I can't see how you can develop a responsible citizenry in this country unless that development takes place in college, unless college is in some way a preparatory school to the full responsibilities of citizenship.

Now imagine yourself sitting beside me as a university official several offices away responds to Question 4 with:

> The attitude of these students, thinking they can run everything—including the university and the country and everything.

That such a vast difference of outlook could exist between vital components—each presumably with interests complementing the other's—of an educational institution as prestigious as Columbia appalled me. Is it a generation gap that is here to stay? Says John D. Rockefeller, III:

> Every generation has had its gap. But it seems unmistakably clear to me that we are experiencing something much more than the age-old rebelliousness of youth. The ferment of today is deep and intense. Although the activists are a minority of young people, it is a larger and more vocal minority than ever before.—From his remarks at the Family of Man Awards Dinner, October, 1968.

Dr. Jean Noble, guidance counselor, City College of New York, writing in *The PTA Magazine* for October, 1968, observes:

> The active rebels may be few, but the truly unconcerned among youth are few also. Wander into a Girl Scout conference, a church school, or any other noncontroversial gathering place for youth, and you will feel the intensity of their concern for meaning in their lives. The more young people question our ways, test their concerns, and find a hostile response, the more alienated they become and the more avid grows their desire to change the society—by confrontation or violence if need be.

Excerpts from the interviews that follow may shock. But consider that each one presented here represents thousands or perhaps millions of students who are expressing the same ideas across the length and breadth of this nation! And they are determined that the things of which they are so justly critical shall not go on. The United States has, in fact, produced Schooling for Revolution.

As you read what these young people are saying, don't get the picture of acid-tongued, wild-haired hippie-yippie types screaming in the streets. Naturally, my interviews ranged over a proportionate number of the more radical by way of balancing the sampling. The youth speaking here are most often clean-cut young men and women who would be "acceptable," even welcome, in any sector of our society, regardless of their manner of hair or dress. They might be the kid next door, or your boy or girl. True, there are among them single-minded and calculating demagogues who seek only personal aggrandizement and the froth of action. But the vast majority of youth are sincere and willing to put forth constructive ideas. Since so many of *our* ideas haven't worked, why don't we listen? Today, youth is a new force to be reckoned with and we are going to have to change the schools fast, or they are going to change them for us. We still have time to choose between revolution and anarchy in our schools——and in our country.

CHAPTER 2

A VAST
DISCONTENT

Sex, war, money—what has the youthful revolt left untouched? How has it affected your life already? How deeply might the revolutionary forces affect your life in the future? What are these forces? Campus gates crash before student violence. Cities are racked by riots. Individual acts of crime increasingly cut down young and old alike. Are these poisons, erupting from the American system as if from boils, or are they the first waves of new thought cresting before the rising winds of American social consciousness?

Tape recorder, asking Question 10:

It is being said that we are living in an "age of contention" —an "age of controversy" between the younger and the older, between race groups, and between various other kinds of groups. Why this sudden outburst—the demonstrations, the riots, the marches, the sit-ins, even the long hair and the funny clothes? Why do you think this is happening?

An alarming number of the people I interviewed across the United States gave a "business as usual" answer. "Just a flurry; it will soon blow over," or "It's all the parents' fault, they should have brought them up better."

Who are these "business as usual" people—these ostrich-heads-under-the-sand? They range from the average business and industry executive through professional men and women (even in education!) to small store owners and the man in the street. Union leaders and members are particularly unwilling to look up from their relatively cozy corner of the Establishment. Although this general unawareness or unwillingness simply to look at what is going on is most prevalent in rural areas, small towns, and in the South, the ostrich heads are liberally sprinkled across the nation, at all levels of society, and often in key positions in established power structures. For example, a banker in a small Midwest community said:

> I suspect that if one would look over the history of our country for many years back, one would probably find many aspects of history that somewhat resemble our present-day activities, with the riots and civil disorders and marches and that sort of thing. I can just recall a couple of incidents, I suppose, that would be similar to what we see today. For instance, I remember Coxey's Army that marched upon Washington, it was a marching organization at one time. I think I recall from history at one time they had a Whiskey Rebellion as they called it. These were activities that somewhat resemble what we are seeing today. So I suspect that these modern-day movements and marches are really nothing new to history.

And the superintendent of a relatively innovative school district in Pennsylvania commented:

> The activities of today in that respect are not really too much different from the activities of that respect that have gone on over the centuries. There has been the rise of the common man, the inherent desire to be oneself, we go back to the Magna Carta, the French Revolution. We can go back

to dozens of times and eras when people conducted themselves in the same way. The Boston Tea Party was a type of
demonstration. Today is no different than it has always
been. The people moving up to take the place of the older
people think they can do it better. They protest against
what's happening. Racism is no different in this country
than it's been in other countries in the past. We are living—
man is actually an animal of conflict. He makes every con-
cession he can to organize and to work together, and yet individual opinions and individual attitudes can make quite a
difference in what he does and what he would like to do. I
don't really feel we're in any different era than we were before, except that I as an individual am looking at it in a different age level than I did when maybe I was protesting, and
so on.

The nursing supervisor of a large Catholic hospital in the
East said:

Essentially I don't think this is a sudden outburst. I think
every generation has always had conflicts between the
younger or the older, has had causes to become interested
in and to carry on. I just think that it's being given quite a
bit of emphasis and that this is typical of every age.

The ostrich heads say it was ever thus. The problem today
is simply too much publicity. What do others say?

Many of us are disenchanted with law and order. Some of
us are disillusioned. I think that little if anything can be
done in American society because the whole power system
cannot allow it, and some us us feel that even if Eugene
McCarthy is elected, little if anything can be done, that he
cannot change the basic power structures of the American
way of life here and abroad. So we are fighting for revolution. At the time now it is nonviolent. Maybe it will turn
out to be violent.
[An SDS (Students for a Democratic Society) leader, Columbia University, male, white, twenty-five; four months af-

ter he was arrested in the Columbia campus violence and bloodshed.]

The politicians—they come to the minority groups, especially the Negroes and the Puerto Ricans, happen they need votes. They come to us and they promise us this and they promise us that, but once they are up there they forget about us and that's it.
[A New York City high school dropout, female, Negro, sixteen.]

I think they are trying to seek their own recognition, their own satisfaction, and an outlet for their own individualities.
[A West Coast truck driver, white, forty-six.]

I think that our mass media have to—as well as our teaching group—have to lead the people into the right directions. Otherwise they will just do as some leader says and it will be a mass looting, a mass killing.
[A New York City teacher, female, white, thirty-nine.]

It's happening because we cannot enforce the laws that every God-fearing country should have.
[A college fraternity housemother, University of Southern Mississippi, white, sixty-two.]

I think partially it's a result of the war in Vietnam. I think the students and other young people are confused about the war. I think they're rebelling against it.
[A transcontinental airline stewardess, white, twenty-four.]

I think this is happening because it's—all the government programs, give-away programs. It's too easy to obtain money without working, and without working they have too much time on their hands to get themselves involved in riots and what-have-you.
[A Minnesota road-building equipment dealer, white, fifty-two.]

The youngster has a tougher time getting a job now because of the stringent laws and insurance, and so they have

less to do. The family is not as dependent upon them to
bring home some of the bread money. I'm not sure what
the answer is. The young person's market place has all but
disappeared because of the complex nature of the society.
So I think it's basically they have less to do than we did
twenty years ago or forty years ago. They don't have the
work that perhaps we did. They have more time to think
about what's wrong with things.
[A California merchant and city councilman, white, thirty-nine.]

That's a rough question. I—only God Almighty can answer that one.
[A man in New York's Central Park; sometime bartender;
white, forty-five.]

Violence may be only beginning. Politicians promise, but
nothing happens. People are seeking individuality. No, people
are sheep-like; they simply follow a leader. Too much law and
order—not enough law and order. Too much money; too
much time on their hands. They can't get jobs—have time to
think about what's wrong with things. And God only knows.
If, indeed, these increasing outbursts are poison, will the boils
paralyze the patient? Or, if they are new waves of social consciousness, what does social consciousness really mean? What
does it mean in terms of deeds and acts, in terms of the needs
and wants of men—*all* men—and the opportunity for each to
work, in keeping with his mental and physical ability levels, to
pursue these needs and wants? What does it mean in terms of
man's almost schizophrenic struggle to be, on the one hand,
an individual, and, on the other, a *member of society?*

"From each according to his ability; to each according to
his need," said Karl Marx. ". . . men are . . . endowed . . .
with certain Unalienable Rights. . . . Life, Liberty and the

pursuit of Happiness," says the Declaration of Independence of the United States. Yet neither communism nor American democracy has given more than token substance to these keystones of self-realization. Neither has put within the reach of all men self-realization *both* as an individual and as a member of society.

What kinds of changes are needed? How drastic should they be? ". . . Life, Liberty and the pursuit of Happiness. Whenever any Form of Government becomes destructive of these ends, it is the Right of the People to alter or to abolish it, and to institute new Government, laying its foundation on such principles and organizing its powers in such form, as to them shall seem most likely to effect their Safety and Happiness." Must change come through anarchy, or can it come through evolution? The seeds of both are in the air. Which ones will find fertile ground? By listening, we may find the evolutionary way toward change rather than the road of violence and anarchy. What are the people of these United States saying? What is the problem?

As Question 10, "Why do you think all this is all happening?" came off the tape, an eighty-year-old millionaire California real estate developer threw up his hands and pushed his chair back from the massive mahogany desk. . . .

You just asked me a very tough question to answer. Every age has its problems. We look in history and see the development of Christianity, for example. And the struggles between the various dogmas and differences which still plague the church, not as much as they used to. We have seen countries overrun by conquest as Rome was. And new people, and new citizens—a new way of life. What we have in this country today I don't think is unusual. It's happened before. But it is a problem. I can't understand, quite frankly, the hippie movement. I don't know what the kids are trying

to express or what they're reaching for. I hope it isn't a last-
ing matter because it is, to my mind, very unattractive to
say the least.

But he has very definite ideas on black-white relationships.

As regards the problems of the black people, this is something that we have to face sooner or later. I do not go with
the feeling that we are responsible for the activities of our
ancestors or for anything that was considered proper a few
hundred years ago. This question is a realistic one that
we're faced with now. And I don't want to take time now
to give my personal opinion about this very important question other than to say that the black people have every opportunity that we have, and that we should do everything
we can to teach them how to take advantage of the opportunities that are open to them. But, on the other hand, I see
no reason in the world why there should be forced integration. Let them go along side by side with us and compete in
a friendly way, and in time integration will take care of itself. But you can't hold a gun up to a man's head and say,
"Love me." That isn't the way things develop. It isn't normal and it won't get anywhere. In fact, it's unfortunate that
the minority—the violent minority—of the blacks today
are doing all of the blacks a great disservice and hurting
them a great deal more than they help. Give them—they
have the opportunities—give them more chance and more
help in taking advantage of them, and the rest will take
care of itself.

Even the best minds often veered sharply away from the
heart of the question, "Why is all this happening?" All in all
the youth themselves seemed best able to stick to the question
and come up with answers stripped of so much of the verbal
underbrush I found in the responses of so many adults. Lissa,
a sixteen-year-old white student, sits down with me in the
chemistry lab of the high school in one of the larger cities of
Mississippi.

Well, as far as the students are concerned, I think the children are growing up faster than they used to. I know, I listen to my parents and I'll be taking a course in school and my mother'll tell me, "Well, I didn't take such things like that till I was in college." And I think we are taking more and harder schooling, and competition is so great these days that I think we are having to grow up faster than the other children had to. Parents see a sixteen-year-old boy and it makes them feel that, well, he's only sixteen. But I think when you consider that in just two years he'll be going to Vietnam, that maybe he's a little older than they think he is. And I think it's this lack of communication where the parents don't feel that the children have ideas worth expressing that they bring out these conflicts. And these boys and girls want to be heard and listened to a little bit, so they put on these weird costumes and all so their parents will pay a little attention to them.

A thousand miles away in Washington, D.C., Arthur, a fifteen-year-old black youth, left his classroom and walked with me down the dimly-lit corridor of the school building housing summer session. I had gone to the class to ask for volunteers, with the principal's permission. His mother is a "salad girl" in a restaurant and his stepfather a "house man." As the tape asked Question 10, the eighth-grader let himself go:

I think the main reason why this is happening is because mostly everybody feel that they want freedom. Like the young people that's rebelling against the older people. They try to say, like my own mother, she always tells me, "When I was your age this and that, and however, I used to do such a thing." But they don't realize that all this was in a different generation. That was when they was coming up. Things have changed, a whole lot of things have happened since they was coming up, and you try to compare somebody today with somebody of yesterday, that's not going to work. Because everybody is different now. Things have changed, a whole lot of things have changed. Things going to keep on changing.

Are all youngsters against the Establishment? Or do they go along with what they see other youngsters do just because they're both youngsters? Diana, a sixteen-year-old white student in a predominantly Negro Washington, D.C., high school, represents many others of both high school and college youth.

I think this is happening because people have been too lenient. I think the law in itself has been lenient. Parents have been too lenient. People have gotten away with so much they think they can just walk in and take over. Take, for instance, teenagers and their parents; I mean, running away from home, smoking pot, popping pills or taking pills, and all this—and they say it's a form of rebellion. It's not, really. They just want kicks, they want something new. Because they've had everything. They've run out of things to do. It's just dumb. And races, I mean, I don't see any color in people. They're all the same to me. And yet there's so much fighting and things between the races because so many people, they'll see one person and they'll judge them on a whole. They'll say, "Well, this person is like that and so everybody is," but this isn't true. You have to know the individual. And even when you do, you should never judge. You should never judge anybody. And I think there's so much crime today because there's not enough done about it. I mean, take, for instance, during riots. I mean, they didn't try—well, I know for a fact the first day or so people weren't apprehended and taken to jail or anything. They just stood around and let them go. And—different things. I think people aren't strict enough and they don't enforce laws enough. And they're not standing up for themselves, I don't think the country is. That's about it.

*   *   *

She was wearing a baby-blue micro-mini skirt over baby-

blue tights. She looked sixteen . . . well, twenty-one. She was
Jewish, thirty-nine, unmarried, and a biology teacher in a
New York City high school. For her the reason was:

> The permissive attitude that we've developed in the past
> number of years. I saw that as I was going to college. Many
> of the young people marrying felt that they should allow
> their children freedom of expression, and those that have
> allowed their children too much freedom of expression and
> have not been around to take care of them, I believe, have
> had this rebellious type of child.

Three thousand miles away, in a tiny rural California community (population 375) a forty-seven-year-old general
builder and contractor and father of two sub-teens answered:

> The first thing I will say about why the long hair, the
> clothes, and this is that the children now are the products
> of parents who have not had the one most important thing
> that those children want as they have been growing up,
> and that's the time of their parents. Most of these children
> seem to come from well-to-do families where the parents
> have just said, "OK, here's five dollars. Go enjoy your-
> selves." But they've had everything they wanted except the
> one real main thing and that's love and time. And now
> they're just out trying to rebel about—they don't know
> what they're rebelling about.

A prominent Chicago attorney with a daughter in college
said:

> I think that the conflicts and the tensions that these reflect
> have always existed in one form or another. The clothing
> may differ, but the material is the same, the body under-
> neath it is the same. Because we are more people and be-
> cause we have created a more complex society for our-
> selves, these conflicts and tensions assume a sharper focus.
> And there are more accentuated frustrations which there-
> fore produce more violent reactions.

"No, we've no real trouble in our schools," said the super-intendent of a small, Deep South school district. When asked to put his finger on the answer to Question 10, he did his best:

Probably there are a number of factors which has created this. And I believe as far as some of the problems which we have had go back to the family. We go back a few years and we'll find that the war babies are young men and women now. At that time, both parents were away from home working, and they were brought up with some keeper. There was no discipline, there was no family life. When disciplinary methods tried to be used to try to get them to understand the part that they were going to have to play in the family and in the school, in the community, they probably rebelled against that. This rebellion has continued to increase over the years. Then a second factor may be the schools. We have failed to provide the educational opportunities for these youngsters. Maybe we have never been able to challenge them. Being young and eager, they were looking for excitement and they have gone to other places which may have been unhealthy for them, but they got what they wanted, or rather what they thought they wanted, and they have used that and it has created, well, I don't know whether this is a good term, animosity toward the older group. They may think that our way of life, our methods that we use, they may be out of date, outmoded. Another factor might be the publicity. The youngsters who are craving excitement want to get in the limelight, want to get their name in the paper or see their picture on television. These are just a number of factors that has created the problems which we have today, and I don't know if we could say there is one, two, or three, and put them down consecutively. I have to say that there are a number of things that has caused the young people to think like they do today and act like they do today.

In a rural Gulf Coast high school—no long hair; no mini skirts—I got two answers. First Henry, age fifteen:

Everyone seems to be trying to get more modern. Actually, how most fads like this get started, I believe, is a person that maybe has an inferiority complex and they start something new or either . . . Well, actually, it all goes back to a religious point of view. It's the fulfillment of the Bible because it speaks of all this in the last days.

Then a girl classmate:

The world around us is constantly changing and so are the people. These people feel that it's time that something's changed in the way they're being treated, and also this is true of the younger people. They feel it's time that they had their voice and this is their way of getting it—the sit-ins, the riots. It's not all right, but it's, it's the way they think.

During most of the interviews in this sleepy little kingdom by the sea I had the distinct feeling that they were talking about the world "out there"—just beyond the freeway—as a foreign country.

Nearly a thousand miles away, in the Appalachia country of Virginia, a twenty-five-year-old waitress in a roadside restaurant ("we have country ham and city ham") also talks in terms of "they."

Well, I think that people like that, I think they see if they can outdo the other people, you know. Like clothing, they try to dress odd and they say, oh, well, if I do this nobody else won't, and they just start, you know, go on up. And I think they have a, they live in a state of their own mind, you know, to do what they want to do. And the people, they say, well, the people, see, they think I'm doing, you know, and that breaks them on up, publicity and all that.

A sixty-three-year-old half-Indian union laborer in a small West Coast town laid a simple finger on "the itch you can't scratch" that came through more subtly in many other interviews.

Well, this is just my opinion for this. It may not be a very intelligent opinion, but I think these atomic bombs we got
stored away, other countries got stored away, I think people think that we most any minute will be blowed off the
face of the map, so why, so I think they think, why
shouldn't we go ahead and make all the nuisance of ourselves we can, or get all the fun out of life we can, even if
we destroy, why what of it? I think the atomic age, that
some think that they may die at any minute so why, I think
that's the main thing. Put it on the atomic age.

One morning a prominent leader of the steam fitters union
in a large Eastern city led me under giant cranes straining sky-
ward, around piles of cement, past blinding welding torches,
and into throbbing engine rooms to pull construction workers
off their jobs long enough for several highly satisfactory interviews. Halfway up a set of unfinished stairs I stopped. My
twenty-eight-and-one-half-pound tape recorder kit had me an-
chored to the spot. As I stood panting, the union leader
looked back and smiled. "Well, anyway, the questions you ask
are good for the men. Makes them think." What they thought
in their separate interviews was not necessarily what their
leader thought. For him the answer to what was happening
was an open-and-shut case of outside interference:

My idea of why it's happening, from what I could see and
from what I read and the people who are involved, that this
is a way for the Communists to move into our society.
They've tried it every other way they possibly could. First
tried it through unions and couldn't make it. Thought
they'd be able to take them over and weren't able to make
it. They started with wars to weaken the United States,
have a war in all different parts of the world and we're in
all kinds of controversy. They still weren't making any
headway. Now I think they've hit upon the real way to
make progress.

She was plainly dressed, a housewife in a small Arkansas town. At forty-five, she had three children in school and college, had herself been to college three and a half years. Her husband was a typical small-town shopkeeper.

I think it's happening because there's so much attention being paid to it. It really isn't new. I don't think you have hate between your races as much as you have hate between people—hostility between people. It's really nothing new at all, for the majority of people like to pick on the minority. And I feel like if you can educate people to—but still, when you get real educated people, they take the uneducated as the minority, so you really—until you kind of make people kind to each other, education or what-have-you, you won't, you know, affect it.

And there you have it—too much hate, too little kindness; the majority picks on the minority; it's the Communists; the hippie movement, distasteful, hope it doesn't last; publicity craving youth; lack of parental love, parental permissiveness; law too lenient; atomic bomb threat; fulfillment of the Bible —why *is* it all happening? Why this vast, seething discontent, not only gripping the United States but exploding world-wide? I believe the reasons given by the people, and by most people, are merely symptoms of the real problem: the battle of the haves vs. the have-nots.

In the United States "the rich get richer and the poor get poorer." On the planet, the gap between the "developed" and the "developing" nations gets wider. Where will it all end? In *The Lessons of History,* growing out of their monumental forty years of work in producing their ten-volume *The Story of Civilization,* Will and Ariel Durant point out two pathways:

The concentration of wealth is a natural result of [the] concentration of ability, and regularly recurs in history. . . . In progressive societies the concentration may reach a point where the strength of number in the many poor rivals the strength of ability in the few rich. Then the unstable equilibrium generates a critical situation, which history has diversely met by legislation redistributing wealth or by revolution distributing poverty.[1]

The Durants speak historically of rhythmic concentration and redistribution of wealth and poverty, and so we may well be at that point where some apocalyptic event will touch off an attempt on the part of the have-nots to redistribute the wealth by violence before we get around to doing it legitimately. In any event, the problem today is compounded in that this term "have-nots" not only includes the dimension of poorness but also the several dimensions of disenfranchisement as suffered by the young (military service but no vote, for example), the black, and other minorities (inequality in work, education, housing, and so on). Today we have not only the problem of redistribution of wealth, the effect of which can only be fleeting, but even more difficult, the redistribution of power—power to decide who gets what of the good things of life. Will the Establishment give up some of its wealth and power soon enough—voluntarily, or will it have both taken away by savage force? Perhaps we need to listen to the beat of that "different drummer." Will we give more than "ear service" to the young, fresh ideas of the counter culture, or will we let young dreams die—and pay the price?

CHAPTER 3

WE'VE ASKED
FOR IT

Since the beginning of time the young have had disagreements with their elders. Taking issue with teachers was even encouraged by Socrates, who goaded his students into the thoughtful kind of back talk that was to become known as the Socratic method. Since the origin of the university concept in the twelfth century students from time to time have expressed their displeasure with discipline, curriculum, professors, and so on. But these were relatively mild and ineffective protests, hardly noticeable to an outsider, and of short duration. They hardly compare to the highly visible demonstrations and the month-after-month confrontations that have headlined our newspapers and filled our TV screens. There is no precedent to the running battle of more than five years between dissidents and authorities at the University of California at Berkeley.

What is this new thing that prolongs student protest? Where have the students gotten this new sense of power, importance, rightness that sustains their efforts? There is little doubt that the phenomenon will grow, with or without violent overtones, until we have come to some answer, in consultation with the young people themselves: a clearer—and perhaps a more human—answer than we have come up with to the question, "Schooling for what?"

In my more than 33,000 miles of travel I interviewed 512 high school and college students in thirty states located in all four major regions of the nation. Because of my random method of sampling in each location, I firmly believe that the students I interviewed are representative of the over 14 million high school and 8 million college students in the United States. Their responses to the ten questions built around the main query, "Schooling for what?" tell me that the great majority of these 22 million students are deeply concerned about what they are getting in school—and what they're not getting. They are concerned about the social forces our schools represent—and those they do not represent. In short, students are revolting against a nineteenth-century answer to the question, "Schooling for what?" in today's electrotechtronic age and the impending twenty-first century.

In Chicago a high school junior girl in a fashionable private school, white, sixteen, had this to say:

> As much as I hate to say it, I think students are upset because of school, because of the education that we're getting now. I think before the education process was to teach you a bunch of facts and you just swallow them. Now they tell you the facts, but you have to do something with them. You're not taught just to swallow ideas; you're supposed to evaluate them yourself the way you are being taught. And so, if you apply it to life and you look around at things, what society's composed of, and you see so much wrong and you don't want to swallow it and accept it.

It would almost seem as though our schooling has been *too* good. It has been so good that youngsters at all levels, in the view of most adults I've taped, are better informed than ever before. In the words of one top-drawer business executive, "Kids are smarter than I ever was at their age. They know more and they can do more—and they think more." It is as though we have raised up a monster in our midst. We have trained them to think about what they hear, to evaluate what they see, and now because they are doing just that—and using our own measuring stick—we are in an uproar. We'd like to turn them off. An eighty-one-year-old real estate developer and financier whom *Fortune* magazine called "one of the nineteen grand old men of business" reaches for the panic button:

> I think we're getting a little far afield from actually teaching the useful things to children—the discipline and the sort of thing that we were subjected to in the old days. I'm not sympathetic with the idea of kids wearing trick hats and having societies in the schools and the sort of folderol that we see evidenced on all sides. Children get to demanding too much and expecting too much, which is evidenced often in the colleges where they riot in objection to everything that's going on and want to take part—in fact, they want to run the show. I think that we should have more discipline and less liberty of action and freedom of thought along these lines.

We have filled young people with more knowledge than ever before, and now, when they begin to use it to evaluate what they see, we rise up with righteous indignation and reject them as revolutionaries. And now *they* are asking us the question, "Schooling for what?" and getting nothing but old, trite answers: for food to eat and clothes to wear. Thanks to technology today—technology built by the hard work and inventiveness of our generation—youth has enough to eat and wear in increasing abundance. Also thanks to technology, they have time to sit back and think and ask about values. And they're not buying a lot of what they see.

For perhaps the first time in human history there is a large body of individuals of youthful vigor, of superior schooling, and whose life support requirements have been provided so abundantly that they can turn their attention from making money to concern for others—and for the quality of their own lives as related to others. We have hatched these curious creatures in our own incubator and we can no more put them back where they were than we can put a chicken back into the egg.

Less than 10 per cent of the students found school to their liking, judging by their answers to the questions, "Can you think of ways to make schooling better?" "What do you like most about schooling now?" and "What do you like least about schooling now?" The concerns of the remaining 90 per cent were largely centered around the irrelevancy of curriculum and courses, the diploma race, poor teachers, poor teaching methods, useless grading and testing practices, lack of individualized learning opportunity through use of modern technology, lack of opportunity for creative activity, and many statistically less frequently expressed concerns. None complained about the often outdated, ugly, unfunctional buildings in which I interviewed, or dimly-lit, shoebox classrooms, or poor school lunches. Instead, they were concerned about fundamentals, about learning—the opportunity to learn.

In the colleges and among thoughtful high school students there were varying degrees of concern that schooling at all levels has become the tool of an industrial-military complex bent on sustaining itself rather than seeking the greatest good for the greatest number. This concern was most strongly felt by students of the humanities and social sciences and to a lesser degree by those in the "natural" sciences (physics, chemistry, mathematics, and so on). The concern was felt least of all by students studying or planning to study business administration, engineering, and other areas of applied science and technology.

In the main, there was generally less complaint about schooling in rural areas, where life is still conducted more in the nineteenth-century manner—where children are still something to be seen but not heard. But the United States is no longer a rural community. In the cities and the suburbs, where 90 per cent of the students live, the twentieth century is a fact of life with the twenty-first coming at a headlong rush.

To Question 4, "What do you like least about schooling now?" a seventeen-year-old California senior girl, herself a good student, replied grimly:

> Most schooling represents an authority figure trying to alienate thoughts and ideas from living and trying to segregate it into little, unassociable classes.

Two thousand miles away a zoology senior at the University of Tennessee answered the same question:

> I think the thing that I like least about schooling is the pressure and the emphasis put on grading these days. A student has got so much pressure on his mind, and he's gotta make a grade. Universities that are starting the new pass-fail system, I think this is a step toward improving this pressure that is on students right now about, "You gotta make a grade. Your mother and daddy gonna disown you if you don't make a grade, if you don't make good grades." I think grades make a student most of the time study pretty hard, but when there's so much pressure on a person that they gotta make a grade, they don't even think about learning somethin', they just got to sit down and cram all the knowledge they're supposed to know for this particular course, cram it all into their head, and end up forgettin' ev-

erything that they ever learned or were supposed to have learned in this course just by having to make a grade.

Back on the West Coast a sixteen-year-old high school boy said what he likes least is

The classes in which a teacher stands up in front of a class and throws a bunch of information at you and you're expected to take notes on it and memorize it for a test. I think this is very boring. And also the class where you're, well, the whole emphasis is on grades and not really what you accomplish or learn, since you can forget something as soon as you go out and you can still get an A in it.

In New York City a Columbia University graduate student in sociology finds, even at the graduate level,

. . . required courses in which you have no choice and where there—you just get mass taught, and there's really —it's very hard to involve yourself personally in what you're learning, especially with subjects which may have little relevance for your interest.

A journalism sophomore in a large mid-South university also finds mass, machine-like treatment and lack of identity revolting.

The fact that when I go to class I'm number 39B in row five, seat seven. I'm simply not a person. I'm now simply a number instead of a person.

A nineteen-year-old journalism student at the same university:

The testing system. The simple fact that you go into a classroom. . . . They are really not interested—it's not feasible when you have to teach 18 to 25 thousand students for the teacher to be interested in knowing what you learn. You simply record in your mind a list of facts and then you're tested. All they want you to do is regurgitate these same stated facts.

A twenty-four-year-old political science major at Howard University in Washington, D.C.:

Again it comes back to this matter of dogmatic things. I've had some teachers where evidence's changed as to what they're teaching, and you try to show them where this new evidence has come in, they've stuck solely by the book. Or they take the very distinct attitude: I've got mine, you get yours, forget it—and are nasty about it. And it's frustrating, because you know better, but it comes up to the matter of grade. He's right; he's got his. And in order to get a grade out of him, you got to go along exactly with his program.

A Chicago housewife with a daughter at college:

I believe that schooling has become too mechanized, too much of a factory-type situation, and that the students, at the universities in particular, do not have enough contact with their instructors. I also feel that the pressure on the students today is what is making the young people react the way they are.

Stifling of ideas: an invitation to revolution? This seventeen-year-old Deep South senior may think so:

What I really like least is a certain, a type of class where you have to go and you're told to learn a certain thing and you have to learn this thing and that's all. Where your opinions should be that of the teacher and actually they're not really tolerated, and discussion is not encouraged. You're just supposed to follow the course or follow what the teacher says and not be independent or not do anything in class other than what the teacher says to do.

After four years on the diploma treadmill the son of a former San Francisco newspaperman summarized what I heard countless times in my interviews with high school and college students across the nation. In spite of the fact that he had attained the highest grade-point average of any graduating senior in the College of Letters and Sciences at the University of California at Berkeley, he opened his Phi Beta Kappa acceptance speech by saying that it was not worth it. He went on to describe how he had become a mental machine, composing papers at the rate of 1,000 words an hour, doing required reading at thirty-three pages an hour, and feeling "more enchained than a Russian factory worker in the 1930s."

The fact is that in 1957, after Russia launched Sputnik, American boys and girls were consigned to a concentration camp, a labor camp in which of each was demanded his mind's blood in the deadly race for grades. Even if this jittery reaction was justified as a technological showdown with communism, today, with big-power technology more nearly equal, can we any longer justify this prostration, almost prostitution, of our youth to have a national orgasm?

For five years or so after Sputnik high school and college youth plodded on like so many faithful donkeys. Then, as their backs were piled higher and higher with things to be learned, and their gait lashed by the Establishment, from plodding to trotting to a dead-heat run, some stumbled and fell. Student suicides shot up, dropouts soared, and the hippie movement was born. Others simply stopped, turned around, and faced their whip masters with a simple question, "Why?" Receiving no answer, they reared up on their hind legs, threw off their pack burdens, and began charging their tormentors. Said a nationally famous professor of psychology:

> I don't think at the present time students have much reason for doing what they're doing. They do it primarily to avoid the consequences of not doing it. I think that's what all this revolt in education is about.

Are schools still pushing youngsters down a lock-step track to "get to page 153 by Christmas" because the school board bought the books and students must "cover" the pages? Ask the students:

> I think the fact that too much of the learning process in high school is a matter of regurgitation of facts, of memorizing without having to understand, of accepting facts from a teacher and not really thinking about it but just giving back these same facts on a true-false or multiple-choice test. This all, I guess, is part of the idea of I think schooling should teach people to think rather than just give them facts.

The vast majority of students with whom I talked—all but a few of the most passive—were unanimous in criticizing the unrealistic way in which they are being asked merely to cram information into their heads. Often the more intelligent are simply opting out.

Any organism pushed beyond its natural limits is bound to revolt. Perhaps the human organism has more tolerance for pain and more endurance beyond pure physical stress than any other, simply because man is a thinking being. He has accomplished unbelievable feats of physical and psychological hardship when his reasoned tenacity kept him at the task long after his body said "no." But he has to have a reason; the effort must have some relevance to his life.

> The thing which I think I like least about schooling now is the lack of relevance to present problems. I just said that in education one studies the past, but it seems to me that in education at the present moment there is little, if any, criticism of the past, and this can be done through an examination of the present. If we, for example, studied American history, and studied the present current events and concerned ourself with the war in Vietnam, with the Black Liberation Movement, the radical deficiencies in the American way of life, we would be able to better understand the past and to criticize it, and we would be more critical of

America's history. We would not believe that things suddenly
went wrong in the last five years. I think that the thing I
like least about education, as I've said, is this lack of rele-
vancy to the present situation, to the Black Liberation
Movement, to a radical criticism of the American way of
life and the consideration of other possibilities of existence
in the twentieth century.

How would you reply to that twenty-five-year-old English
Ph.D. candidate I interviewed on a major Eastern university
campus only weeks after he had engaged in a campus take-
over resulting in violence? Do his ideas sound like those of a
madman? Will the Establishment—which, through boards
of trustees, controls what is to be taught in our universities—
listen?

In the past, those who saw no value in schooling merely
dropped out. Today, many young people are doing the same,
but many more are staying in to fight for the kind of schooling they visualize as more relevant to life. Whether they know
it or not, they are harking back to John Dewey's philosophy
that schooling should *be* life, not *preparation* for life. A twenty-five-year-old graduate student working for an advanced degree in education at a large Eastern university put it this way,
in spite (or because?) of the fact that his father is a banker in
a small Texas town:

> I'm interested in—what I like least about schooling now is
> the fact that, that the values behind education are not being
> questioned. It's the lack of questioning of values or the sort
> of broad acceptance of technological values in education.
> We tend to, our universities are structured to the needs, it
> seems to me, are geared to the needs of industry, govern-
> ment, etc. All this is in Goodman and Kinisten and people
> like that, but it's worth reiterating here. The idea that I'm
> getting an education so that I may fit into the structures of
> society is nice insofar as I'd have a niche. On the other

hand, an education is to be more than that. It's supposed to
teach me something about my world and teach me to relate
to it, instead of being a cog in it—or in its machinery. I'd
like to see universities that are independent of government
agencies and independent of industry, sort of pure universities, universities that are communities of scholars, where
people learn what they feel is relevant to them rather than
mere research-type oriented courses. Also, there're all sorts
of values that need to be brought up that are serious that
students never get to study that should be, that should be at
least gone over. Rather, the surface of them at least should
be scratched, questions relating to the science, the values
that the metaphysics of science gives us, versus the old humanistic values, and maybe other values that, that could be
ushered in by other metaphysical systems of thought.

Even high school-age youngsters, once content to go with
the system and ask no questions, are becoming deeply concerned by our often Janus-faced values. One eighteen-year-old
in Carmel, California, said:

I don't feel that it [schooling] really does enough in giving
you things that will be essential to your living in society.
Say the fact that four years of English are required, the fact
that you can communicate well and use correct grammar is
important, yet at the same time there is no real requirement
for something like humanities. Although civics helps, it still
isn't, to me, really enough. There are—I feel that the
school reflects our society in that our society is moving
more toward the sort of dollar goal idea, and that although
I don't like it, I think schools do reflect this somewhat in
how when I hear a teacher say, "Do this well because it will
help you get a job, or you can make money from doing
this," where it should be, "Do this well just for your own
sake, for wanting to do it well."

An eighteen-year-old senior girl in the same class, who is
already experiencing school from the other side of the counter

as a junior teacher's aide, looked wistfully out of the window
of the little office and told the tape recorder:

> There have to be so many changes made, for filling your
> own requirements for life and for filling the responsibilities
> that the society in which you live has set for you, and basi-
> cally just to get along and to live. It's just a requirement
> both spiritually and put on you by your society.

If the schooling seems so ill-related to the life of a white,
middle-class girl, how does it seem to a twenty-one-year-old
black eleventh-grade girl dropout with two children, who has
decided to put her pride in her pocket and try it for a second
time around? Will she be able to take another dose of the
dream world handed out in the name of "curriculum"? Or
will she be turned off forever in her quest "to go on to better
living"?

> The school system in the District of Columbia, I feel that
> they could improve the schools, they could improve the
> textbooks and give—they could improve the textbooks and
> give the students more materials. The textbooks that they
> have today, teaching in the District of Columbia, are not
> equipped with things, the modern trend of today. You
> teach, say, for instance, you teach *The Scarlet Letter* which
> is a book that was dated down from year to year to year.
> Now in this day and age you're still reading *The Scarlet
> Letter* in the eleventh-grade English which I took last year,
> going into the twelfth-grade English this year. And they
> have many textbooks like this, that are backdated, and
> they're not keeping up with the materials that you need for
> today, nor to go on to better living.

A twenty-year-old University of Denver junior—daughter
of a prominent mortician—easily identified the well-set-in
rigor mortis of schooling today.

> What I like least about schooling would—I would have to
> answer that question in the context of the school system it-

self. And that would be, as I said before, that it stifles and suffocates and strangles free expression. And, I think if we're talking in the area of school system, as far as on the college level, I think that schools are run too much on tradition, too much on what was done when it [the university] was founded in 1866, not in what's happening in 1968.

It was an old tenement building across from the university. I presented my credentials, arranged in advance, through the speaking tube. The buzzer signaled the door lock free. I pressed the heavy latch, swung tape recorder and brief case through the massive, ornate door, and moved down the dark hallway past a series of lighted openings. Here were old bedrooms filled now with mismatched desks and tables, typewriters and mimeographs, and walls hung with charts. In the oppressive heat of July in New York, especially at four-thirty on a Friday afternoon, what were all these youngsters—perhaps twelve or fifteen of them—doing huddled over papers, gesticulating at charts, or clutching coffee mugs as they talked in small knots? Through the door at the end of the hall chairs clustered around an old dining-room table apparently awaiting a conference. At that moment a keen-eyed youth, tousled but clean, called, "I'm in here. C'mon in."

"Are you the leader of Students for a Restructured University?"

"I'm J———. I'm one of them, yes."

After the usual ten-question formal interview, I asked, "Were some of you folks in the recent gate-tearing-down and building-occupying act and so on?"

Yes, we have several people on the staff who were involved in that, and I think the feeling about that is if those people hadn't done what they did, we wouldn't be here now. The system here at Columbia, we have a record of many years, of students presenting their grievances to the administration

through one channel or another and having those grievances absolutely not even responded to, much less answered. And the situation got to the point where we simply
had no recourse but to take illegal action, an action which
many felt was the only thing they could do because they
felt there was nothing else that could be done. And, you
know, I know the press has been very bad against us for
this. But here at Columbia I think now there is going to be
change. And I can't see any other reason to point to for the
reason why there is going to be change except that those
students did go into those buildings, and they stayed there,
and they said, "We can't take it any longer." And about
one-third of the students sent representatives to the strike
coordinating committee. I think that shows how widespread
the feeling of alienation from the powers that be, and of
alienation from the program, the educational program here
at Columbia, and from the political influence, the political
stands that this institution has taken vis-à-vis IDA [Insti-
tute for Defense Analysis] and vis-à-vis the Harlem
community—I think that's a sizable indication of the alienation of students from this institution. The only way I can
see of getting out of this crisis is for students to be given the
power to be responsible in large part for those decisions
that shape their daily lives. We're here four years, some of
us, longer or shorter, others of us; this is our relevant community. We want to be able to help in the governing of that
community.

"You referred awhile ago to the interest of political and Establishment bodies being more served than the interests of the
student body. Would you elaborate on that? I read that there
are so many defense grants, research grants, that professors
don't have time actually to be with their students as professors. Do you feel this is one of your objections?"

Well, it doesn't touch me personally because there aren't
many English professors who are called upon for defense

contracts. I think a more relevant thing along that line is simply that a good many decisions are made about what contracts to accept—are made by that small group of men, the trustees, essentially businessmen, men who don't live in this community, who don't involve themselves directly with the ongoing life of the university.

"And they're serving the economy rather than building the values you think of as life?"

I think we have many disagreements with that small group of men about what a university should be. I think many of us feel that a university is not preeminently a business concern, and not preeminently an arm of the government, responsible preeminently to the government. That its business is the education of students and the education of faculty through the teaching process. And attention to this business will provide our society with the greatest social benefit it can have, and that is an informed, intelligent citizenry capable of assuming responsibility in these times.

A flash of lightning and a thunderclap punctuated our conference. A torrent of rain swept through the soot-strangled window screen smudging my notes with the city's polluted blackness.

"If you'd like to sit out the rain here, you're welcome, but Mr. W——— is here now and I've got to go. They've been waiting the conference for me."

I thanked J———. In spite of the completely tape-recorded interview, I had many notes to make. By near dark the rain had spent itself to the point where I, raincoatless, could venture into the street to hail a taxi. As I reached the corner, I turned to see a black-umbrella-ed figure emerging from the same door I had just left. His course took him to my corner to await the light.

"Are you by any chance Mr. W———, the university board

member who was meeting with the students in there?" He was.
We introduced ourselves.

"Have they got a point?" I asked.

"They've got several good points. They're really quite reasonable when you sit down and talk with them. But when I take the word back to the board, I know what will happen." A gust of rain drove us back under a sheltering doorway.

"What will happen?"

"They'll say we can't do those things. It will make a lot of the university's patrons very unhappy—and they're the ones we depend on for funds to keep the university running."

"Where do you think it will all end?"

"Right now I can't say. Something's got to give. I just wish my fellow board members could sit down and talk with some of these people as I have."

"Why can't they?"

"Busy, you know. Well, I guess it's let up now. I've got to go."

As the black umbrella bobbed away under the street lights, the tape of J———'s voice began unwinding in my head, loud and clear:

Certainly the democratic system here in America is failing to be responsive to the pressures from people. We've got to learn to find new ways of having the mechanism be responsive to the people. What we have is protests all over the country from one underprivileged class in one way or another. We have the whole problem of Negroes and poor people in the urban areas of the cities who've been ignored for so long, who've been put off for so long with insufficient responses, who have been patted on the head for so long, and who finally—now that they've finally started to get somewhere—want it all now. And I think one can hardly blame them. In a way, the students of this country are another underprivileged minority. On the one hand, we're among the

most privileged classes that has ever existed on the face of
the earth. We generally come from wealthy or at least mod-
erately wealthy upper-middle-class families; we have everything handed to us, in a way, on a silver platter. On the
other hand, behind this whole marvelous, indeed in many
ways luxurious, façade there are all these pressures on us to
lose our humanity, to become simply cogs in the societal
machine. And we are not taken seriously as citizens of the
communities in which we live, that is to say the university
communities. One of the great problems is that we haven't
—our humanity hasn't caught up to our technological development. Our wisdom of what do do with the machines
that we've created hasn't caught up with us. We haven't yet
understood how to govern ourselves as individual human
beings or as societies. People in positions of power can
make terrific mistakes, and therefore one wonders whether
or not power should be concentrated in few hands. I think
President Johnson is a perfect example; the President is the
one who declared war against North Vietnam, not the Congress, and certainly not the people. The established centers
of power function for their own advantage and not for the
advantage of many of the repressed areas of our society. I
think there's a lot of turbulence because, as I've implied already, there's a great shift in values. And there are many,
many sets of values that any individual can choose from.
You can divide it along generation lines or you can divide
it along race lines or wealth lines, but you have different
segments of society which hold to specific sets of values
which are not at all the values other segments use. And you
have different groups of very, very sincere, dedicated people who simply can't understand each what the other is saying, what it's all about. Middle-class white America still
doesn't even understand the faintest thing about what it
means to be a Negro in an urban area. I think we're starting to understand, maybe, what it means to be a Negro in
the South. Progress in these areas is still possible. I think
the McCarthy movement, the anti-Vietnam war movement,
at least shows that America hasn't died yet; at least shows

that the attempts of the sort of impersonal motion of society toward mechanization, impersonalization, standardi-
zation, uniformity, conformity—all those ugly, ugly words
—is being resisted, that we still have some health left in our
society, and certainly I have a great deal of anxiety in the
society, and certainly I have a great deal of anxiety in myself, because we have to learn so much so quickly and we
have to change so fast. Otherwise, the whole thing's just
going to blow up.

Schooling for what? Why have we reaped this fallout?

CHAPTER 4

NEVER BEFORE...

Why these outbursts—demonstrations, riots, marches, sit-ins, the long hair, and the funny clothes? Never before in history has there been any parallel to the rising tempest of the young-old, black-white conflicts of today. Add these two to the ever widening gulf between the "haves" and the "have-nots" and you have a volatile mixture, awaiting only a match to set it off. Let's look at the explosive facts with regard to the young, particularly in the United States. Never before have there been so many young, with so much schooling, with so much affluence, so much personal and sexual freedom, with such an affinity for each other and a sense of alienation from their elders, and with so much time on their hands to sit back and think about what they are seeing.

1. *Never before* have there been so many young, or so many young in proportion to older segments of the population, or such a swift rise in the number and proportion of the young.

In the fifteen years between 1960 and 1975 the population (actual and projected) of fifteen to twenty-four-year-olds shows an increase of approximately 15 million or 65 per cent. During the same period, for forty-five to fifty-four-year-olds the figure is approximately 3 million, or an increase of only 15 per cent, while thirty-five to forty-four-year-olds will actually decline in numbers by one million, a decrease of 8 per cent. Thus, during the years 1960–1975, the sheer quantity of the young will increase more than four times as fast as the quantity of their elders.

In 1975 the total of *three* generations of people, the entire range of twenty-five to fifty-four's, is not even double that of *one* generation of fifteen- to twenty-four's: 77 million (rounded) versus 40 million. Put another way, the whole trend is going counter to even our recent past history—a scant twenty years ago. The 1950 population figure showed nearly three times as many twenty-five to fifty-four's as there were fifteen to twenty-four's: 63 million (rounded) versus 22 million. Under the headline "The World Needs More Adults per Child," Margaret Mead says in an interview:

> I'm not worried about the world becoming like one great packed elevator stuck between floors while everybody starves to death—yet. I *am* worried about the more immediate fact that every country in the world, America included, urgently needs more adults per child. . . . Our population is out of balance and could easily become more so, as riots develop in parks meant to be used as playing fields, as students are crowded into huge impersonal lecture halls and teachers grow more desperate in overcrowded classrooms, as our cities swarm with uncared-for children. The relation between children and productive adults is askew in the United States, and in the rest of the world.[1]

2. *Never before* have so many young had so much schooling.

In 1925 less than a third of all pupils in grade five stayed in school to become high school graduates. Even by 1950 the stay-in figure was only about one-half. But ten years later, around 60 per cent graduated from high school.

In 1950 we spent 5½ billion dollars (rounded) to provide
schooling for 25 million elementary and secondary pupils
(kindergarten through twelfth grade). In 1964, with only 65
per cent more pupils, we spent nearly 400 per cent more (41
million pupils, $21 billion). By 1969 we were spending nearly
$38 billion on 52 million pupils. In slightly less than a twen-
ty-year period our expenditure rose from $259 to $750 per
pupil per school year. In 1920 the figure was $64.

In 1950 only 83 per cent of fourteen to seventeen-year-olds
were in school. By 1966 the figure was 93 per cent. For the
same years, eighteen- to nineteen-year-old stay-ins increased
from 20 to 88 per cent and the percentage of twenty to twenty-four's more than doubled, from 9 to nearly 20 per cent. All
along the line more young people have been staying in school
for a greater length of time.

3. *Never before* have so many young people been kept in a
state of dependency for so long.

As we have seen in Number 2 above, never have so many
young had so much schooling. The years spent in schooling
are, for most, dependent years, years in which the student
looks to his parents or some other source to provide life-giving
food and shelter while, at least theoretically, he pursues his
studies. For centuries, until the very recent past, the vast majority of youth joined the work force in their teens. The young
male's normal aggression instincts were healthily drained off
in providing an independent living for himself, and shortly
for a family. Between his aggression instincts, his life needs,
and ever-needed success in fulfilling them, he developed "ambition."

But since World War II all this has changed. Machines are
doing more and more work previously done by human hands.
Suddenly there is more time, especially for the young, whose
usual induction into society has been years of menial, unskilled work. Almost overnight we have begun keeping nearly

all of our youth in school—hence dependent on us—well into their teens and, for increasing numbers, into their early and even mid-twenties.

Aggression and dependency are dynamically connected. The more a person remains dependent on others, the more aggression builds up within him. If you are dependent on another person, you are in the power of that person; you see his power as a restrictive influence—from which you must break out. By keeping youth dependent overlong we have fostered the build-up of an abnormal amount of aggression while depriving them more and more of the opportunity for its normal, constructive release. Instead, the release has come via such protests as long hair and funny clothes, demonstrations, sit-ins, and—increasingly—violence. By refusing youth the vote, and by various other ways of isolating them from political, working, and social activity, we have given them a ready target for their built-up aggression. Add to these factors the deprivations inherent in being black, Mexican, Puerto Rican, or Indian, and you have these youth aggressions compounded. The wonder is that there has been so little violence—so far.

4. *Never before* has youth had so much time on its hands, yet so little outlet for useful, independent physical activity so necessary to develop and refine a feeling of self-reliance.

In the mid-1930s nearly two-thirds of all pupils who entered the fifth grade dropped out before the end of high school. Most went to work. During an eight- or nine-hour day, six days a week, they had little time on their hands. Today, with 93 per cent of fourteen to seventeen-year-olds remaining in school, most teenagers leave school with three or four daylight hours and all day Saturday and Sunday on their hands. Farm chores, household tasks, and odd jobs for pocket money have disappeared in mechanized, urban living. But the young remain—and in ever larger quantities. The time not spent in useful work used to be filled with hours exploring the woods, fields, and streams. What ever happened to the vacant lots with endless games of baseball and no-holds-barred football? Bulldozed into subdivisions, laid out in row after row of deadly dull tract houses, they are no more. In yesteryear a youngster was pretty much able to find his own excitement without the help of parents. Today, it takes an unusually resourceful parent, and one willing to put in a great deal more time than most do, to guide the release of young energies in the maze of our constricting environment.

5. *Never before* have so many young had so much affluence. And money is power.

> In the time it takes you to read these lines, the American teenager will have spent $2,378.22. In 1965 the teenage market estimate was $13 billion a year. Viewed in the old-fashioned way, this market has expanded by about $3 billion annually within the past two years and is expected to be well above the $20 billion mark by 1967. And those statisticians who count the youth market—the age range of thirteen to twenty-two rather than fifteen to nineteen—say that it has already reached about $25 billion.[2]

When did you first hear the word "teenager"? Actually it wasn't until the 1940s that we gave this vague no-man's land between child and adulthood a name. And the name bred a subculture—a way of life. Hallmark of the new way of life for the burgeoning youthful millions was a groping versatility: They wanted to try out everything in their own way. For one thing, they wanted to read about themselves, to see what other teenagers were thinking and doing. Old-line publishers would have none of it, and it took Eugene Gilbert, himself barely out of his teens, to start the first magazine written by youth for youth—*Seventeen*—in 1944. Sensing something big, commercial interests sent researchers into the field to find out what youth wanted to spend its money on. To zero in on the new market, new advertising media were needed. By 1967 there were fifteen full-fledged magazines aimed directly at youth, among them *Teen Talk, Ingenue,* and *Jet,* the last exclusively for black teens. Today these broad-coverage magazines are flanked by dozens of special-interest publications such as *Hot Rod, Surfing, Skin Diving, Sky Diving,* and so forth, not to mention those of religious youth organizations. Between parents who would rather pay off in money instead of time and affection and the earnings some enterprising teenagers were able to make, youth set the nation's cash registers jangling at a new pitch. What does it mean—the new billions commanded by youth in the market place? It means new power and influence for a segment of the population—white and black— that until a scant generation ago was only seen and not heard.

6. *Never before* have the young had sexual freedom.

The young, confronting the thrust of nature within themselves, can only turn to each other. Before the pill, certain sex mores were necessary to avoid unwanted pregnancy; yet magazine advertising, TV, verboten sexographics, and the Barbie Doll launched the young early on the American sex scene. Now, with this retainer wall of unwanted pregnancy blown down before their eyes, the young are trapped in mixed feelings. Like children turned loose in a candy store, some are eating themselves sick. Others, remembering parental warnings that too much candy will make you sick, are torn between appetite and admonition. Many undoubtedly can see such parental lashings as "I never did such a thing when I was your age" as thinly veiled hypocrisy or even jealousy of parents "born thirty years too soon." Often this shrugging off of a burning issue by parents has driven youngsters to new extremes. In terms of decision making, the young are carrying a heavier burden than ever before.

7. *Never before* have so many young had such easy access
to drugs.

We used to read of drug addicts and quietly relegate these
people to a nether world. Now that world is coming right into
our schools and into our homes as increasing numbers of
youth, and even elementary school children, driven out of
place in the real world, seek inner-space thrills through mind-
blowing drugs. Said one teacher of thirty-three years' experience, and very much in contact with youth of all ages: "The
young have always wanted to touch fire. Now they want to
handle it."

Furthermore, it is no longer a big-city phenomenon. Even
the smallest, "nicest" towns are not immune. In the spring of
1968 a survey at the high school in a small resort and residen-
tial community in California disclosed that 24.8 per cent of
the students admitted to trying drugs ranging from marijuana
to LSD and heroin. A number were on the verge of being
hooked. In the same period, several fifth-grade boys were discovered sniffing glue, and model shops in the area were re-
porting a run on the stuff. The coordinator of a drug information center in a Western community of 50,000 told me that at
least 80 per cent of all high school students have tried drugs
by the time they graduate and between 30 to 50 per cent are
habitual users of drugs ranging from marijuana on up. "Dope
is so easy to get now," she said. "There's an eight-year-old
drug pusher living down the street from me. How can you cope
with a thing like that?" Psychedelic parties combining the
multisensory mind-blowing effects of drugs and violent doses
of light and sound are now so numerous they are no longer
written about. "It's no worse than you adults and your alcohol," one teenager told me. Nor has the over-thirty example of
pill-popping psychotropic mood-change drugs—tranquilizers
for "down," amphetamines for "up"—been a helpful one for
the young.

The milder drugs, such as marijuana, are becoming increasingly available. As demand grows, smugglers step up the supply. Many people are finding it easy to grow the weed at home. That any bright high school chemistry student can make LSD has been known for some years. Glue, "bennies," and other drugs make inner-space travel available to all. The *Journal of the American Medical Association* noted the latest fad in psychedelic drug use is smoking catnip—and perfectly legal. According to Dr. Basil Jackson of Milwaukee and Dr. Alan Reed of San Francisco, the effects of catnip are similar to marijuana, and often as strongly hallucinogenic as LSD. Catnip grows wild, is legal, and sells for sixty cents an ounce in any pet store versus ten dollars to twenty dollars an ounce for marijuana purchased on the sly from a dope pusher. For today's increasingly affluent young, acquiring drugs is becoming easier. Many may get their start with the readily available supply of currently faddish drugs now in the family medicine chest.

It would be helpful to many of the young if they could have sat with me as I interviewed at the Correctional Training Facility—actually a penitentiary trying hard to live up to its name—in Soledad, California. I recall a twenty-six-year-old man serving five years to life on a dope charge. When I asked him about the upsurge of violence and crime, he said:

> Well, I think the reason this is happening is because a lot of teenagers doesn't have anything to do and really doesn't know what they could—in other words, they could get in trouble from doing certain things that they are not aware of, and I have found out for a fact that my biggest problem is narcotics, and that I think a lot of teenagers, beatniks, and etc., drugs play a great role in violence, and I think that in the future I am going to stay away from dope drugs because I know it has gotten me in trouble and I'm pretty sure it will get many others in trouble, especially teenagers.

At the end of our interview I couldn't help asking him, "What kind of thinking brought you here?"

Well, my thinking—see, I don't have a record. I don't have any record at all. I've never been in jail before. I've never been in any institution, but like I was saying, drugs got me sent. I came into contact with a lot of dope peddlers and more or less I developed a habit or I thought I needed drugs, and . . .

"To help you sing?" I suggested, as earlier he had told me of his efforts to become a singer.

No, well, sometimes I was lacking in communicating with certain people. In other words, it caused a little conflict to me that I, I thought that I would, I could meet the qualifications by using drugs, whereas now I see I don't. I don't need drugs at all because I sing better and I think better, you know, without drugs. And when I was introduced to drugs it was something, shall I say, just new and it got out of control. I got out of control, that's why I'm here.

8. *Never before* have so many young lived so closely together.

In colonial America the average density of persons was one per square mile; in modern Chicago it is 15,000 per square mile. Well into this century over half of the American people still lived on farms dispersed across the countryside, while most of the rest of us lived in small, uncrowded towns. In 1870 there were only three cities of more than 300,000 population—New York, Philadelphia, and St. Louis. Now there are forty-two. Today 70 per cent of the people live on 1 per cent of the land. As an increasingly large proportion of the population youth finds itself equally compressed.

In addition, youth has been subject to still further concentration by being herded into huge factory-like high schools and colleges. In 1940 the average high school enrolled a little over 500 students. Today the average high school has well over 700 students, with many big-city plants bringing together 5,000 or 6,000 young, vital individuals into one seething mass. In Erasmus High School, Brooklyn, New York, where I interviewed, every day approximately 5,500 youngsters of secondary school age—a population equal to one-third of the towns and cities of the United States—are jammed into the area of a city block.

Intense and abnormal personal contact can bring about several phenomena, some of which may nurture rebellion by students (or any human beings, for that matter). Anthony Storr, a noted psychiatrist, in his book *Human Aggression* writes:

> Where overcrowding does occur, . . . it increases aggression between animals, which may either lead to their fighting each other to the death or else to their succumbing to stress diseases. The latter has been observed, under natural conditions, in the case of a certain species of hare which, from time to time, increases its own population too rapidly. The result is that large numbers of the animal succumb to a disease which appears to be the result of stress. Overcrowding is also common in zoos, and may lead to fights to the death, partly because the vanquished animal cannot escape from the victor, and partly because the restriction of the environment leads to an increase of aggression.[3]

Is it not reasonable to believe that, simply as an animal of higher order, man suffers equally from the stresses of over-proximity? Add to this the normal, healthy aggression of youth and you have an explosive force that must go somewhere. Obviously, it will be directed first toward anything perceived as a bar to freedom of action—mental or physical. And the phenomenon knows no color.

Another result of overproximity is the ease and speed with

which ideas can be communicated and snowballed into mass response. Imagine, in earlier days, trying to get 1,000, 1,500, or 2,000 or more students to assemble in demonstrations when these students were dispersed over dozens or scores of square miles in ten, fifteen, or twenty or more schools. Today the same number of students can assemble at eyeball distance in minutes, on campus after campus, presenting a show of aggression and power never before possible.

9. *Never before* have so many young been aware of the young in other parts of their own country and in other countries of the world.

Directly in front of me, awaiting his turn to board the airport bus at the East Side Terminal in New York, was a gaunt young man laden with hiker's backpack and a not-too-clean rolled-up blanket. I made it a point to sit beside him. We were both bound for San Francisco. An interview? "Well, I haven't got much to say, especially about schooling. I was thrown out of one and I dropped out of another." Where had he been? On a hiking tour of Europe. Ended up as a cave dweller on the island of Crete. He was seventeen and self-possessed. For the past two months he had hitchhiked and bicycled from London to Istanbul and back to Paris, stopping off along the way "just to see how the people really are."

Even a few years ago youngsters were relatively isolated. They came and went at their parents' pleasure, few read newspapers because all the news was about the adult world, and TV sets were a rarity. By 1966, 93 per cent of all American homes had television. In 1967 Telstar was bringing world-wide happenings, live, into the living room. And not only has the accent on programs been going more "young" each year, but because the young have been making an increasing amount of news, they are able to see each other on TV at opposite ends of the planet—students rioting in Tokyo or rebelling in Strasbourg—not to mention the evening run-down on college and high school demonstrations and violence across the United States. The young know that student rebel-lion is not simply "USA," but a world-wide uprising of youth questioning the values of their elders. Once relatively alone with their thoughts, or at best airing their views at dormitory or fraternity house bull sessions, the young now shout them to each other across the land and around the world. The hope-less feeling of "What can the few of us do about anything?" has turned into a feeling of power—the power of numbers. And the young are quick to seize on modern technology to put their power to work. Bull horns and P.A. systems have be-come the standard equipment of student groups. Ways of at-tracting the cameras of TV newscasters spread the word even further, and the airplane—what with youth fares and hand-outs from home—can converge thousands of youth on a sin-gle city in hours—witness Chicago, 1968, the Woodstock "happening" of 400,000, and the November march on Wash-ington in 1969.

Youth has always had a way of keeping their elders off bal-ance by doing unexpected and often more creative things than we'd like to give them credit for. Now it comes in mass doses —with world-wide reinforcement.

10. *Never before* have so many young been so exposed, collectively, to the presence of so many social ills.

I can remember "the poor people" who lived down by the tracks and the little "nigger-town" shacks during my growing-up years. And, yes, we who were fortunate enough to live somewhere near "the right part of town" felt sorry for them. But we didn't know it was like that all over. Today the plight of the have-nots, the blacks, and other not-yet-enfranchised Americans is there for all to see in magazines, newspapers, and on TV.

Television: purveyor of useful knowledge and entertainment, or curse-ridden exemplar of the violent life style and the instant solution? Dr. S. I. Hayakawa, acting president of San Francisco State College, speaking at a dinner of young businessmen in Monterey in 1969, said that television suggests "instant solution for upset stomachs, for your unpopularity, for your inadequate sex life. It's full of messages that promise instant solutions. I wonder if a whole generation feels there must be an instant solution to racial discrimination in America." And yet there is nothing unnatural about the anguished impact of social ills on idealistic young minds. Suppose we had been aware of what the young people know today?

11. *Never before* has youth faced such an acceleration in the amount of knowledge being generated.

Perhaps you've seen the fascinating facsimile edition of the *Encyclopaedia Britannica* originally published in three volumes during 1768–1771. Its 2,459 pages, written by 109 contributors and containing slightly over 2,000,000 words and 160 copperplate engravings, represented a compendium of man's knowledge a little over 200 years ago. The 1968 edition of the *Encyclopaedia Britannica* has twenty-three volumes containing 36,000,000 words researched and written by more than 9,000 men and women. Far from claiming it to be a compendium of the world's knowledge, Editor-in-chief Warren E. Preece writes: "The utility of the *Britannica* will be in direct proportion to its ability to meet, and indeed to stimulate, man's need for knowledge." Commenting on the knowledge explosion, he says that the editors

are aware that one of the lessons derived from 200 years of encyclopedia publishing is that arrogance ill becomes those who deal with knowledge. Within its history, the *Britannica* has reported as scientific "fact" that the atom is the part of matter subject to no further division, that uranium is of value only as an additive in the manufacture of ceramics. Knowledge and the "facts" based upon it are never static, and it is not the function of an encyclopedia to be a volume of permanent "truths."

Elsewhere in the current *Britannica* it is noted, "Currently as many as 6,000,000 and more words may be reset each year." That's nearly three times as many words as contained in the original edition of *Britannica*. If this is any measure, then man's new knowledge each year is three times all that he knew 200 years ago. Put in another way, only two centuries ago man could put all the knowledge he had accumulated in fifty or sixty centuries down in approximately 2,000,000 words. Today it takes three times that many words to record what he learns in a single year!

... 90 per cent of all scientists and engineers who ever lived are still alive and practising. ... At a minimum this means that most of the goods and services that sustain and shape our civilization have been conceived or perfected by the contemporary generation. The material world is almost entirely new; the world that is emerging is bound to be newer still. And now it is suggested that the rate of technological change may be approaching the exponential, ushering in a permanent condition of newness, world without end.[4]

And as if today's kaleidoscopic changes were not enough, take an over-the-shoulder glance into Marshall McLuhan's crystal ball. In the early 1969 announcement for his *Dew Line Newsletter*, McLuhan listed some of the topics to be considered in forthcoming issues:

The Computer data-bank as the dissolution of private life.
The satellite as the end of Nature.
Galaxies as art forms.
The artist as the antennae of the race.

The substitution of man-made environments for biological evolution.

The end of the visual organization of knowledge and experience.

Song as slowed-down speech. Instrumentation as speeded-up speech.

Pot and LSD as chemical simulation of our electric environment.

Why the message will be dropped in favor of the effect.

The disappearance not only of writing but of speech.

The end of the split between business and culture.

The end of history via the computer.

Jokes and humor as the infallible test of grievance areas in a society.

Games and sports as live models of existing procedures in business.

Why the "backward" countries will inevitably dominate the Western world.

War as the effort to recover an *old* image of identity and purpose.

Why our first TV war has ended the boundaries between civilian and military life.

Why the prayer mat shall replace the Cadillac.

Violence as the quest for identity.

NASA as an obsolete program.

The Future of Convalescence. (Anesthesia applied not only to surgery but to total recovery.)

The computer as the LSD of the business world.

War as education. Education as war. Clothing as weaponry. (Fashion as the bore war.)

Why there is a return of horoscopy in the electric age.

The end of the Stock Exchange via the computer.

In his 1968 annual report President Nathan M. Pusey of Harvard University pointed out that the young are not alone in their concerns about world problems. "None of us is unaware of or unmoved by the manifold troubles which confront us at home and the apparent inability of establishment institutions to make adequate quick response. There can be no question here of a generation gap." The explanation that society is moving into a period of fundamental and widespread changes President Pusey regards as "overdramatic." "Nonetheless," he continues, "I must concede the possibility that our colleges and universities are only among the first of institutions to be shaken by an all-encompassing sea-change now occurring around the world—though I hope not."

12. *Never before* have the young been exposed to such a wide range of religious views.

Depending on the accident of birth, one used to bear the label "Baptist," "Catholic," "Seventh-Day Adventist," or some other religious "faith," and that was usually that. If one religion was better than another, it was taken for granted that it was your own. As for the religions of the other parts of the world, well, they were for the heathen. It isn't that way for the youth any more. They are finding out that Buddha was for hundreds of millions what Christ was to Christians. The young are reading the Hindu Upanishads alongside the Christian Bible and finding each an ennobling experience. They are reaching out to taste religious beliefs other than those they were born and raised in.

The current battle to "secularize" the church is largely one of youthful thinking versus establishment thinking. Those favoring secularization take the view that man is living in *this* world rather than for some *other* or later world. Secularization sees man as an increasingly mature and responsible entity on this planet. It is not surprising that Zen Buddhism, for example, is gaining such a following among the young. Zen disavows arguing, theorizing, sermonizing, or trying to explain. Rather, it urges the follower to find in himself the answer to any question raised from within himself, because the answer is where the question is. While many of the young explore the mysteries of Oriental transcendentalism over coffee, drugs, or simply trying to live in another world, others prefer a more "formal" version, Soka Gakkai. Known in the United States as Nichiren Shoshu of America (The True Church of Nichiren), the sect grew from 30,000 in 1965 to 170,000 four years later. More than three-quarters of its converts are of non-Oriental origin. Chanting Buddhist sutras while kneeling on the floor, the devotees develop a fervor that runs the gamut from the old-time "holy rollers" to the Moral Youth Rearmament. In Japan the movement has 16 million followers and its Clean Government party is the third largest political entity within the Diet.

Seeking metaphysical communication through simple closeness, groups of hippies may sit quietly in a circle looking at each other or at nothing. Occasionally a home-grown guru will lead the group in a mystical, mind-expanding Hindu chant of one long strung-out syllable, "Ommm-m-m-m-m," that seems to rumble up from their very toes. "We can get high on our own vibrations, and it's beautiful," one girl in a granny dress told me.

The intense wish of the young to certify religion by means of experience has led increasing numbers to the practice of Yoga. Originally one of the "six systems" of Indian philosophy, Yoga combines serene bodily movement with exercises in relaxation, concentration, and meditation, the goal of which is, in today's language, to turn the individual on to a new self-awareness and a blending of the Self with the Great Ultimate Power in one harmonic relationship. "I used to think drugs were the only way to turn on," one heavily bearded youth told me, "but Yoga is better. It's a natural way to get high, and all things natural are spiritual." That Yoga is a do-it-yourself thing is part of its appeal to the young as they reach back through layers of materialism to find their true American heritage.

While some young Americans look to the ancient and contemporary East in their quest for faith in something beyond themselves, others indulge in the occult—witchcraft, numerology, astrology. Still others are bringing new form—and often considerable informality—to the stereotype church.

In a very real sense today's spiritually hungry young are reliving the strivings of the New England Transcendentalists, especially during the intensely active years of 1830–1835. Spearheaded by Ralph Waldo Emerson, Henry David Thoreau, Margaret Fuller, Theodore Parker, and others, the Transcendentalist movement represented not only a battle between the younger and older generations of that time but also a major rift in American culture. Like the Transcendentalists, today's young are learning that in a variety and richness of religious experiences there can be found affluence of the spirit as well as of the body.

13. *Never before* have the young been exposed to such a wide range of political views and actions.

Absolutism, anarchism, chauvinism, collectivism, communism, conservatism, individualism, liberalism, nationalism, nihilism, socialism, syndicalism, aristocracy, democracy, monarchy, oligarchy—nearly everything but gerontocracy (the thing they are fighting) is being looked at, thought about, and tried, in one way or another, by the young these days. But instead of these classic labels, budding political philosophies are carrying such names as Students for a Democratic Society, The Third World Liberation Front, the Yippies, Castroism, Che-ism, Maoism, (Eugene) McCarthyism, Young Americans for Freedom, LUV (Let Us Vote), Black Power in various manifestations, plus a host of others. Then, of course, there are the Democrats and the Republicans, as well as the emerging Wallacites—the last most recently under the convenient acronym NCASPAIPAPIPCPCPCP (The National Committee of Autonomous State Parties known as the American Independent party, the American party, the Independent party, the Conservative party, the Constitution party, the Courage party, and such other political parties as desire to affiliate with this national committee). Belatedly, the major political parties have opened their ranks to youth—or else.

Once content to read and take tests in "civics," students are now taking to the streets to get the feel of group power—its potentials and pitfalls. Goals may vary, but the anatomy of student rebellion in college or high school, in the United States, Canada, Mexico, Great Britain, France, West Germany, Spain, India, Pakistan, Japan, and various Latin-American countries is much the same.

Up till now there has usually been little connection among groups on various campuses using the same name. While there is a token national headquarters of the Students for a Democratic Society, the groups using the same name in New York and San Francisco may, for example, have no common list of grievances or even common methods of operation. That some of the militant organizations may have "outside help" from organized communism is the subject of much discussion. In any event, the lone-wolf outlook of many local student groups is changing, reflecting Benjamin Franklin's ancient admonition, "We must all hang together or we shall all hang separately." This is true among the anti-Establishment dissidents as well as the pro-Establishment counter militants. Young Americans for Freedom, organized in 1960 in the home of William F. Buckley, Jr., conservative publisher-columnist, claimed nine years later to have 30,000 members on 500 high school and college campuses. The YAF aims to uphold the Constitution of the United States and to "oppose collectivism, socialism, statism, and other utopianisms which have poisoned the minds, weakened the wills, and smothered the spirits of Americans for three decades and more." For the YAF, the

Young Republicans have lost their punch. In the spring of 1969 Dennis Bogdan, YAF president at City College of San Francisco, said that his organization was "in a death struggle with the radicals of the left and the socialists." One item of a list of organizational suggestions to members exhorted, "Never be satisfied. Start working toward your next triumph immediately after you've pulled off your last one. Stay lean, hungry, and determined to make your club, organization, or yourself the most powerful in your community." A few weeks previously the YAF had confronted the SDS on the Stanford University campus, turned their own techniques against them, and knocked out the SDS march to close down the Stanford Research Institute.

Seeking to back up their beliefs with ballots, LUV, the brain child of Dennis Warren, twenty-one, a pre-law student at the University of the Pacific in Stockton, California, seeks the vote for eighteen-year-olds. In only a six-weeks period in the spring of 1969 the movement grew from his own campus to 327 college chapters and over 3,000 high school divisions. In spite of Capitol Hill's long-standing policy of sending eighteen-year-olds to war while denying them the vote, Warren is confident that LUV will conquer all.

In politics, religion, sex, money, life style—in almost every segment of life—the young have come up with a whole new ball game. To those who say, "They'll soon get over it," I would like to point out that many of the young whom I have interviewed are quite aware of this possibility and are busily making sure that they don't slip into the hypocrisies of their parents and become simply wards of the Establishment. Moreover, the upcoming teenagers are going even further in questioning the *status quo* than did their older brothers and sisters now in upper high school and college.

Almost all of the adults among the 1,000 people interviewed were aware of one or more of these "never befores," but no one person seemed aware of more than a few of them. Very few share my opinion that the young today have reached a stage that is new in the history of man. Whereas before, youth protests have occurred in occasional, short-lived, and isolated flurries, today they are continuous, sustained, and world-wide. If not formally interconnected, they are mutually reinforcing in that almost all the youth of the world are now instantly aware of each other's thoughts and actions because of TV, radio, the press, and the airplane. Always before, youth has had its fling, only to meld into the *status quo* accepting society's values and abandoning idealism in the satisfaction of the biological urge through marriage and the struggle for daily bread. Today the pill brings sex without marriage and daily bread is taken for granted. Does this mean that the young have been released to pursue values higher than the mere satisfaction of the biological urge and food, clothing, and shelter? Or does it mean they are riding the whirlwinds of destruction? What do they want? Schooling for what?

CHAPTER 5

WHAT DO
THEY WANT?

We have seen that the young are asking for more self-determination—all the way from the middle school years through the university—more of a say in what they are to learn and how they are to go about it. "Why," they are asking, "do we have to study this many pages in this book when what I want to know is in that book, or some other book, or to be gone out and looked at, or simply experienced?" And what are some of the specifics that are irritating clear-thinking young people as they regard our present schooling in the light of logic and what we have taught them to be worth-while human values? Here is the essence of what I have heard in hundreds of interviews at the high school and university level.

> You have driven us through all these years of schooling motivated by *fear* instead of by the joy of learning—yet you talk about love. You have made us work for grades instead of learning or caring about learning—yet you complain that we lack motivation.

> You have taught many of us to cheat, since you would not let us admit that there are certain things we could not or

would not do, because we are individually different—yet you preach about personal integrity.

You have herded us lock-stepped through one classroom after another and we have seen almost half of our fellows fall by the wayside, scarred by failure for life—yet you speak of equal opportunity for all.

You have made us take courses which will make us cogs in the industrial machine, not caring if it were something we wanted to learn—yet you tout the sanctity of the individual.

You make us take tests to compete with each other so we can enter the dog-eat-dog arena of the Establishment— even as you advocate a world with more kindness.

The young see these manifestations of adult hypocrisy as the symptoms of what ails society in general, especially in the matter of work. I recall one California student's definition: "School is a mouse race that gets you ready for the rat race."

This is what they think we've created in the world of work, and they are bringing a different set of attitudes to the scene: Instead of asking about a job, "How much can I make?" they're asking, "Will it be interesting work, and will it enable me to contribute to society?" Instead of quantity, they are asking about quality: "What is the good life for me as an individual, and as a member of society?" They're asking questions we older folks have perhaps stopped asking, but which need asking and answering if human beings are to continue to inhabit the planet Earth. For example: why do the so-called civilized countries operate on an economy of scarcity in the midst of abundance? Why are there millions of bushels of wheat stored in U.S. granaries and millions of pounds of butter stored in Germany's refrigerated warehouses while nearly half the world's human beings go to bed each night hungry? Why is a young man eighteen years of age in the United States old enough to be drafted into the Army to fight for his country, yet not old enough to vote until three years later—when he may be dead? How can a whole race of human beings be kept out of society just because their skin is black? Why does it seem that the older generation, the Establishment, wants to give young people the skills of reading, writing, and arithmetic only to make them cogs in a machine that makes the rich get richer and the poor get poorer and has been doing the same thing for centuries?

There is something both grim and refreshing about the young people today. They are telling us they're not going to continue to grind through meaningless courses, grub for competitive grades, and take home irrelevant report cards. And they're beginning to pack power. For example, the National Association of Elementary School Principals has just called for abolition of report cards. Five years ago these same school principals would not have dared! But the young have struck the spark. Another item, the PTA—Parent Teachers Association—was a good idea but too often a dead organization; but something new has been added, and along with it a chance at new life. In several high schools the PTA is becoming PTSA—Parent-Teacher-Student Association—as students seek a voice in changing schooling into something more meaningful and relevant to life in today's world. Neither are they awed by people in high places: The young have toppled more than one college president, and in 1968 they brought down a President of the United States!

For some even that isn't enough. They want to see that the revolution gets started—they want anarchy, overthrow of the state. "Our job is to break down society. We're not responsible for a plan to rebuild it. Anything would be better than what we have now." These rank anarchists are few, but they exert a force all out of proportion to their number. Students stay pretty much tuned in, and the anarchists have the ear of the vast majority of the student body. What may begin as a handful staging a sit-in, take-over, or other attention-getting device can, if the cause makes sense, develop into a drama involving most of the campus, with the faculty joining in as well. Furthermore, with today's technology, a handful of determined fanatics, strategically placed to push the right buttons at the right time, could effect a coup and—without outside help— plunge the nation into chaos. Over 70 per cent of our population lives in only 135 cities. With only a little outside help, the U.S. government could be overthrown. No one who has seen the underground press of the young radical left can doubt that violence, even armed violence, is almost an obsession with them. The front page of one issue of the SDS publication *New Left Notes* carried a sketch of two crouching men with guns and cartridge belts. The caption read: "We are advocates of the abolition of war, we do not want war, but war can only be abolished through war, and in order to get rid of the gun it is necessary to take up the gun." Arms have already sprung up on the cloistered university campus. Arms have spoken more than once in the streets of our cities. Training in the use of arms will not have been lost on black men returning from Vietnam if they find nothing is changed. Schooled in the violent arts as no generation of blacks has ever been, they could constitute a formidable force in the streets of America.

Yet for every young anarchist there are hundreds of high school– and college-age activists who are putting forth constructive ideas and are willing to work for them. Many of these, their revolutionary zeal fanned by the prospect of exciting action, have in the past joined the ranks of the anarchists. Their rapidly rising expectations in the face of snail-paced change—or no change at all—turn them to the anarchist route against the Establishment, even as the black man has turned to violence as the only way to arouse whitey from his lethargy.

The young today are like a horse which—sensing a rattlesnake out of sight of the rider—suddenly rears up on its hind legs and refuses to continue in the direction it is being driven. Balking at danger it only senses, the horse saves its own life and the rider's. The younger generation seems to have developed this sixth sense.

What they are pointing up is that the time is *now*—or it may even be too late. They have found out that we won't listen to them talk about it, so they have taken to acting it out. In place of reasoning about war, they are striking. Instead of joining us in our racial prejudices, many young whites and blacks have begun actively fraternizing. Rejecting a society that stores up grain and pays farmers for not producing while one-sixth of the nation and nearly one-half of the world goes hungry, many have developed a new life style of sharing, expressed in its extreme by the hippie commune. To escape further depersonalization by our huge knowledge factories, many have dropped out of school. Instead of increasingly living by the numbers spewed out by computers, many have sought an unorganized way of life. Refusing to accept as inevitable and necessary man's spoliation of his earth, many young are now mounting a crusade against pollution. No longer guilt-ridden about sexual desires and their fulfillment, the young are taking advantage of the new science of birth control to turn sex away from a pure animal function toward the beauty it can be (leaving it to their elders to squabble about sex education!). The moderate use of drugs is seen by the young as no worse than a moderate consumption of alcohol by their elders. But the elders' hysteria on the matter of drugs makes even mild experimentation just one more way for the young to turn their backs on a society which has kept them waiting outside. Disenchanted by party politics and largely ignored by both Democrats and Republicans, the young may yet come up with a new political life style which gives them a number of real options instead of only two—Tweedledee and Tweedledum. To take just one political example, the young have a great deal of difficulty understanding our relations with Red China. They wonder why, in the words of Senator Edward Kennedy, "The world's oldest and most populous nation and the world's richest and most powerful nation glare at each other across the abyss of nuclear war."

Central to the younger generation's complaint is the older generation's attitude that "everything's going to be all right. Just you wait." Today the young can see perfectly clearly that cybernation has turned from creeping to running, that pollution has grown from a theory to a deadly fact of life, that the Establishment is a great deal more concerned about winning the war in Vietnam than fighting any war on poverty, and that promises made to the black man—like "good intentions"— have only been used to pave the road to hell.

But is it so much a question of generation gap as a peculiar contradiction in the United States? From its beginning our nation was a blend of liberal politics and conservative attitudes toward property, religion, and family life. This curious blend enabled us to build up wealth second to none in the world. It brought us food, clothing, and shelter in ever-increasing quantities, and today the young have these life-support elements in abundance. We produced these benefits by "working hard" and "saving up," we tell them. In the process, however, we too often neglected our spiritual and bodily senses and forgot about the beauties that could be experienced and expressed with them. And today, even as we rush headlong "to provide more for my children than I had," the very benefactors of our efforts turn on us to ask: "Are you really doing it for me? In your own hurry to produce more and more things, you have said to us, 'Stay out of the way so we can get the job done.' What job? And where are we supposed to go?"

Are we working so hard so we won't have to think? Is our addiction to hard work, to hurry, scramble, and rush driving our youngsters to pot, heroin, and "speed"? Where are we going? Is this what *we* went to school to learn? Is this what we're sending our children to school to learn? Schooling for what?

"We see no reason," they are telling us, "to keep on learning how to produce more and more *things*. We've got enough *things*. You've got enough *things*. What we're concerned with is the quality of life we don't have and you don't have, even with all these *things*. You have no time to discover and use your God-given senses. You have no time for beauty.

"Another thing that bothers us is that while you have these material benefits in increasing abundance, you watch indifferently as others get less and less. How can this be when you are supposed to be living by such mottoes as 'Do unto others as you would they should do unto you'? That's not all. You seem to take the fact of individual differences in human needs and wants as a license to *use* people instead of providing an opportunity for everybody to do the things he can as an individual and as a member of society.

"Yes, you have your philanthropic organizations and your foundations. But do the Community Chest and the United Fund really do anything but salve the Establishment's conscience so it can exploit even more ruthlessly the prostrate bodies of those they use or eliminate them from society by automation? And do your corporate foundations, for the most part, do anything but give the Establishment new ways of concentrating power?

"Sure, you have sent us to school nearly all our lives and

you admit we've learned more about things than any generation before us. But we also have learned that you are paying
no more than lip service to the high-minded ideals you have
instilled in us. It's about time that *you* learned what the American Way of Life is really all about. And if you won't change it,
then we will—with or without your help."

While we attack them for their hedonism, irrationality, low
regard for the technology and ethic that built the affluence
they now enjoy, they retort with the observation that the supposedly most rational and technically accomplished society
the world has ever known has led only to repression, racism, a
meaningless jungle war in Southeast Asia, a polluted environment at home, and a killer-pace life style whose icon is the
dollar sign. The truth is that the young people crying out for
change are not a threat. The real danger to America comes
from the radical left and the radical right who owe their re-
spective growing strength to the fact that we are not listening
to the young.

Members of the radical left—the SDS and its several fac-
tions, for example—come from middle and upper-middle-
class homes and have been suddenly disenchanted with the society from which they sprung. Most of them have elected to
live in near poverty partly as protest, partly because they
spend relatively little time in money-making activity. Their
disenchantment seems to stem from the conviction that their
families' affluence has come about from "exploitation of the
masses"—i.e., the working class. Ironically, it is some elements of the white working class, who are among those that
SDS would like to rescue from exploitation and on whom they
count to overthrow the Establishment, that seem to be turning
to Wallace and the radical right, protectors of the *status quo.*

Is the Establishment itself the radical right? Or does the Establishment simply use the radical right to keep from being

toppled by the radical left? Does it encourage a rising radical right against the time when it may need its actual physical support against radical left violence? Or is the Real Establishment—those few who hold the ultimate reins of the power structure—merely waiting around for the radicals to kill each other off—ready to step in with a benign smile to lend money for reconstruction when the shooting stops and the burning is over?

And what about us, who are "we"? You—the reader—of course, may be a member of the radical left, the radical right, or one of the chosen few of the Real Establishment. The odds are, however, from the standpoint of mere numbers, that you are one of "us"—those of the lower-middle, middle, and upper-middle classes of any race or color, who work for a living, have prospered more or less according to natural ability possessed and energy expended. We are the people often too busy to look up from our own work to see what is going on around us or, if we do, to take time to find the meaning of it for ourselves. But when the violence erupts, it is we who will be caught in the cross fire between the radical extremes. Even worse, we may find ourselves taking sides irrationally because we have not taken time to think things through and talk things out.

What or who, then, is the Establishment? Is it the government? Not necessarily. Corporate management? To some extent. The military? Possibly. What else? The university? To an increasing extent, as it becomes more and more the handmaiden of corporate management and the military. "We"—us? To the extent that we participate in, or go along with, the Establishment's socially irresponsible behavior which continues to build itself at the expense of others. But the Real Establishment is that other Mafia—those who concentrate wealth as a passion, perhaps for much the same reasons a criminal robs and kills—the combination of a psychotic need to get back at society and the need to prove one's self at all costs. Both have this in common: both prey on society. According to Ferdinand Lundberg in his book *The Rich and the Super-Rich,* all of the nation's productive private property is owned by the upper 10 per cent of the population, *and* only 1 per cent of the population owns more than 70 per cent of it. There are now more millionaires in this world than ever before. And there are billionaires who barricade themselves in mansions surrounded by barbed wire and vicious dogs. One such has holdings that bring him an estimated income of $300,000 *each day.* These people have used the techniques of this post-industrial, cybertronic age to maintain an economic system by which the rich get richer and the poor get poorer. Not only do they bleed society for their profits but they scheme and connive to keep from paying any of the blood money back to nourish the society from which they drained it. In 1968 nearly 400 of these people arranged their affairs so they did not pay one penny of income tax. Legally? Of course. Law and order for whom? The men of government become a part of the Real Establishment to the extent that they make these things possible—and, perhaps, profit personally.

While not using the word Establishment, John Gardner, in his new book *The Recovery of Confidence,* gives us a good description: "That complacent lump of self-satisfied Americans who fatten on the yield of society but never bestir themselves to solve its problems," and ". . . the powerful men who rest complacently with worn-out institutions when they have it in their power to redesign them." Isn't it time we demanded of these men that they spend at least as much time thinking of ways to put money back into society as they do taking it out? Isn't this what the young are demanding, are even willing to fight for? It is what I heard often during my interviews with the more thoughtful young. Compare my findings with those of *Esquire* magazine. Each year the magazine's editors convene a "College Board," a group of young men to advise them of the latest trends in campus thinking in such matters as clothes, girls, and jobs. Participating in the 1969 conference, along with university students, was a group of top-echelon businessmen. Describing the experience as "shocking" to the "over thirty" in attendance, Arnold Gingrich wrote in the October, 1969, issue that three hard questions emerged from the session. The young men, chosen from representative campuses across the country, wanted to know from the corporation executives present:

"1. What is the purpose of your business besides making money?
"2. What sort of creative challenge does your company offer a young man?
"3. How is your company involved in making this a better world?"

Whether we question their sincerity or not, the young people see the storm signals, and they know that time is running out on the Establishment. The battle between the haves and have-nots is taking shape. "Of course," you say, "things are getting worse, but the government is working on them, and if it ever comes to real violence, the government stands ready to back up the forces of law and order." True. But this is Band-Aid thinking when the patient is dying of cancer. The same circumstances that have permitted the overconcentration of wealth among the few have necessitated the concentration of the technology that controls it. We should learn from the famous 1965 blackout of New York. Remember, it was caused by the "malfunction" of only one small part of the control system in only one location. A small group of anarchists, guided by an even smaller group of technically informed but disenchanted young intellectuals, could sabotage the vitals of a large city in a matter of hours. Synchronized, it could happen to many of our large cities at once. With utilities, transportation, and communication out of action and repair crews kept at bay with a few well-placed guns, the Establishment might find itself unable to do anything but accede to demands that could only be further destructive to the nation. Are we going to let the Real Establishment continue to drive us along the path of destruction?

We, the great, usually silent, middle, have, as the psychiatrists would say, a "free-floating anxiety." We're "concerned" but we never quite come to grips with such questions as "What should we change?" or "What kinds of things should we hold on to?" Instead, we leave it to people "who have more time." Most often this turns out to be the seasoned politician. It is interesting that Webster's Unabridged Dictionary devotes fifteen lines to defining "politician" and that the largest portion of it describes a politician in such negative terms as "shrewd," "crafty schemer," "motivated by narrow and short-term interests as contrasted with the long-term welfare of people." Webster's contrasts "politician" with "statesman," describing the latter in terms of "leadership characterized by wisdom, breadth of vision, regard for general welfare. . . ."

Many of us know young men who have "gone into politics" with statesmanlike views and ambitions—only to become hacks of the Establishment. Many other young men, some brilliant, have simply looked at the political scene and said, "What's the use?" Accordingly, they have buried their visions and applied their intelligence, wittingly or unwittingly, to building up Establishment power structures. This means that political offices are too often filled by incompetents—people who are not builders, not men of vision, but merely hangers-on. Occasionally statesmanlike individuals are elected to public office. But their numbers have been so few compared with the hacks that their power is often inundated. Sometimes they are assassinated because their power threatens too much change. If there is anything the hack politician dislikes it is change. He likes to find the safe, high ground and play king of the mountain. He knows that is the way to get into the Establishment, and the bigger the politician, the closer he can get to the Real Establishment, where his bread is not only well buttered but turns into cake.

So what can "we" do? One thing is to make sure that we aren't being used by the Real Establishment as a buffer between them and the mounting fury of the have-nots; or that we are not merely the glue that holds their worn-out system in place and sticks it back together in the same old way when a piece falls off. Another thing we must do is to listen to both the radical left and the radical right and help them to get together for more talking out and less shooting out. Perhaps the SDS types and Wallacites have much in common. We should try to explore with them the extremities of their views and where they might lead if followed to conclusion. By talking out first one alternative then another, we should be able to help develop a perspective that can set the stage for getting on with the job of bringing the American Dream up to date.

Many of the young of all ethnic groups, white, black, Spanish-speaking, Oriental, and so on, have worth-while ideas on what ought to be changed and how to go about it. But will we listen? One fifty-year-old woman, a Detroit auto industry executive, who had just visited Colorado University, where her son is an instructor, told me:

It was a revelation to me and I think it is to any older person who sits and not only watches them and sees the long hair and the funny clothes as you mentioned, but listens to what they're saying. If we don't listen, we shouldn't criticize, and if we do listen we won't criticize most of them.

I would put it more strongly: If we don't listen to the young and the blacks, we are "going to hell in a handbasket." At this point in time in these United States, the old order must change, or very soon there will be no order at all. Perhaps even now, as we tread the brink of destruction from without and from within, we are nearing the threshold of a world more beautiful than we can imagine. The way will not be smooth. It may even be rougher than it has been—more demonstrations, more violence, more crime in the streets, more of the young copping out of society even to the point of forming a counter culture. We may experience more of these centrifugal forces that divide and separate. Only then may the way be opened for counter forces to begin—the cohesive forces of fusion that could start men on an upward spiral once more. Is it possible that no unification is possible until separation has reached its greatest extreme?

It was a rare sunny September afternoon in New York. Along Fifth Avenue, the very heartland of the Establishment, flowed citizens in full finery. A figure on a distant corner held a sheaf of oversize magazines. As I approached, I made the figure out to be a hippie-type character with a nondescript face, wearing faded dungarees, a shawl, and beads. From the cover of the slim magazine the inquiring eyes of a little girl looked into mine and I stopped. The name of the publication was intriguing: *American Avatar,* Summer, 1969. I paid a dollar for a copy, turned away, then turned back. "Are you by any chance on the staff of the magazine?" The face was no longer nondescript, as its owner—a girl—replied, "Yes, I'm one of the writers. We feel we should do more than just write,

so we come to the people and talk with them, people of all
ages. We *try* to talk with them. It's so hard to talk with the
older people sometimes."

"Like me?"

"Well, you seem to be a little different."

"Thank you." After learning her group was based in Boston
and wishing them luck in their publishing venture, I sought a
cup of coffee and a chance to look over my purchase.

In the lead article, "No Solution to Revolution," Wayne
Hansen, twenty-four-year-old managing editor and a Harvard
dropout, pointed out that the generation which created the hy-
drogen bomb is fixed in its way of life, in its conceptuali-
zation, in its language. These people cannot change. He freely
admitted that the depression forced the parent generation into
purely material concerns, and that the material development
they created has allowed their children freedom from these
limitations. But their sons and daughters are a whole new
race: They seek self-expression rather than security. As yet,
the children have no language of their own; they are still
trying to use the external language of their fathers. Because it
is only an external language—not the inner language of
communication—they will never change the parent through
it. The new language, the new form of self-expression of the
young, will be created as a result of opposition of their parents to the reality of their new life style.

Perhaps the young alone, prescient in their freshness, can
formulate what may well be a significant "law of human progress" and here I'd like to quote Mr. Hansen directly:

> Every forward step of humanity was impossible before it hap-
> pened. All that we know is that through separation and opposi-
> tion a new language, a new way of life evolves which is limited
> only by the extremities of the two opposing forces. *To produce
> the greatest possible creation, therefore, we must first produce
> the greatest possible separation.* [Italics added.]

We are now in the midst of a world-wide period of upheaval and oppression. To a sensitive idealist it is a time of such universal agony, he must pledge his total understanding to alleviate it. Seeing the mistakes of the past and hoping for an early solution to end the bloodshed of a Vietnam, the hopelessness of a ghetto existence, and the inner emptiness of an affluent society, he has no choice but to align himself with any movement toward change. The conservative pragmatist sees only the destruction of his values and his society, the hard-earned results of his own years of discipline, sacrifice, and self-denial, being threatened by irresponsible forces which can offer no concrete plan of what they will achieve. In the center of this opposition, men are being forced to align themselves with ideas, positions, and actions beyond the scope of their own personal desires.

With these forces separating further and further every day, with men being continually thrown back upon themselves and forced into acting from the depths of what they hold most dear, the time is coming when every individual will be absolutely real, when words and concepts will be unable to mask ulterior motive, when everything will be reduced to exactly what it is, and only then will there be room on earth for entire and true creation.

I have listened again and again to the actual voices of some of the 1,000 people I have interviewed on tape. I have listened especially to the young, trying to hear what their voice inflections, their real feelings, said to my inner being—how our values really compared. Are we really so far apart? I believe the young are saying, "Yes, we have dreams of a better world, and we want a chance to do something about them— and we want your help. After all, these are *your* dreams!" So why do we resist the new generation to the point of turning them off and severing communication, at times to the point of inciting their violence?

Actually, the younger generation and the older need each other, and in my interviews I have found they deeply want each other. Youth with its blind spots, without enough experience to see the kinds of compromises needed if man is to live with man, wants a fill-in from those who have learned the value of a certain amount of oil to keep the machinery running. Youth needs to have to sweat and compromise a little. We older, on the other hand, need the fresh ideas and approaches to problems—to living itself—that can come only from those whose perceptions have not yet been dulled by the abrasive forces of a high-tension society. Establishment adults need actively to seek ways of letting the young—black and white—in on the game of life. The young today have the same need to experience "the real thing" as their forebears did in pioneering days, when by the early or mid-teens one was able to ride, shoot, farm, and otherwise play for keeps. The youth of the old days could not complain his life was irrelevant, meaningless, or useless. He had a piece of the action, and he knew it. We've taken all this away. Now, we are saying to youth, you must stay in school until your early or mid-twenties, "preparing" for action. Consigned as they are to this pseudo-life for so long, is it any wonder our youth are exploding? Do we think that because we now provide higher education for so many, their red corpuscles have dried up?

Contrary to what is becoming a stereotype of the young—the hippie cartoon character—youth wants to work. But because youth jobs are so hard to find, too often they can't work when they want to. Union pressures don't help either. It's bad for white youth. It's worse for blacks. A survey by the Bureau of Labor Statistics in spring, 1969, found that one out of seven white teenagers in the nation's largest metropolitan poverty area was idle. For blacks of the same age, it was one out of three.

What is needed is a new concept blending working and schooling so that the youth can feel himself playing a needed part in the main stream of society instead of being kept waiting hungrily in the wings while the drama of society passes him by. Motivation? In a study program geared to work, the student doesn't ask, "Why do I have to learn 'this' or 'that'?" He knows why, because he uses his learning to get on with the job. Motivation is built in. Why are there only a handful of such programs? Why are we forcing so many young people into a counter culture that feeds on disillusionment and drugs? Why do we continue to produce a turned-off generation that could be turning on with meaningful work-connected schooling?

The young vary in their wants as they vary in their mental and physical capacities to interact with the environment. Some merely want a job to gain some degree of economic independence. They will accept, even prefer, the kind of repetitive work now becoming extinct through automation. I recall interviewing a fifty-four-year-old Chicago elevator operator, who had started at the age of twenty-one in the same building. Nearly thirty-three years later he was about to be replaced by a robot. Where are jobs like this for people like that now?

Many of the young want more variety in their work. Some thrive only on a continuous daily challenge. Now think about this: With libraries full of studies of human behavior—psychology, sociology, anthropology, political science, and so forth—can it be that we really don't know how to arrange a society so that most people are doing the kinds of things they do best, contributing to each other the kinds of things they need, as individuals and as members of society? Even primitive tribes manage to do that! With their experiments in communal living, the young are turning their backs on conventional economic theory and the Puritan work ethic and turning to primitive models for more of what they want. For one thing, they're finding a way to take responsibility for their own lives. For another, they are relating to each other on the basis of respect for what each person is as well as for the unique thing he may contribute to the life style of the commune. As a leader of one commune group in Boston told me, "We didn't start with a structure. We just started living together because we liked each other. We have worked out what you might call rules and structures as we found the need to. We've been going two years and now there are eighty of us. We expect to continue to change as we go along. We can't be static like society out there."

In Las Vegas the game is rigged. The house is going to win. If you play enough times, you're bound to lose. But we play roulette or blackjack or craps for fun—win, lose, or draw. But suppose you were playing the game of life knowing that the more you played the more you would lose? And suppose the game wasn't fun either? That's much the way the young feel about the game we've got going. No win and no fun. Is it any wonder so many of them are simply saying, "Deal me out. I'll take less of the material accouterments of life as long as I have a chance to do my own thing." Perhaps not too strangely, in our secret longing to break out of the strait jacket we've so carefully laced ourselves in, more and more of society at large is picking up on the ethic of "doing your own thing." Look at clothes. Many of us have finally gotten up the courage to be a little more colorful and casual in our dress, even in business! Beards and long hair are now not so much protest as the "in" look. Today's fashion advertising shows Madame in the most glamorous of Establishment environments, wearing what would have been sneered at as a "hippie costume" only yesterday! Perhaps there is hope for all of us.

What do they want—the young, the now generation? They want to get in on adult life and privileges at an earlier age than ever before, and they are, indeed, more ready for it today than any previous generation. But they have to do it the way they see it. Moreover, they want less hypocrisy on the part of their elders. The matter of hypocrisy was raised by a young panel member at a recent conference on "Finding Meaning in the Generation Gap." Another panelist, the celebrated anthropologist Margaret Mead, answered, "Hypocrisy is not all bad. It takes a little hypocrisy to oil the wheels of civilization." Whereupon a tow-headed youngster of sixteen stood up in the audience to reply, "Well, a little hypocrisy may be all right—if you older folks would just let us younger folks in on some of it."

As to the question of "What Do They Want?" an editorial statement by Mel Lyman, editor-in-chief of the *American Avatar,* answers the question in much the same way as the most thoughtful of the hundreds of young people I have talked with all over the United States. Perhaps it not only speaks for the young but also to the question "What do *we* really want?"

The "Establishment" in this country is the most lenient establishment in the world. But still it needs changing. The revolutionaries in this country are the most demanding people in the world, but they are a product of this country. Only in this country could such a wondrous revolution take place. Everybody's right and everybody's wrong and somehow everybody seems to want the same thing. This revolution is the test and the fruition of true democracy, of the people, by the people, for the people. There is spirit in the air again, and without a world war yet! That is encouraging. We are not uniting against an alien power, we are uniting against each OTHER! Not even North against South this time, even that won't work any more, we are virtually eliminating geographical warfare, we are fighting man against man, we are fighting for something bombs can't buy, we are fighting for LIFE! America is getting stale, we are fighting for LIFE!

CHAPTER 6

BLACK-WHITE OR YOUNG-OLD GAP?

Never before have so many young doubted the values of their elders—and said so. And the doubting is not confined just to student militants. A sixteen-year-old Washington, D.C., high school senior girl puts it bluntly:

> Well, this generation has been taught, you know, that there shouldn't be any phonies or anything, and then suddenly you find that the whole, everything is phony, I mean adults are phony. They say one thing and they mean another and they say that America's the greatest country, you know, and here we have all these problems between races and they, they don't listen to you and, and I guess that's why, you know, you just get frustrated, and I guess it's come out more in this generation 'cause there's been a sort of loss of interest in, in money, you know, and before this, in the fifties, they were always interested in money and getting ahead, and now we're ahead and we're supposed to be at the peak, you know, affluence and everything, but you know, really we're just as bad as we were when we started, it seems, because everything is phony and the world's all a mess. I, I guess that's why we're revolting so.

At the other end of the country, in Carmel, California, another high school senior girl reacts to Question 10: "Why is it all happening?" She was not too coherent—not because she lacked intelligence, but rather because the question struck something deep within her eighteen-year-old psyche. Her finger found the on-button of the tape recorder. Her pale face, without a trace of cosmetic, was trance-like as she answered:

> The rebellion against the home, against the adults—I think kids are beginning to realize that life is not based around money, around the materialistic objects. That life is the beauty around you and the physical and the spiritual-type things, that it's not so much a present from somebody. It seems that kids today have a feeling that instead of let's say a gift, a very warm hug would be just as meaningful. I think kids are rebelling against the materialistic society which our parents stand for. And about the race riots and all, I just think that it's time that we, instead of sitting around, that we do something instead of just sitting back. And kids want and they will get, and it's very hard to say, like nonviolent and so on, I think that you'll even find like with Martin Luther King's death that the kids mourned his death, but it's not so much that what he stood for was peace and getting it peacefully, and if you have to you will take. That's the answer that we want, and we will not sit back, we will take. And I don't mean that in a violent-type way, but we'll get it.

*   *   *

I would not have expected to find this kind of thinking in the setting in which I interviewed him—in the backwash of the digs of near-hippie Harvard militants. But then I am over thirty. Question 10, you will recall, focuses on our present age of contention and controversy in which the black-white and young-old gaps seem to be widening, asking, "Why do you think this is happening?"

> This is one I could talk a long time on. This is—it's been said that there has been a generation gap which has always

existed and that the liberal tendencies in the young gradu-
ally become conservative tendencies and the children's
children are in the same position that their fathers had been
in. I don't think this is necessarily true. I think there is reason
to think that a steady progress is being made of a kind. I
think that the generation of parents today are the generation of the depression. They had as a generation an over-
riding goal which was that their children should want
nothing. And that, the largest part, as a whole they accomplished this goal. They did so by sacrificing certain
things to expediency, to what they would call realities,
while on the other hand continuing to voice the ideal of
thou shalt not kill, brotherhood of man, equality of man,
and so on. That the children are by virtue of their success
materially uninterested in material success and have learned
those things which their parents taught them to believe,
they're now believing them fully and completely. Their
parents are in the position of either admitting that they
themselves have made compromises that were unnecessary,
compromises which could have been avoided, in their
principles, or they're forced to believe that those compromises must be made in order to accommodate the world.
They must believe that the youthful idealism of their children has to be dissipated if they are to exist. Children believe
they can change the world so that idealism can be worked
out in fact. And if this proves to be true, then those parents
who have spent their lives pursuing what in their own
terms are lesser, more earthly goals, will have been in a
sense rebuked by the lives that their children lead. I think
that this is a real problem, that by living closer to the
ideas which have been voiced in America for years, the
children in a sense challenge what their parents have
found it necessary to do—necessary to buy a second
car and television and so on rather than spend their lives
concerned with the inequalities and injustices in this country. I think, therefore, there is a real possibility that this
generation of young people will grow up continuing to be

concerned with justice and equality, that their children will be taught these things but will feel as great a gap, and that a real change in society will exist. That the parents—the young children of today—can be much more permissive parents because they will have lived closer to what they will teach their children in the schools and in the home, and therefore can allow the children more freedom of decision and so on. This may be idealistic, but I think there are some signs that it's not simply a recurrent cycle.

There is unquestionably a generation gap in the white population. Is there a similar lack of communication and common purpose between black youth and their elders? In the recent past there has been. Today, however, more and more black adults, even those who have "made it" to middle-class economic standards, are beginning to move away from their don't-upset-the-applecart attitude toward tacit support, if not outright encouragement, of their young along activist lines. A forty-five-year-old black attorney in San Francisco, with an LL.B from the University of Wisconsin, invited my wife and me to his home. After some informal conversation in the living room with his wife and two sons, Mr. H———— and I retired to the dining room for our formal interview. On the question of dissent between the races and between generations he had strong feelings.

Let me say that I don't believe this is just beginning to happen. I believe it's been coming a long time and we laughed about it behind our backs when blacks were trying to get a better deal through legal means. We were offered some piecemeal handouts to tide us over. These long-haired kids that we now call hippies are derivatives of something that we used to call the beatniks who used to tell us that society wasn't meeting their needs. We used to laugh at the beatniks.

These college kids who're having the sit-ins and rebelling
against their administrations are the same kids, or are hand-
downs from the kids who used to do the panty raids somewhere getting their frustrations off. We didn't see these things
when they were happening. The only time society really no-
tices something is when there is a direct confrontation.
Today there is a direct confrontation. The young have realized this fact, whether we like to admit it or not, they realize that the only thing we older people will look at and understand is some kind of conflict. So they decided to bring
it to us right where it's at, as they like to say it. And this is
what is happening today. This isn't something new. These
people have been asking for changes for a long time and we
refused. We've refused and we've refused and laughed and
said, "Oh, these are just youngsters. They'll grow out of it."
But in this day and time, when people are getting more—
there was a time when they were asking and they had to
worry about security, but there are so many people with so
much security today that there isn't that big worry about security as there was before. Today people are more worried
about human rights and this is the reason it is coming into
the open now. The problem has always been there. It isn't a
new problem. They've been asking for changes. They've
been asking for the right to do their thing for a long time.
Now they're going to get it, whether we want them to have
it or not. I think they have a little more guts than we did,
that's all. And I'm glad they have, really.

Later, interviewing his sixteen-year-old high school senior
son, I found an attitude of defiance mixed with resignation
that seemed more concerned with the hypocrisy of the older
generation than with black-white relationships.

Well, the black people want to be free, and they feel that
they're not free, and they're not in the South where there's
lynchings all the time, and, well, people—they just aren't
free and they want to be. It's not just the blacks, it's many
people, and I—the kids these days, they want to change,

but I feel that it will never change. It will always be the same, as long as our parents are teaching us this way and we'll be teaching our kids the same thing when we get old, too. We fit into school and it teaches us the history of war-like people and all, and the government sends us to Vietnam to shoot up and kill people whereas in our churches they teach us thou shalt not kill and thou shall love thy neighbor, but still we go—they send us to Vietnam and we kill and kill.

A black high school principal in Washington, D.C., after extending me the courtesy of interviewing a number of his nearly all-black student body, granted me a personal interview. He came to the counseling office where I had been assigned working space for the day. Sitting down, he waved a hand apologetically at the broken windowpane that had been letting in a bit too much of the outdoor air to compete with the heating system. "Sorry about that; guess it happened last night. We get around to them as fast as we can. Even these bars don't do much good. But it's a part of what's happening."

"Why is it happening?"

I feel that this is happening as a result of slow, very slow change, and also due to the lack of adequate communication. I also think it is a stage of development where people in their search for change, in their search for a variety of things, are moving and searching and often pushing in an effort to become involved, to become included, and so become accepted in a way that they will get a better life, not only for themselves, their unborn children, but to participate more fully in what they feel is rightfully theirs. Now, I want to be on your record to cite that there are individuals that are going to an extreme with this, individuals that often do more harm than good, individuals that are not

truly dedicated to change—positive change. I think that
these people are extremists and should be identified as
extremists. But there are those that are speaking out and
are acting out in a variety of ways to simply say to the entire system that we have not been heard, we have not been
considered, and we are attempting to speak now in a variety of ways that are not always condoned, that are not always acceptable, but it is a means of communication, and I
sincerely hope as an educator with a great deal of faith and
belief in people and hope for a better tomorrow, that
through these sit-ins, demonstrations, through these efforts
that are made often to the extreme, that out of it all will
come a better world and a better tomorrow for young and
for old to live, work, and re-create together, for the sake of
not only ourselves, our unborn children, but for our own
salvation as Christian men and women.

A number of other responsible black people, like this
school principal, decry the violence on one hand yet on the
other believe that direct physical confrontation is too often the
only thing that will get the black man within speaking distance of the power structure. His words came out fervently,
almost like a prayer, but his attitude of quiet conviction left
no doubt as to where he stood and where he would have to
stand if the chips were down. As the interview ended, I re-
called the somewhat less prayerful attitude of a twenty-six-
year-old Oakland, California, black militant. While not himself
a Black Panther, he was sympathetic to many of their actions.
I had asked him, "How can we do more talking and less
shooting?"

That would be great. It would be great to sit down and
talk, but generally I find that the power structure don't
want it like that; they're not ready to give in.

The Washington high school principal introduced me to his
head guidance counselor, a delightful fifty-year-old black

woman. At the end of our interview I asked, "Is there a generation gap among people of your race?" There was, she
thought, then began musing over the "why."

> I'm not sure I know why it's happening now. I've often
> wondered why it hasn't happened before. I think maybe it
> might have started partially from a racial point of view,
> with the Negro children who, in the society in which they
> have lived, have been subordinated so much and have
> wanted to revolt and could not—have not revolted. Their
> parents haven't, and they look at their parents and say,
> "How can you take this?" This is a part of their feeling that
> "I would revolt against anything that I don't like." So they
> begin to revolt or to fight back at society, just like they
> want to fight back at anything that they were not happy
> about, and then others have joined in with them until now I
> don't think that it's racial at all. I think it's just a general
> revolting among the younger generation about anything—
> about the courses, about how long they have to go to class,
> about the rules and regulations, about how they have to
> dress.

Julia, a black seventeen-year-old senior in the same school,
doesn't quite agree. It's much more than courses and rules and
regulations. There is little question in her mind that today is a
different world from that of her elders and requires different
response on the part of the black people—and young blacks
are willing to give that response.

> I think young people today are getting more and more
> away from the idea of everything your parents says is right.
> And they want to be different from their parents because,
> well, I think all along people have criticized their parents.
> You might feel that they think they're right, but you don't
> necessarily agree with them, and many people today just
> don't think that you have to agree with them. And so this is
> why the long hair comes out—because you want to be dif-
> ferent from your parents. And the riots came, I think, when

a race of people were united, or just kept getting closer together and started instilling pride, but it was mostly the
unity, because I'm sure a lot of the parents disapproved of
the people going out, the teenagers going out and looting
and acting like this. But it was something from within the
teenager, something that the parents don't have because the
parents haven't been brought up in the same surrounding or
environment, the same situation we live in, and we just feel
that you can't live in the situation today with the same
ideas or customs that your parents used in about the last
decade.

Another seventeen-year-old said simply:

I think this is happening because times are changing now
and people are changing and the older people aren't ready
to change with the ideas.

To get at the very crux of the likenesses and differences in
the generation gaps in the white and black populations, I
sought many viewpoints—North, South, East, and West—
among both races. "Are the young whites protesting for the
same reasons as the young blacks?" I asked an eighteen-year-
old Brent, Alabama, Negro coed in her first year of Alabama
A. and M. College.

There might be some similarities, but the basic reason I
don't think is the same. Most black students' rioting and
demonstrating is because they have been denied the right of
civil rights, human rights, they have not been allowed to
really be a human being, but something less than a human
being. OK, the white students and their rioting—their rioting and demonstration is more a protest against their elders.

I asked a seventeen-year-old black youth in Columbia, Tennessee, about to enter college in the fall this question: "Do
both black and white young people who are rebelling want the
same thing?"

I really don't believe they want the same thing. I think the
black people want to be respected. I think they want more
—they're trying to look for better opportunities. The hippies or whatever, I really don't know what their philosophy
is.

To the same question an eighteen-year-old New Bern,
North Carolina, black youth, a freshman at North Carolina
A. and T. whose father was a brick mason, put it this way:

Well, so far as the white demonstrations, I think the white
youth of this country, I think they're mainly demonstrating
because they're fed up with this society and they are trying
to advocate a change. And the black, their main rebellion
is centered in the fact that they're not included in this society.

After attending the Sunday-morning services with the
mixed black and white congregation of her church, I interviewed the lay minister in charge of this Presbyterian experiment in San Francisco, a forty-nine-year-old black woman
with three children of her own. She had a way of putting
things simply:

I sometimes think there is quite a bit of unity between the
black and the youth because they don't have the same generation gap as the white and the youth because they are in
about the same place. You see the black people, they didn't
know anything, they didn't have anything, and they've
never been anywhere, they've never done anything, so they
don't have this unlearning. All we learn now is new, because we never knew anything before. We've never been in
that society, and that's one of the differences between, say,
the white youth—they're dropping out. We want to drop in.

A nineteen-year-old black college freshman attending Florida A. and M. University gave this variation on the black-
white generation gap happening:

The hippies, as they are called, they're trying to get away from the old structure of society and they want to be individual and do what they want. And the black community, they're trying to become a separate part and not just be something that's thrown in society as—I don't know what you might call it, but just something that's just there—not separate and not recognized.

"Do you mean there should be a separate black community?" I asked.

No, I don't think there should be a separate black community, but I think they should be allowed to mingle as they please and to be recognized in government and business.

Moving northward, I talked with a nineteen-year-old black youth majoring in economics at Lincoln University in Pennsylvania. His father is a janitor and his mother does housecleaning.

First of all, when you say recent riots, one thing, well, I'm a black student and so I'm thinking in a sense as a group. Black people, at one time we were down. Black people—well, we went along with things as they were. But a few people, say the late Martin Luther King, had an idea that things could be better. First it was just him that started out with Freedom Rides and things like this, but now it's getting bigger and bigger. And people—I think it would take time, but people just can't see this. They can't understand why, if we're citizens of the United States, we cannot have the rights now. I think this is why riots come about. People are just tired of living this way now that they believe that things could be better.

A public relations director of a thriving Arkansas business, white, age sixty, and school board member for eighteen years, sees things a little differently. When asked to compare the white and black generation gaps, he dwelt simply on the black-white chasm.

I think the basic cause of our riots was—the government's at fault. They have convinced the Negro that he has been mistreated so bad, and I will grant you that I feel like he has been mistreated. But it's a structure that's been going on for 100 years and we can't change it overnight. I think it's an educational program that will take time to grow into it. I think we'll finally get it fairly well settled, but the— they have convinced them that they have been mistreated so bad and I've heard some of our big officials say that they don't blame them for getting out and rioting. As long as they know they're not going to get in trouble for doing it, they're going to do it.

His solution to the problem echoed that of many of the Deep South Establishment.

And I'll say this, that I think in the end the South will solve the race question to the satisfaction of the nigger much better than they will in the North. One thing, it's because I think we understand them better. We have lived with 'em. We called ourselves segregated, and yet in the South you'd find them living in—both families in the same block, and it's always been that way in my lifetime. Now, we didn't go to school with 'em and we didn't go to church with 'em, and we didn't invite 'em to eat with us, but we were with 'em a lot, we worked 'em all the time, and we were with them, and so I think basically we understood 'em. Now, I do think that the nigger has begun to hate the white race much more than they have in their life. But I believe that we'll end up curing that.

When an immovable object meets an irresistible force, what then? Contrast the above entrenched representative of much of the Solid South body politic with this young, black coed sociology major at A. and T. State University of North Carolina. Her mother is a maid in the Greensboro city school system. During our informal talk following the interview, I asked her: "Do you think the protest of the white college student is the same as the protest of the black of similar age?"

Basically, yes, perhaps, in that both have been denied a
chance to fulfill themselves as they see it. And I think that's
where it ends. Because your college students are protesting
a traditional way of life. They want reforms, you know.
And we black people want a complete change because we
feel that reforms are not going to get it. I think that the college protest movement is asking basically for reforms
within the institution. They might be radical reforms, but
they don't want to completely throw away the institution of
education; they want reforms within the educational institution to make it better. As black people, we feel that it
might be necessary to do away with several institutions because they have not fulfilled their promises.

She went on to speak of political parties and labor unions.
She was more than aware of the efforts by labor unions in the
skilled trades to keep blacks out of their ranks, "to keep the
good jobs for the white man." She was familiar with the case
of Anderson L. Dobbins, who had tried for four years to get
into the electricians' union in Cincinnati. Finally a federal
judge found this black man as well if not better qualified to
engage in his trade than most of the union's white members.
Sometime later, preparing to interview union leaders and
rank-and-file members of various trades, in Pittsburgh, I
found that nationally Negroes hold only 2 per cent of the
800,000 best-paying construction jobs and a mere 7.2 per
cent of all 2,900,000 building crafts jobs. In Pittsburgh, the
Mayor's Commission on Human Relations found that blacks
made up 49 per cent of the laborers' unions of the city while
Negro membership in most of the other Pittsburgh building
unions was less than 2 per cent. In 1968 the government
"jawboned" the eighteen major AFL–CIO construction unions to agree to take "affirmative action" to find and admit
more qualified blacks to membership. During my interviews
with both union leaders and members I found those in the
construction trades tended to sweep black unrest under the

rug as mainly Communist inspired. In September, 1969, tired of "talk, talk, talk," angry crowds of blacks marched through Pittsburgh attacking white workers on construction sites with bricks, stones, and bottles. In the scuffles that followed, police arrested more than 200 in a scene that introduced a new tactic—demonstrators and police spraying each other with Mace. Shortly thereafter black leadership announced plans to force work stoppages on millions of dollars' worth of construction work throughout the nation until unions do indeed take the promised "affirmative action." Meanwhile, building costs soar as a "shortage" of skilled construction workers forces up wages. How long can the institution of the labor union continue if it perists in ignoring social realities? The younger generation of both black and white is becoming more and more concerned about refurbishing or replacing institutions that are not showing themselves flexible enough to meet changing human needs.

During the course of many interviews with young white militants the cause of the black people came out as a major concern. Here an SDS member sets forth dramatically the radicals' position:

> Many of us are concerned about the black liberation movement. We feel that this country cannot claim to be the country of liberty and justice when for 300 years a minority group has been enslaved. In the twentieth century, beside genocide there is psychological murder, and I believe that the United States has performed psychological murder and castration upon 20 million people.

"Do you think that the college students are expressing themselves for the same reasons that the blacks are expressing themselves?"

> Perhaps. I think there is some connection, but there are also some differences. Some white radicals find it difficult to relate to black movements because the black movements,

the black liberation movements, believe that the white radicals or activists are not really serious, that they don't have a
basic stake involved in what is going on. The people in the
black liberation movement are extremely militant and are
very, very serious and committed because they're fighting
for their lives. The idea—which the Black Panthers use—
of a colony, they're fighting against the mother country—I
think is a very correct analogy. These people, in a sense,
are really fighting for liberation. And this fight for liberation brings them into direct conflict with the system, with
the power structure.

And a feeling for what underlies black militancy is not confined to militant whites nor to hippie types. This California
small-town high school senior said:

> But most of these demonstrations and things like this are
> caused by the black militants and the people, the black peo-
> ple, that really don't know anything else to do but fight, but
> cause trouble. I mean, they can have demonstrations and
> they can be peaceful and they can say what they want to
> say and do what they want to do. But unless they fight and
> cause a lot of trouble and cause a lot of damage, none of
> the white people are going to do anything about it. I mean,
> they're going to say, "Well, they're going to be peaceful and
> they're going to talk and they're going to talk about all this
> stuff, well, we'll just let them talk. We won't do anything
> about it." And then the black people get upset about it,
> they get mad and they figure, "Well, we'll fight. Maybe we'll
> get some action that way."

Of course there were those who simply reflected the traditional atmosphere which they have breathed. This high school
senior girl in an adjoining small coastal town—white, seventeen, and daughter of a famous country club golf pro—
shrugged:

> The riots—I don't understand them myself. I've tried. I
> can't understand why the Negroes do do these things like in
> Watts or back in New Jersey. I just don't understand.

A former deputy director of the Community Action Program of the Office of Economic Opportunity, the man who sat beside me addressing the tape recorder, had just come from his charge in Chicago. He was deeply involved in a project in that city's all-Negro South Side. His concept of his role as director of the program was to "get out there and get with it." As a result, this thirty-two-year-old white man had established a vital empathy with blacks in all walks of life—from ghetto to middle-class residents. He was full of their feelings as he talked with me, following our formal interview.

For the Negro child, the cultural heritage that he inherits at birth, by definition, denies his individualism. His heritage of slavery, his heritage of welfare, his heritage of poverty, his heritage of always having someone make decisions for him. The Negro in the ghetto is always having someone make decisions for him. The social worker and the welfare department, the school counselor, the guidance counselor, the truant officer, the teacher, the principal, the policeman on the beat—someone is always making decisions for him. Very, very seldom is he ever consulted about what he thinks. As a matter of fact, I've met many, many kids who don't even have a concept that they're entitled to think anything about their future, literally that.

A highly placed white official in the Detroit Skills Center, located in a former U.S. Tank Arsenal in that city, told me:

Many people who were not aware, really, of what it was like on the other side of the fence then began to see, you know, actually things happening. And even within the Negro community I heard the other day that one of the real resentments about the whole area, about the pot boiling and things exploding and so forth, has been the resentment on the part of many Negroes that in this country we would have to resort to legislation to do this. I mean, there would be a feeling that this was the right thing, why do we have to have legislation when really in the essence, when you look

at it in a calm, cool light of everything, why do you have to
have legislation to give some rights to people who are people, because their skin was not the same as the majority?

We often credit the young with more than average intelligence today, but this young black woman of Fort Lauderdale,
about to enter college to study speech therapy, shows not only
remarkable insight into her own race, but deep compassion
for the white man.

People need to see that white people and black people can
live together, can get along, and it's going to take a lot of
strength on the part of the whites as well as the blacks to
bring this about. Most people say it's going to take a lot of
patience on the part of the black person. I think it's different. I think it's going to take much more patience for the
white person. The reason I say that is because the white
person can't really understand how we feel—they haven't
been through what we've been through. They really don't
know. They can imagine, but you just can't imagine it.
There's no way possible.

A New Orleans black woman holds that prejudice is a
two-edged sword, especially in the hands of the older generation:

There's a lot of prejudice in the black race, and that's why I
can't—I have great fights with colored people because of
this thing. They say no white man should be prejudiced, yet
there is so much prejudice and spite there. It's too contra-
dictory. White people would say, "Colored people are nice
but would you want your daughter to marry one?" Colored
people will say, "White people are all right, but would you
want your daughter to marry one?" It's the very same
thing, exactly the same. People aren't that different.

If parents would stay out of it, everything would be all
right, says this twenty-year-old LaFayette, Alabama, Negro.
He speaks not only from a background of a recent B.A. degree in sociology, but as an instructor in the Upward Bound

program for black underprivileged youth. "Do you think we have a more serious gap between old and young or black and white?" I asked him.

I would tend to think that the worst problem is between the young and old. Because you can take two young people, you can take a black kid that's fifteen years old and you can take a white kid. No, I take that back. You can take a black kid, I'd say nine years old, and take a white kid nine years old and you can put them together and they'll play together beautifully. They'll go to school beautifully. As long as their parents have not tried to instill this hatred within them, this is the main thing. This is the trouble with the white race. The parents get involved in everything. If they would just stay out of it, everything would work out beautiful.

A sixteen-year-old black youth in Harlan, Kentucky, echoes the same idea. I talked with him on the steps of the town library.

I believe this is not all the kids' fault. It's mainly the parents. Say the white people, they bring their kids up that a Negro kid is something bad, and that it's wrong to associate with 'em. And the Negro parents, they bring their kids up that they want to try to help them to do better and so there's the conflict right there. The Negro kid is striving to do better, and some—not all, now—but some of the white kids are trying to lure them down, so there's the conflict and that's why they have riots and stuff like that. Me and my friends, white and colored alike, we get together real good.

I asked a white man of fifty about the black-white-generation gap. He was a school textbook publisher's representative and traveled widely in the South-central part of the United States. He seemed most concerned with the black-white problem:

Marches, demonstrations, even riots? Why are we having this sort of thing? Well, I think we've tried to legislate something that is very, is a very difficult thing to do. We're legislating something that people are reacting to emotionally and we're working at it from the wrong angle. For instance, the race prejudice is an automatic thing with a white person even though he may intellectually recognize the equality of all men, the rights of every human being, but there are little things that he's grown up with, such as little white lies. "That's a dirty black story you told. Black is dirty, white is good." It's an almost automatic reaction. It's a sort of conditioned reaction to black. That is, within the core of his emotions that the—that he has not been trained to react to a black person, but the color black is part of his conditioned reaction. How about devil's food cake and angel's food cake, white or black? Black suits for funerals, white suits for summer, for play, for joy; the bright, white cheerful room, a black, dark ugly room. These are things that a person grows up with all his life, and then suddenly he must recognize that here are human beings that are black and with as much rights as he has.

Will white attitudes change enough to prevent further violence by the black people?

I don't believe that there's going to be much that's going to prevent further violence. Now, I think that in time this will level off, but I don't think that it's going to be probably in our generation. I think that because of the frustration that the Negro is bound to feel, that he is going to react to frustration, and there are many areas of the country where he cannot help but feel frustrated because of the attitude of the white community toward the black. I think as this gains momentum we may find—although violence may not be in such great masses or great numbers—that it will probably become a—this reaction to frustration may become a sort of a way of life.

In Pittsburgh I had asked a forty-one-year-old Negro secretary of a building maintenance union his version of militancy among Negroes. When I asked a direct question about the black-white-generation gap, he turned darkly thoughtful and proceeded in measured words:

> The riots, the marches, the demonstrations as related to the generation gap? Personally, I feel this is part of the education process that our younger people have undergone which has been denied to some of the older people. The younger people realize that the freedoms that we speak about do not exist for everyone, and as a result we have demonstrations. As the people become more intelligent, or have more education, they will demonstrate until freedom is acquired by all. This country was built on demonstrations, peaceful and violent demonstrations, and until we have freedom for all, we do not have freedom for anyone.

It appears that while the generation gap among whites is widening, the gap among blacks may be narrowing. The Establishment now faces not only the growing militancy of the young white and the young black, but also a black race reinforced by a larger sense of community between its younger and older generations. Will it heed the message of this twenty-six-year-old black man interviewed in the Detroit Skills Center, who, in my opinion, sums up the way the young themselves feel. He had experienced the clutches of the law, had been "turned around," and was now in a training program that would not only complete his high school diploma but lift him from steel-mill laborer to the trade of tailoring. As editor of the Center's 1,500 students' newspaper, he was more than ordinarily in touch with the thoughts and ideas of those around him. He spoke quietly, reaching back through his relatively short but full life.

> I know how I viewed the riots, these marches and sit-ins, and I was in favor of all of them. Just why, it's not so much clear to myself, really. I know the way I felt when I heard Martin Luther King make his speech, and Malcolm X, and I felt that black people had been denied a chance for so long, deprived of an education to develop. And something

had to be done. It's been built up and held inside for so long that it just came out into a form of riots, marches, demonstrations. It was a group. Some wanted to riot, some wanted to march, they all had their own belief on what was the best way to go at building a recognition.

"This thing has gone so far in a certain direction, do you think it can go so far that the movement will begin to hurt itself?"

No, I don't believe so. If we were going to hurt ourselves' movement, I feel when Dr. King was killed, Kennedy was shot, Malcolm X was shot, then it would have been just about destroyed, if black people and concerned whites just felt that it wasn't worth it. And those that were opposed, I feel they would have took advantage of that.

"Do you think there has to be more violence before enough white people wake up?"

Hopefully, no. After enough violence, the problem is out in the open, and I don't see any further need for violence. If we consider ourselves intelligent people, as we say we are, then I feel that we will sit down and do something about these problems in the form of working in conjunction with each other.

"Is it in the hands of the young, black and white?"

Yes, I go along with you on that. This is one of the reasons why I admire these hippies with their long hair. I don't have any real great love for whites, the older whites. But the young ones, I feel that they are aware of the problem, and they're going to become in control of this power that their fathers have now. I feel through association with them and developing ourselves educationally with them, and especially those that have the leader ability, we're more able to understand each other by just a mutual conversation and our beliefs and our wants and our desires. They can understand. I feel once this here younger generation becomes in position to make changes and develop new ideas, it should be much better—a much better world.

CHAPTER 7

Sex and *SEX*

_____

Since our dialogue is on "schooling for what?" and our concern here is sex education, we might begin by asking a fundamental question: Sex for what? The word "sex" used to denote the anatomical differences between man and woman, but it has come to mean doing something with them. One could say now there is sex and SEX—sex for having babies and SEX for fun. That there may be just a little more to it may be seen in Desmond Morris' book *The Human Zoo*. In a chapter entitled "Sex and Super-Sex" Morris delineates ten different functional categories of sexual behavior, documenting each from observation and studies made of both the human and animal world. The categories can only be listed here, but I can assure you the full text makes eye-opening reading. They are: procreative sex, pair-formation sex, pair-maintenance sex, physiological sex, exploratory sex, self-rewarding sex, occupational sex, tranquillizing sex, commercial sex, and status sex.

The aim of Question 9 was to find out what a wide range of individuals of all ages and both sexes say in regard to sex education. The question was: "If you believe we should have sex education in the public schools, what kinds of things should be learned?" The tizzy into which the subject of sex education has sent parents and schools is reflected in the story going around of two youngsters taking their report cards home from school. One says, pointing to a mark on his card, "Gosh, will my mother be worried; I made an A in sex education!" Of the people I interviewed, the young want it, the older question it, some 10 per cent are against it, and about 3 per cent offered no opinion. Those against had an average age of thirty-four years. Half were located in the South, half in the North. More males than females took a dim view of sex education; older males took an even dimmer view. Among the protestors, approximately 60 per cent were Protestants, 25 per cent were Catholics, and 15 per cent Jewish or "other."

If there is to be sex education, what is to be learned and is school the place to have it? Approximately 42 per cent want sex taught mainly as a biological process for the purpose of procreation. Some would limit the study to merely learning the proper names of the organs! The farther one moves into rural areas—the Bible Belt—and among the older and less educated, the more one finds that sex education should be purely biological if it should be given at all. On the other side are the young crying for help in an age when sex assaults the eye and the ear from all sides, a condition the older of us did not have to live with. We do not really know how we would have reacted in our teens and early twenties if our normal youthful sexual curiosity and drive had been reinforced and amplified by the rampant commercialization of sex. Also, had we had sex education as a part of our schooling, we might not have today's prurient sex cluttering the media. In short, we of the adult generation now in power have brought on the need for sex education. The majority of those whom I interviewed are in favor of it in at least some form.

Are those who would withhold it practicing the keenest self-deception and the cruelest educational deprivation? Consider the remarks of the Rev. Arthur A. Froehlich, pastor of Maitland Bible Presbyterian Church announcing a speech by Edgar C. Bundy, executive secretary of the Church League of America at the Central Florida Rally of Bible-Believing Pastors, Parents and Young People in Orlando, Florida, January 11, 1970:

> On this occasion, Bundy will expose the subversive forces of the sexologists and sex pushers and tell what they are doing to our children in the public schools, in cooperation with the churches here in Florida and elsewhere. Stress will be made on the means we can utilize to counter this awesome tide of Godless materialism and gross immorality which is sweeping across the country, coming into the classroom, the church, and into the privacy of our very homes. A report will be given on the progress of the lawsuit against the Orange County School Board for exposing our children and youth to "sex pornography." Bundy has just come into possession of a most secret report on the progress and process by which the enemy is determined to enslave and capture our nation.[1]

In the interviews that follow three "conscientious objectors" to sex education give their reasons:

Sex in school? That's one thing I never learned in school in my life, anything about sex. It's what my parents told me, that's the only thing I know of. After, when I was up in the age where I was, just when I was ready to get married, they told me all about sex and all about love and everything else. But that would be out of the question to answer that one for schools. Because that's where they do a lot wrong. Learn about history, geography, and all that stuff in school instead of sex.
[A fifty-four-year-old, second-generation Italian janitor in Detroit.]

I don't know why we think that we have to have a big sexual education in school. I think a general knowledge. We have kittens that come to school, we see that they have babies. I know that when I was going to school we had no formal sex education. I don't think any of us suffered. I don't remember raping anybody in my life because I was confused. I think we're running into problems mainly because I don't know where you're going to draw a line and find out who's going to teach us sex education, how far you think you want to go. I can't personally think right now why I'd want anybody teaching my children sex education other than the general knowledge such as, sure we could show them a pregnant woman and explain that she's going to have a baby, and that they're going to have a little baby in their house. I'd have to know what you felt, or who felt we would need on sex education as such, where are we going to start, or where are we going to end on sex education? I think a general knowledge that we have boys and we have girls are fine, that they grow up and eventually the woman can have a baby. Maybe my knowledge is very weak on this.

Again I say we didn't suffer or seem to suffer when we were growing up and it wasn't because of our education at home. Who would be qualified to teach sex education? Certainly not a medical doctor who's more frustrated than most people in the world. Certainly not our teachers. I think we'd have to be awful careful with a sex-education program and keep it to a very limited field. I believe that if you intended to be, if you intend to become married or something then maybe we could go into something different. I think it's very poor.
[A thirty-two-year-old fireman in San Jose, California.]

I don't believe it should be taught in school. I think that it's something personal that shouldn't be brought out in public.
[A sixteen-year-old black eleventh grader (male) in Harlan, Kentucky.]

The Victorian outlook is no respecter of ages. If you *must* have sex education, keep it clean, keep it simple, and above all keep it away from SEX.

I believe in a very, very limited sex education. In fact, I'd say that I believe that sex education should go to the extent of what is already being taught in biology class and in psychology class. The new program that is now being started in the schools here I am against, and I think that only the bare basics of sex that can be taught in these two classes I mentioned should be the only parts in it.
[An eighteen-year-old high school senior (male) in the village of Ocoee, Florida.]

First, I must admit that I am still of the old school. I still feel that sex education should be taught by the proper individuals, the doctor, the religious leader, and perhaps the parent if he can bring himself to that. But certainly not by teachers who are not qualified. Also, this should not begin in kindergarten. It should begin, if at all, at about the sophomore or junior year in high school.
[A fifty-five-year-old manufacturing plant comptroller in Detroit.]

If it's going to be taught, they should teach the basic sex, because usually the kids who learn about it, their parents don't teach 'em, they get out on the streets and learn about it—and they should just teach the basic sex.
[A fifteen-year-old eleventh grader (male) in Baxter, Kentucky.]

Typical adult confusion and ambivalence over what should be taught in sex education are reflected in the response of this forty-four-year-old dean of a Bible college in California:

Sex education is always criticized from the standpoint of values, the teaching of values. Schools have been criticized on the one hand for teaching wrong values, on the other hand for having no values, and so it seems schools have become pretty gun-shy over the whole value business to the extent of saying that they don't teach values. Regardless what they say and what they do, values are being taught, even though they are not being taught overtly. I think sex education belongs in the schools, but it should be taught, I would think, on a purely biological basis. Furthermore, I think the schools and the churches need to work together as a team, the school go on teaching the purely biological and the other one bringing in the particular value structure that that particular church feels should be added to this aspect of education.

Contrast the dean's thinking with that of one of his nine-teen-year-old coeds:

I think that at the age of puberty boys and girls should be taught what is happening to their bodies, the capabilities that they have for reproducing life. They should be taught the actual mechanics of sexual intercourse because they have no other way to learn them. Children should be taught some of the deviations from normal sexual patterns such as lesbianism, homosexuality. Children should be taught that sexual deviation is more a disease than it is a crime or something like this.

Nor does the twenty-nine-year-old student body president at the same college see eye to eye with the dean.

I think the majority of young people are aware of the ana-tomical aspects of sex, although this should not be ignored in a complete sex education. I particularly would like to see stressed the individual psychology of the male and female living closely with each other. I think that the man and the woman should be aware of the subtle clues that if they were aware of and could accommodate then more radical symp-toms of maladjustment could be avoided.

Some of the young would like to get their sex information at home, but they have mixed feelings about parent capability and willingness.

It's very difficult for me to answer that question because I have two different ways of thinking about it. One is that I think that sex education should be taught in the home, not in school, for the simple reason that many people, rather

students, that would listen to it at school might take it lighter than they would if they had it coming from their own parents. And by learning it at home could be a disadvantage as well as an advantage, but I think learning it from the parents would be stronger than taking it lightly at school.
[A nineteen-year-old junior college student (female) in a small California town.]

I believe that this is one place where the school has taken over the responsibility of the home, and even if some homes, the majority of homes, are failing in this, I believe it's no business of the schools to try to take over this.
[An eighteen-year-old high school senior, son of a postal clerk, in a rural Southern town.]

Sex education is the responsibility of parents, but because our parents are not educated so often, the school has had to take over this area, because of the many disasters that have come because parents were never educated. Because the schools have to do this, they really have to teach everything to the child he needs to know because some parents don't tell their children anything.
[A nineteen-year-old college junior (female) from Santa Cruz, California.]

The gap between what some parents do and what they should do can lead to tragedy. Consider the following:

The parents don't tell their children because they just don't feel like they could—they're embarrassed by it. I think that children, when they're in high school, they should know all about it [sex]. One reason is because other kids are going to tell them. Say, for instance, a sub-freshman, an eighth grader, enters high school and a sophomore, a tenth grader, starts telling him all this stuff about dating and petting and sex relations with boys, this just gets a person, they just don't know what they're saying and they believe them. They say, I think I'll try it, you know. Well, they go try it,

say a girl will, and she'll get pregnant. She just didn't know what she was doing because she's gone out with an older boy and he's known all the rules and all the ways to talk her into it . . . they go out with a boy for the first time and he says, well, now here's a pill, you take this pill and nothing will happen. Well, it's been done, it was just an aspirin.
[An eighteen-year-old high school senior girl in Virginia.]

Those favoring sex education in the public schools (the majority) do so for a range of reasons as wide and varied as the individuals themselves.

Most thing is birth control. Yes, I think that you should be able to, you know, be able to control it without, you know, going all, you know.
[A twenty-five-year-old waitress in a roadside restaurant in Appalachia.]

Because of the increase in promiscuity nowadays, I feel that students at a young age in school, high school, should be taught about birth control. Most of them know about reproduction. I feel they should also be taught about venereal diseases which occur, from what I read, in quite a number of cases in high schools. This is pretty bad and it could be avoided with the proper education to the students.
[A twenty-three-year-old male marine biology major at Moss Landing, California.]

I think that we should have sex education taught in our school where we can better equip our youngsters when they have gone to the age that they will be matured, that they will know the things that they are getting into, druthern to take someone's word for it and get in trouble like most of them do.
[A forty-five-year-old man, black, in Pittsburgh, twenty-three years a janitor.]

Yes, I do believe they should have sex education in the schools for the simple reason that there has been a great

moral decline in our society over the past few decades. I
believe that sex education in the schools could help slow
this down and could possibly even almost bring it to a halt.
We really need sex education, because without it I believe
this world, or the United States will, like the great empires
of the past, fall through moral decay, from the inside, not
from outside sources.
[A seventeen-year-old boy, a high school senior in New
Port Richey, Florida.]

Well, I believe the unvarnished truth should be learned when
the children are real young, because they make such a myth
out of it and make it seem to be such a bad and immoral
thing that it causes more harm in the end than it caused
good. And children, when they are young, they young and
innocent and they tell the truth. I don't see why the truth
couldn't be told back to them about life.
[A fifty-seven-year-old black man learning building maintenance skills at McNamara Skills Center in Detroit.]

I think we should learn the basic biological organs and
structures, the physiological mechanisms, so to speak. In
addition to this, we should have some method of open expression by young people, among young people, open discussion. Whether or not this should take place in a sex-education class I don't know, but that would seem to be the
logical place. We shouldn't just talk about biology. We should
actually get into some of the attitudes and taboos that deal
with sex.
[A twenty-seven-year-old (male) coordinator of educational
experimentation in Apalachia.]

If we have sex education in the public schools, the kind of
things I think that should be learned are how one should
get along with the opposite sex decently and how they
should act in public and when they are alone. And I think
that both sexes should learn the opposite sex's body and the
things that we have to go through in birth and the process
of having children and stuff like that.

[A fifteen-year-old high school girl in a small Southern town.]

I'm not even sure I know what sex education means. I guess if it means biology, anatomical structure and reproductive process, I don't think It makes much difference whether it's learned in the school or not. It's learned somewhere, and wherever it's learned it probably has little relation to the real functions one is involved in in any meaningful sex act.
[A forty-year-old director of educational research programs in Pittsburgh.]

Of course I do believe in sex education in the schools, and we've had recent experience with that—providing a course in sex education which has been rather violently opposed by 10 to 15 per cent of the parents because they feel it has been an invasion of privacy. One of the greatest objections that they've raised against the course is the fact that it is too explicit. This seems to me to be an absurd criticism. A psychiatrist who prepared and delivered this course certainly convinced me beyond any doubt that in being explicit, in, for example, showing diagrams of the human anatomy, or drawings of the human anatomy rather than diagrammatic renderings of this, that you answered the child's question of what the size of the organ in question was in relation to the rest of the body and where it came on the body. A diagram doesn't do this. I'm also convinced that the child hasn't the prurient interest in these things that an adult has, that the greatest barrier to sex education is the fears of the adult, not the innocence of the child. So I believe that sex education should begin early in schooling. I think that it should become increasingly more sophisticated as you go up the grade levels, but I think by fifth or sixth grade it should be rather explicit and should not leave the child to go to his peers for answers that he wants to his questions.
[A forty-nine-year-old ETV (educational television) executive in San Francisco.]

I would think that a general program would not be too practical. I would think that there should be a different program for rural and urban areas, and I think these programs should be rather tailor-made to the type of environment children come from. I think a general sex education program would not be too practical.
[A forty-seven-year-old Big Sur, California, sculptor.]

Well, we do have sex education in the public schools, whether it's formal or greatly informal. The facts are pretty much open to most people. What I could hope would be learned would be some awareness of the place of one's body in the total personality development, and what its use or misuse can do to the rest of the personality. I don't know how to teach that. I don't know where to find teachers who have some sort of balanced conception of this. Perhaps factual information in the elementary and junior high schools, and then some chance of dealing with a human being who has lived somewhat and is not afraid of himself or others.
[A fifty-seven-year-old principal of an Oakland, California, experimental high school.]

The facts are that there are very few adults, either in or out of the teaching profession, who can stand up before a mixed group of adolescents—or even parents—and talk openly, clearly, and without embarrassment on sex, sexuality. I have found, however, that most educators are not only willing but anxious to work with parents in developing some form of sex education to relieve needless suffering on the part of all concerned. This teacher has a number of ideas worth exploring:

Certainly the biological information should be learned, but then most of that's already taught and all but the dullest student can make the translation from the biology of most of the animal kingdom. I think much more important so far as sex education is concerned is attitudes toward sex. What attitudes the students should have. And then, of course, you run into the old problem of, well, the community has an at-

titude, the church has an attitude, and so what most schools do is back off the problem entirely. Perhaps this could be solved by letting the students themselves discuss the various attitudes toward sex and draw their own conclusions, or letting various members of the community and parents come in and discuss this with the students. But certainly all the biological information can be learned very quickly. It's the attitudes that need to be changed, and I don't think many of us have the answers as to what these attitudes should be. I have answers for myself, personally, but I don't know that those are the answers for someone else, and I don't know that any parent would want to give my answers to his children.
[A thirty-six-year-old head (male) of a big city high school English department.]

I found a number of school administrators who were utter realists, like this one:

My basic philosophy is that you can't fight a problem by running away from it. If you're going to offer sex education in the schools today, there's only one way to handle it and that's to tell the truth. You've got to give the program as it is. For students when they start asking questions, or any child from three to four years old on up, when they ask questions they need to receive answers. I don't believe we can beat around the bush in giving these answers, or paint a flowery picture which isn't so. I believe in approaching it on the same tone or level that we would be if we were discussing what we're going to have for supper this evening. It's a normal process and therefore it ought to be taught as being a normal process. One of the biggest issues today is, do you teach just the bare facts of reproduction or do you bring the moral aspects into this, too? And I think that this is what some of the people in the nation are getting concerned about. But let's face it. Parents say, "We're doing this at home, this should be a home situation." But statistics will prove that this isn't being done in the home. Now they need to get it someplace, and if they don't get it at home

and they don't get it in the church, then where are they going to get it? I don't believe we can teach sex education without teaching some morals along with it.
[A thirty-two-year-old assistant principal (male) in the rural South.]

While not a parent, this young adult questioned the value of sex education, but not for the usual reason:

I really don't necessarily think they should have sex education in the public schools. I think it should be just out in the open. People shouldn't really try to hide sexual things. People tend to keep sexual things a secret. People make each other try to make people ashamed of sex. If you remove this idea of being ashamed of sex, then a person will be able to be more satisfied with sex and he would be able to identify with sex without running into any problems. So you wouldn't necessarily have to have it taught in schools on an intellectual level, you wouldn't have to be identified. That's the bad part. This comes back to this group attitude. Everybody's supposed to fit within certain requirements on sex. You're supposed to act a certain way, and if you're teaching it in school, once again you're losing out this individual thing.
[A twenty-three-year-old black college senior and student activist at Fresno State College in California.]

That is a very broad question, very difficult to narrow down. There definitely should be a type of sex education. This, of course, may have been too scientifically designed in the past, but we can't present sex education without relating it to the total, whole picture, and you must also relate it to the real meaning of love. And thus, of course, you get into the philosophical range, and you should be working with the parents of the community so that it is not something artificial and something devoid of connection with their own family life.
[A thirty-seven-year-old female associate director of instruction in a big-city school system.]

When should sex education begin? The vast majority of those who expressed themselves on this said it should begin in elementary school. A very few gave the idealized answer, "when children start asking questions." They did not, however, go on to elaborate how this could be done in view of our present mass-instruction technique. But what would prevent us from taking a leaf from Hamburg, Germany's sex information by telephone? By simply dialing the telephone (Sex 2-1212?), adult Hamburgers can get a tape-recorded explanation of several sex-related subjects. The service became so popular with adults that Dr. Klaus Zylmann prepared a "birds and bees" version for children. "Parents say the telephone presents the subject with the proper technical approach, free of emotion and coloring," says Dr. Zylmann. "It has a special ring of authority because it is delivered by an expert through the electronic medium." He added, "Since sex is obviously here to stay, I think it makes sense to treat it like the weather or any other natural phenomenon." With today's inexpensive tape casette recorders, language laboratories, and other devices, not to mention the advent of computerized information retrieval systems, why couldn't we do likewise, bringing students together periodically for discussion, sharing of learning, and motivation to go back for more information?

Demonstrating our national shyness on what is perhaps the fundamental issue—birth control—only a little over 3 per cent of all interviewees made any mention of birth control, or the need to incorporate it in sex education—this in spite of the fact that the population explosion is now our number-one problem. It should be added, however, that nearly 32 per cent, when questioned specifically, did agree that birth control should be included in the study of sex.

When I discovered that Detroit had two high schools exclusively for pregnant girls, I asked a number of people, both in and out of the school system, whether sex education in the schools might not have averted the need for these particular schools. Here are the comments of one of the city system's administrative staff:

Recently I had to write an article on two schools that we're pioneering in Detroit in sex education. One of the sad things I learned was that these two schools had been built for pregnant high school girls, but there wasn't a single high school girl in them. They were all junior high school girls. Which means, at least to me, that sex education has to begin probably in kindergarten and first grade. I think youngsters are horribly mixed up today because all the mass media pushes sex at them as soon as they can learn to read, and even before that when they can look at pictures. As long as sex sells a product, we're going to be saturated by it in our kind of capitalistic society. And we haven't learned to come to terms with it. And as a result, many people don't have the knowledge that they should have about the sex act and especially the consequences of the act. At the board of education we're constantly interviewing pregnant girls who tell us that their boyfriend told them that they had to prove their love or he would leave them and then he would give them a pill and tell them that this would take care of everything. Now, if they had knowledge, they would know that a single pill taken an hour or two, or sometimes ten minutes, before intercourse wouldn't prevent pregnancy. And it's this lack of knowledge that makes it a tough subject to handle. And I think the worst thing we've done in our teaching about sex education is that we have put it on a rather cold, clinical basis. And you can give all the reasons in the world why you should or shouldn't do something, but sex isn't a very reasoned process. It's a highly charged emotional thing. And you could know all the reasons why you shouldn't do this thing at a particular time, or what the consequences would be, and you could actually be reading the book while going through the sex act and your emotions would overcome your intellect at that particular time.

Now in Detroit we have a situation where parents have stormed into the schools and we really don't know what to do. Half of them want us to teach more sex education and teach it earlier and the other half is saying, "No, don't teach anything about sex education because you have spinsters teaching this course. They don't know what they're talking about." Or, "You have people teaching who are not trained for it." Or, "This is against our religion."

I asked him, of those who are against, what percentage think it's done badly and what percentage say it's against their principles?

Well, I couldn't even begin to answer that question. I have no idea as to the exact breakdown. I don't think we've done a study. I think we go back again to the highly charged emotional climate. To take it one step further, many of the parents who are upset about sex education are upset about it not because it's being taught to mixed classes, for example, where male and female are getting instruction at the same time, but because, very frankly, of the race problem. Many people don't want this subject taught in Detroit where you have close to 60 per cent Negro children in the schools. They feel that this is a subject which is already on the youngster's mind and that this merely adds information.

"The crossing over of black and white in sex relations?"

Yes, that's right. It's a very hot issue in most of your large cities. For example, for the first time we have white and black students of the opposite sex, uh, parading in public. And many of the oldsters resent this. They've never seen it before. Many of them feel that "it's all right to be nice to them, but I wouldn't want my daughter to marry one." This kind of sentiment.

"What proportion do not want sex education because it's against their religious principles?"

I think it's rather a small number of people who feel that it's against their religious principles.

"In Appalachia I would say that 90 per cent, maybe 100 per cent of parents would say it was against their religious principles."

Well, in Appalachia you're dealing with the Bible Belt. Here I would think it is almost totally reversed. Most parents are willing for the schools to take over what once they taught in the family, or what was taught in the churches. But with the pill and other birth-control measures, and the constant uproar in the Catholic Church over this, many parents don't actually know where they stand today. They're completely mixed up, and they're hoping that the schools will lead them out of this sexual wilderness.

I asked a fifty-year-old design engineer in Detroit's automotive industry: "Would sex education have made Detroit's high schools for pregnant girls unnecessary?"

I believe it would have cut out an awful lot of experimentation.

A fifty-eight-year-old president of four automotive parts manufacturing companies was asked: "Do you think if there had been sex education in Detroit there would not have been the need for the two high schools for pregnant girls?"

I'm not sure if education would solve this problem. Hopefully it would. Hopefully, at least these people would be educated to the point where if they wanted to indulge in sex or any type of premarital sexual relations they would at least be wise enough to use some form of contraceptive to prevent unwanted children. And I feel that it's up to us now to face this need for contraceptives and quit thinking about them as any type of a taboo, even for unmarried women. Because this is the only way we're going to solve many of our problems. Not only with the population explosion and welfare problems, but a lot of these problems with uneducated society and the militant groups created by this faction of the society.

To a forty-five-year-old black woman attending a continuation school in Detroit I put this question: "Is it better to open high schools for pregnant girls or to have sex education?"

Well, if they could have sex education for those girls I think it would be wonderful.

"Maybe if you had sex education they wouldn't be pregnant."

This is true, that's why I say start teaching material about this at an early age, and then that would kind of knock some of it out.

"You'd have to teach them contraception, wouldn't you?"

Well, if you started teaching them at an early age, say like seventh grade on up, then they wouldn't be so wild when they get in college, don't you think so? Well, as a mother, I am, I have one daughter. She's twenty now, and I think this would be wonderful because, see, I started teaching my daughter this when she was twelve, because I wasn't intending to teach her this, but you have to teach them that now. Because, see, she come in one day and told me one of the girls was pregnant, and the teacher was calling her out, and she had to send her home. Well, I just went on then and told her everything because it was pressing on me right there. So this is why I say teach them from twelve on up. Maybe some mothers wouldn't approve of this, but I say nowadays is more children today, more wild than they've ever been it look like, and they need to learn more at an early age now than they did when I came along.

I asked the sales manager for a Detroit auto parts manufacturer: "If you had sex education in school, would there be a need for Detroit's high schools for pregnant girls? Would there be a connection between sex education and fewer pregnant girls or what?"

Oh, I definitely think so. I think that through better education and particularly, uh, well, let me phrase it another

way. I think a lot of kids today, and a lot of this hanky-
panky amongst the teenagers is done, uh, primarily as a re-
bellious attitude, they want to show they are accomplishing
something and this is one way they can show it. Maybe the
girl isn't as pretty as the next girl or as smart as the next
girl setting next to her, so the only thing she has to contribute toward her achievement or toward her status is by being
free with her love, not realizing what she is giving away. I
think there are probably several answers to this. The young
people today, for one, are individualists. They do not participate in many group activities, it is limited to sororities,
small, um, small groups or organizations. Two, their activities are usually far divorced from their family life and
therefore their action is never looked upon as wrongdoing.

My dialogue with a white thirty-five-year-old Detroit
woman with four children whose job it was to inspect auto
parts coming at her in an endless line, hour after hour, typ-
ified the confusion I met in the minds of many adults in all
parts of the country.

"Do you think if there were sex education in school it
would eliminate some of the need for high schools for pregnant girls?" I asked.

No, because, my opinion is that these, when they are going
too far into sex and that's why these girls are going out and
getting into trouble, they're trying these things. Like some
of them say these books they read, I mean, to me they're
really going too far in the books that they have to read
today in sex. Well, I feel that if they didn't go so far, maybe
that the children wouldn't go that far either. I think there's
more girls being pregnant today than ever, and I think
that's because we are teaching so much sex in schools.

"If they're going to do it, would you prefer to just let them
get pregnant and forget it?"

No, no, I don't mean that at all. I don't, I mean, I don't
think they should be allowed to go out as—I mean, you

can't really blame it all on the school, either, because they let them keep such late hours and that.

"If they're going to do it anyway, then what? Just let them suffer?"

Well, no, I think there should be something to help them. I mean, everybody can make a mistake and they are, like teenagers, they really have their own mind more than other people, I mean, at that age it's pretty hard to tell them anything. When they turn seventeen, eighteen, I mean, they think they're their own boss and this and that and that's it. When they get in trouble, I do think that you should help them. I mean, it's something that's already happened, I mean, no one wants to see their children in that kind of trouble, boy or girl.

"Do you think maybe abortion instead of contraceptives?"

No, I don't think that either. I think—well, it's a real problem and I just haven't thought much about it.

I asked a highly placed official in the Detroit city school system about the advisability of teaching birth control in the classroom.

Well, the subject of birth control is very much a debatable one. We in Detroit are more real in our thinking of that because we have two schools operating at the high school level which we call under the polished name or misnomer of "continuing education." These are schools for pregnant girls who are in the lower teens and on up through the high school grades. And these girls are individuals who either haven't known, or didn't want to learn, or preferred to forget, or were in all innocence caught in difficulties. And so there's a case where it's not a matter of black or white but which shade of gray. Are we going to teach all children, men and women, boys and girls, that there is, there are ways? Or are we going to hopefully depend on the teachings of the home and the church and to some extent to the school, although we're greatly limited by law there and certainly by public pressure? I don't know if I'm prepared to give an answer to it. Maybe it's a case of wait and see, or try and possibly fail. It is being done in some areas. We do not do it in Detroit except in a very remote way, and yet I'm sure that if you were to give them a few simple answers in any class, we'd be amazed at what children know about birth control today.

"Do you feel taxpayers would rather have you put up more high schools for pregnant girls than give birth-control instruction?"

Well, it's a little more complicated than that. Our problem comes not so much from taxpayers as it does from, shall I say, religious fanatics—from people who are shocked from having gone the same way and brought up the same road as their great-grandparents did so that, uh, I think your question is a nominal one but I'm not sure it's quite an accurate one. People don't give thought to some of these things until they come in the tragic language of the press. They don't think—most of them don't know that we have these schools although it's no secret. We've had lots of press publicity on it. They don't think about it until it strikes home or strikes a relative.

"Couldn't the school system ask for a vote?"

They could, and I wouldn't want to predict what the result might be. It would create a furor, based largely on religious levels.

"So let the kids suffer."

Well, that's one way of looking at it.

Contrast that with the attitude of a twenty-two-year-old woman living on the mountainous California coast. A few weeks before my interview she had experienced planned natural childbirth at home attended only by her husband. The

event took place in the room where I interviewed her in their
tiny mountain cabin. Behind us, snuggled in a basket of blan-
kets hung from the ceiling, this new bit of humanity occasionally gurgled her own "word" for the tape. Her mother responded to the question, "If you believe we should have sex
education in the public schools, what kinds of things should
be learned?" this way:

> Physical facts about reproduction and about, well, the
> meaning of sex physically, emotionally, morally, and spiri-
> tually.

Before the means of birth control, the sex act between men
and women had been largely an animal function to reproduce
children. Its regulation was simply by taboo. But as men and
women came to savor the pleasure of the sex act itself, and realize its capacity to deepen understanding and appreciation
not only of one another but of the whole of human nature and
condition, they wanted more sex. Still there were the old taboos, useful in their day but meaningless now that the results
of copulation could be controlled and men and women could
regard the sexual encounter as an aesthetic experience growing out of mutual respect and admiration. As birth-control
methods have improved, sex has become less an animal function than an important part of man's search for the good and
the beautiful. The young are finding this out and are trying
desperately to tell us about it. As in any movement, there are
the extremists and the less sensitive who overreact. There are
the young and the not so young who plunge into sex orgies,
turning what should be sublime into something rather sordid.
Getting wind of these rare events, the pre-pill generation calls
upon its gods and brings the taboos crashing down around
anyone unfortunate to be caught out in the open. So sex is

buried in dark corners and often in inconvenient and even ludicrous settings.

Nevertheless, the young are determined to bring sex out into the sunlight, literally and figuratively. "When it's there, you pay less attention to it," one young man told me, "but when you have it, you can just relax and enjoy it with everything that's in you." Said another, "You adults are so hung up on sex. You make so much of it. It's there, and that's all there is to it." Again, "We used to lie up in a meadow, several of us with our clothes off, just feeling the sun wrap around our bodies. And when we wanted to be together, we'd just turn over, and we were."

In their break for sexual freedom many of the young are no doubt becoming worshipers in a new cult of hedonism, with an almost Dionysian fevor. Consider the "groupies," a new breed of stage-door Janies, who go much further than the simple mass hysteria of Sinatra's swooners and Elvis Presley's fanatics. Frank Zappa, who leads a prominent group of young musicians, defines groupies as girls who go to bed with members of rock-and-roll bands. A twenty-five-year-old girl of San Francisco says that the real groupie has "numerous relationships." In one night she may sleep with several members of the group from the lowly equipment pusher to the head man. Zappa says there are thousands of groupies around the country. There is little doubt that in its extreme forms the hedonism of the young may lead to a laxness that can destroy the very values they seek to embrace. But has the Puritan prudery that clings to modern technological man done much more than make a mockery of many of his values? Why were there 22,467 forcible rapes in 1965? Why has the rate for children born out of wedlock tripled between 1940 and 1965? Why are divorce, alcoholism, and heart attacks on the increase? Why do over 100,000 mainly middle-class business executives get up, walk away from their jobs, and drop out of sight each year because they can no longer stand the pressure? Why, according to the FBI, is crime up 99 per cent in the years 1960–1968? Why has shoplifting become epidemic to the extent that in a swiftly growing number of the nation's stores you now shop with a TV "private eye" surveillance camera over your shoulder?

In his book *Sex and the New Morality* Frederic C. Wood, Jr., devotes a chapter to "The Exploitation of Sexuality"; in a section on "Sex and the Marketplace," Reverend Wood asks:

> Why is sex so easily marketable in the first place? How are we to explain the tremendous appeal of sex on the American market? Its virtual centrality to the American economy? Its power to inspire otherwise irrational buying patterns? The answer to those questions should be as obvious as the fact that the price of food soars in times of famine. There is an incessant demand for authentic sexual fulfillment in our time. Although that demand is stimulated by the sex motif in the mass media, its roots lie not in abundance of riches but in real sexual poverty. Sex sells big because people are starved for it. And the more phony, objectified sex they get on the market, the more frantic their starvation becomes, and the more they buy.[2]

We cry out that pornography is corrupting the young, but do we ever ask who or what created pornography? I recently returned from New Guinea where my studies of education among primitive peoples took me into the back country where schools are bamboo huts with bare earth floors. These people have only recently put on clothes, yet there is no pornography in New Guinea. There is still respect for the natural, human body. But give them time. Pornography, a "white man's disease," will come soon enough, along with other phony benefits of "civilization."

In Denmark it was found that when lewd literature was made freely available in newsstands and bookstores sales fell off to the point of alarming the publishers. Nor does pornography find any place in a nudist colony. Who created pornography? We did—the pre-pill generation and countless generations before us—in our futile efforts to hold onto outmoded taboos —taboos that to the young look like shutting the barn door after the horse has been stolen. It all adds up to one of the major charges of hypocrisy that the young fling in our faces.

One of the more hideous farces perpetrated by the Establishment culture—one that is producing the exact opposite of its intention to keep pornography from the young—is movie censorship. I recently broke all precedent and saw two movies on two successive nights: *Alice's Restaurant* and *Oedipus the King*. *Alice* is about a group of hippie-type young people who have set up a commune in an old church that they have duly purchased in a small New England village. They open a restaurant, a pottery shop, and invite the community to their parties. At times their life style clashes with small-town, middle-class mores, and the results are humorous. The young are depicted in all stages of maturity and maturing, and the viewer is struck by the mutual love and respect these young people have for each other. Expressions of love range from a look, a smile, a hand laid on, a hand taken away, a coming near, all the way to deep sexual fulfillment. Love scenes are tastefully handled, not smirkingly suggestive. Emotions are honest; the action is exuberant, as even townspeople join in celebrations and weddings. The only violence depicted is the leaders' punishment of one of the members caught using hard drugs. Filial love at its highest is exemplified by the hero who constantly attends his dying father. A dawning sense of responsibility is seen in the faces and actions of the young actors.

Contrast this with *Oedipus,* a film adaptation of the Greek tragedy by Sophocles. Here a son kills his father, marries his mother, drives her to suicide, and blinds himself. Bloody violence, disease, superstition, and deception recur throughout the picture. Man is depicted as caught in a web of circumstance, fated by an accident of birth, having little to do with what befalls him. One could only go away with the feeling of "what's the use?"

Now to *Oedipus* came two busloads of girls aged twelve to sixteen or seventeen from a nearby well-known private school. To *Alice* came none of this age bracket, because the picture had been censored "R," Restricted: Persons under eighteen (sixteen in certain localities) not admitted unless accompanied by parent or adult guardian. After seeing *Oedipus,* I went over to where the girls were boarding the bus and asked several whether they had seen *Alice's Restaurant.* "No, I'd like to," said one. "I saw the preview. But we can't get in, you know. Well, we could if we had our parent, but I know my mother would never take me." I asked why they were here tonight. It was part of their literature class, they said.

As the bus pulled away, I stood bewildered in the street. What kind of world is this when we send children to see man at his bloodcurdling worst, then require them to discuss it in class, write a composition about it—all in the name of "literature"—yet keep them away from a here-and-now slice of life showing the young trying to live by the virtues of honesty, generosity, and respect, and punish them if they do try to see it? Our schools spend millions for films on "Transportation," "Birds of the Swamplands," "American Children at Home," and so forth, but when it comes to a contemporary, meaningful subject that could spark real discussion and sincere writing about *real* problems of genuine interest to the young, we withhold the experience—and in the name of morality!

Commune living, such as depicted in *Alice,* involves both physical and psychological closeness. Such a life style would be unendurable by most of us, brought up as we have been to live in today's culture. We prefer to remain at considerable social distance from each other, in a style of relative anonymity. One reason modern man has sought to live in the relative anonymity of the big city is to escape the intolerance of his fellow men. His acts are either not seen or lost in a crowd. He does not need to be concerned about others, and others are not concerned about him. But in having escaped these concerns, he has lost a portion of the world's love, the kind of love that is at once impersonal, yet a warm, pervasive feeling that sets the stage not for invasion of privacy but for communication. Whether simple communication goes beyond itself toward a simple friendship or a deep and abiding love for a man or woman is a matter of personal adventure into discovering one's self in another. It may or may not include the sex act, but the sexual relationship is there. It is a part of a potential for deeper relationships, whether man-woman, man-man, or woman-woman.

Sex education should teach these things; it should incorporate a thorough knowledge of birth control and a sharing—the older with the younger, the younger with the older—of insights into the many dimensions of interpersonal commitment which can attach to human sexuality. Thus it could not only put an end to the peril of overpopulation but also raise human relationships through new opportunities for personal growth toward new levels of goodness and beauty.

To the young, sex is beautiful. It is a way of expressing universal love—a love of one's fellow man. To many of the older

it would be a most satisfying experience if they could somehow break out of the box in which they have been incarcerated by generations before. Whether or not we condone the sex
explosion of the Now Generation, we've asked for it with our
magazine advertising, TV, and so forth. It is one more way in
which they are thumbing their noses at the hypocrisy of the
sexual attitudes and behaviors of Establishment culture.

The sex explosion is further evidence that what both the Establishment culture and the youthful counter culture need is
each other. Sex education should go both ways. Youth needs
to ask questions of those who have experienced sexual relations over a long period of years. They need to know about
the stages of feelings one goes through, of the effects of having
children, of the myriad facets of man-woman relationships.
The conformity culture, on the other hand, needs to be exposed to some of the ideas of the counter culture in order to
open their lives to a wider range of thought and perhaps even
experiences, while yet their bodies can enjoy. Now that the
pill and other devices have banished most fears of pregnancy,
more and more men and women will experiment with just this
sort of thing. The legalization of abortion, when it happens,
not only will extend sexual freedom generally but will give
woman a new control over her own destiny as a human being
—not merely as a chattel of the male animal.

What the conformity culture itself needs is the refreshing new
guilt-free attitude of the young. Otherwise, such experimental
ventures could be needlessly frightening and destructive, instead of being an experience to grow on—a love-expanding
experience in which one learns to include more of the human
race in his tender feelings. Perhaps the conformity culture
can't lie on a sunny meadow experiencing multiple sex, and
this may be where many of the young take the Dionysian ethic
too far. On the other hand, consider the conformity culture

version: the awkward times and places—mindless liaisons in the cramped back seat of a car or a chance bedroom at a cocktail party. "How can this be good and beautiful?" ask the young. If sex is such a God-given thing, shouldn't it be pursued openly? Wouldn't it build more real appreciation between individual human beings? Might it not even develop a deeper loyalty between two people? It is interesting to note that in hippie communes while one principle seems to be free love among the members, they inevitably pair off, I am told, showing not sole concern but major concern for just one other person, while sharing concern and at times sex with others of the group. And all are concerned for the welfare of the children, as though each child had multiple aunts and uncles.

As the present sex-hungup generation declines in power it will be less necessary for men and women to seek anonymity and the ugly dark corner for the realization of sexual satisfaction. It will be possible for people to live more closely together, in smaller communities, perhaps even in communes where, besides material things, sex is shared as a part of the group's moving beyond the concerns of what is simply utilitarian, only pleasing, or merely moral.

CHAPTER 8

INCLUDE ME OUT!

Ever since Adam and Eve were thrown out of the Garden of Eden Western man has been asking himself these questions: Am I an individual—or am I a member of society? Do I want to be included in man's collective insanity or would I be better off simply going it alone? Individual or group? To which do I owe allegiance? Some men have solved the problem by becoming hermits; others have thrust themselves into the thick of humanity for the satisfaction of serving others or being served. Robinson Crusoe didn't have the problem, but he didn't choose it that way. Nor would most of us. Down through the ages man has come up with as many answers to the riddle—the central dilemma of Western man—as there are philosophies and religions.

The approach of the Eastern world was set down by the saints and sages of India in the Upanishads some 1,500 years ago. They believed that a simple and essential reality underlies the superficial multiplicity of things and events. The essence of self is not the body, the mind, or the individual ego. Rather it is the formless and silent being within each person—the Atman, the Soul of the World. Furthermore, the intellect is inadequate for reaching the ultimate significance of life. The Indian philosopher Sarvepalli Radakrishnam describes the concept in his book, *Indian Philosophy:* "As flowing rivers disappear into the sea, losing their name and form, thus a wise man, freed from name and form, goes to the divine person who is beyond all." [1]

The wistful metaphysical concept that individual life is a delusion is in sharp contrast with the tenets of Western religions and institutions, permeated as they are with the cult of individualism. Instead of searching for unifying simplicities underlying the multiplicity of human experience, the West has sought to draw out of man's universal characteristics a greater diversity of individual experience. Many of the young today are turning to Zen Buddhism and other Eastern thought to find a way out of the cocoon of materialism, in which modern man seems to be wrapping himself tighter and tighter as he shuts out attempts by others to impinge on his individualism.

We Americans traditionally have prided ourselves on the notion that the United States is *the* land of opportunity, where the only limit to an individual's possibilities of success is the extent of his talent and ambition. This concept—which Herbert Hoover was to label "rugged individualism"—gave impetus to a vital young nation's transformation from a huge, unexplored wilderness into the world's greatest industrial power in a phenomenally short period of time. In that time the Horatio Alger myth was reality for many, but some took—and continue to take—individualism to mean that no holds are barred, that they are perfectly justified in exploiting or merely trampling the weaker and less talented in their quest for wealth and power. The tragic results of these excesses have become painfully evident—the rape of the land, the pollution of the waters and the atmosphere, the misery of the blacks and Puerto Ricans, the Mexican-Americans, and the American Indians.

Because the "rugged individualism" that helped build our country is now being seriously challenged on the one hand and hotly defended on the other, I put Question 8 to my 1,-000 interviewees: "Now what about the individual? In these days we hear a lot about 'trying to be an individual.' The idea of 'trying to be an individual' is probably not very new, but 'being an individual' seems harder than ever in these times. Why do you think this is so?"

A twenty-four-year-old Columbia University graduate student in social psychology reflects the deep concern of nearly nine out of ten people (88.7 per cent) that, indeed, it is more difficult to be an individual in these times.

> You're damned right it is hard to be an individual in these times, because all the forces of our socialization and the continuing system of rewards and punishments which I alluded to earlier are all geared to making what had started out to be people with the capacity for realizing their individuality into, one might say, robots that function efficiently within our larger system which is most influenced by economic values. So, because, as I see it, our society places the broader economic values above the human value of the individual and his worth and the value of promoting the development of his creativity, we wind up with a socialization process—perhaps the major instrument which takes all the rough edges of individuality and lops them off so as to make a set of uniform-appearing and uniform-acting robots that fit well into the roles defined by our businesses, one of those businesses being our schools. So that we end up with robot teachers making robots out of what might have been human individual students.

I asked him, "What kinds of things do you do to be the kind of individual you want to be?"

> To be the individual I want to be? Well, number one, I've taken great strides toward throwing off the external rein-

forcement as being the motivation for how I think and how I act. I've gotten to the point where whether or not I continue as a student, whether or not I get a doctoral degree, what sort of employment I get, are all at best secondary questions. Maybe they're not even that high on my agenda. And that my primary preoccupation is one of—well, first off, trying to cut through the garbage that has been slapped up around my individuality so as to see what really lies beneath it. And then follow that inner directive with regard to where to go from there. These questions have been dealing a lot with individuality, and I don't want to leave the impression that I conceive of myself as a being operating totally on the basis of a motivation coming from within that does not include considerations from without myself, in particular, does not take into account the well-being of other individuals.

Because part of my religious philosophy is that the creative potential within each individual, including myself, is a part of the same unity, higher unity. At times I've called this higher unity a supreme being, or even a god, in my conscientious-objector statement, but because this is the way I conceive of myself, when I speak of realizing my own individuality and my creative spirit, I deeply believe that this realization will be in a way that promotes rather than is destructive to the same potential within all other human individuals. So that my development as an individual is completely in accordance with the development of all other individuals. This is what I was talking about earlier when I talked about a cooperative orientation, a cooperative relationship with other individuals. It's not surprising now, given this orientation toward myself as being part of the same unity as all other individuals, that I'm an individual with what some people call a very strong sense of social responsibility. That is to say, I'm extremely concerned with the way in which our world is destroying individuals, either physically by dropping bombs on their heads and putting bullets through their backs, and psychologically by conditioning them so as not to think of themselves as being individuals possessing a potential which they can realize from within, but rather robots to follow directives from without. And I also take this responsibility so seriously that at this point I'm entirely ready to forego all the usual rewards which robots in our society strive after, everything which goes along with the degree and the high-paying job, if I can somehow have a significant effect on changing this world environment to be one that promotes individuality rather than destroys it.

Not every mind I met among those agreeing that individualism was more difficult today was as finely honed as this young adult's, who was later written up in *Newsweek* for expressing his individuality by, among other ways, appearing for a press conference in the nude. Nor did many express such deep concern and a sense of personal quest in finding answers to the problem of man as an individual and as a member of society. Among both the younger and the older, in all walks of life, responses were mainly complaints that it was more difficult to be an individual today along with reasons for thinking so.

One-third said it was harder to be an individual because of social pressure to conform. They mentioned such things as fear, insecurity, and a desire to be liked. One out of ten laid the problem to "our complex society." Nearly as many said individualism was harder because of more people living closer together. One out of twenty said that technological advances made it more difficult. An equal number said schools were at fault. Others gave such reasons as the mass media (2.7 per cent), government controls (2.1 per cent), and our materialistic society (1.3 per cent). Here is a range of views on pressures for conformity:

> Because nowadays most people are afraid to be individuals. [A thirteen-year-old eighth-grader on the mid-California coast.]

I don't think the school board, anyway in this county, wants you to be an individual because they set up certain rules and regulations to have everybody look like they came out of a factory.
[A sixteen-year-old eleventh-grader in the same school.]

Because so many people are trying to be like the Joneses.
[An eighteen-year-old black freshman in a mid-Tennessee all-black college.]

Well, I believe that being an individual seems harder now because there's so much emphasis on the crowd. You've got to do what the crowd does, you go where the crowd goes, you buy what the crowd buys. And if you don't, then you're just out of it. You're a square. You're not in. And nobody wants to be left out completely. They all want to have some contact with other people. And this crowd is so pulling against the individual, it's like a war with the crowd on one end and the want-to-be-an-individual on the other. And most times the crowd wins.
[A seventeen-year-old eleventh-grade student in a rural Florida community.]

In this world we want to be socially acceptable. We have a tendency in America to move toward the median and that is in the other direction from being an individual.
[A fifty-four-year-old woman, associate professor of educational psychology at a small college in Mississippi.]

I think that it's very hard to be an individual because there are a lot of things going on that are much easier to conform to. And conformity is always easy. It's only when you are trying to be yourself or what you would like to think of as yourself that you run into difficulty.
[A nineteen-year-old black freshman coed at the Agricultural and Technical University of North Carolina in Greensboro.]

I believe that man is by nature basically gregarious. As a consequence of this, he seeks out sanctions or acceptance from his peer group. Because of this, he is reluctant to en-

gage in any activity or do anything that would cause some undue consternation on the part of other members of his peer group. And because of this, he loses his individuality by becoming a part of a crowd. I think this is one of the reasons we have so much mob violence and mob rule on some of our university and college campuses. Not because a person would really condone what he is even doing, let alone what his friends are doing, but he has to have this acceptance because of the fact that he has not had this acceptance all along.
[A thirty-seven-year-old black assistant superintendent of schools in charge of community education in a small California city, holder of a doctor's degree in school administration.]

Mainly because from kindergarten on they start putting people in groups and force people to identify with these particular groups, force people to make themselves acceptable to groups rather than being acceptable to themselves, so, if a person starts being conditioned to be acceptable to groups, then he loses individuality. And that's why a lot of people don't try to be individuals.
[A twenty-three-year-old black senior student of industrial technology at Fresno State College in California.]

I think it's hard to be an individual because you're never treated as an individual, but always dealt with in a group situation. You have to try to maintain your individuality and sometimes ignore what you're supposed to be doing as a group.
[A twenty-six-year-old mathematics teacher in a small Pennsylvania school system.]

I think that so many people in this country have been literally brainwashed into not feeling pain for other people. So, therefore, they have gone in their own little circuit and anyone who stands up and, say, protests about some injustice more or less is considered a sort of kook. The majority, I guess, don't want to get involved. And I think that we have always been led to believe that everything from our history

books on the United States is always right. And they say it's a land of free enterprise, but individualism does seem to be frowned on if it in any way offends the so-called Establishment.
[A fifty-four-year-old San Francisco housewife.]

I think it's harder to be an individual more than ever before because of the great technological advances in this country, and world-wide, especially computers. They've made the person a number rather than an individual. They've decreased his importance in group functions and the person is not able to communicate very well with each other because, with the advancing technology, society is becoming more and more impersonal.
[A twenty-five-year-old biology major in Syracuse, New York.]

I think it's harder to be an individual for most people because we are all part of a vast machine.
[A forty-eight-year-old assistant fleet supervisor for a dairy products firm in Arkansas.]

It's difficult to be an individual because our big cities are becoming more and more crowded with people because there has been this big migration from the rural areas into the cities, and people have not been prepared to work in close quarters with one another. I think, too, the poverty of these people has caused friction and an understanding of how they might be living better. I think it's difficult to be an individual because of all the mass media that are bombarding us with messages to do this and to do that. Most people see the same TV shows. Many people read the same national magazines, weekly magazines, and so they come up with the opinions of somebody else rather than thinking through what they really believe on the basis of all kinds of different positions and viewpoints.
[A sixty-year-old official in the Department of Health, Education and Welfare in Washington, D.C.]

I think you have to go back and look at the events after
World War II when those people who influence other people
greatly, the sociologists, the psychologists, I suppose to a
certain extent the business community, to the extent that
they take up the ideas of these people, were placing great
stress to the exclusion of most other things on, shall we say,
social togetherness. That we should all cooperate, we
should all work together, we should all do this, we should
all do that, and if we didn't, somehow or other we were
freaks. In a way I suppose this was a good movement because it counteracted, perhaps, the extreme in the other
direction. However, we are now coming to realize, I think,
that most actions and most accomplishments are the actions
and accomplishments of individual people. They are very
seldom the actions and accomplishments of society except
as the society reflects the actions of the individual people.
[A forty-six-year-old educational consultant in California.]

I think it's rather hard to become an individual when you're
in a society, as the American society is now, where people
are placed in a niche in large corporations. I think that,
say, in the pioneer United States, a person could become an
individual as a craftsman or in whatever he so desired,
whatever field he so desired to seek out. But in this present
society where, unless a person definitely has artistic talents
or wants to be a free-lance type person, he's probably going
to be starving if he doesn't feel like relying on large industry or business of some type.
[A twenty-three-year-old college student, an industrial arts
(vocational training) major in Evanston, Illinois.]

Well, I think there's several things involved. The typical
nineteenth-century individual, the entrepreneur being the
leading example, the self-made man, the self-directed man,
is no longer needed that much by society. And society now
requires or likes the man who fits into intricate corporative
structure, who accomplishes a task which involves careful
and smooth human relations as much as anything else. The
individual, which is partly a way of saying the eccentric or

partly eccentric, doesn't fit smoothly into complex machines composed of human beings. And in order to keep this large, complex machinery, bureaucratic machinery, going you need, uh, malleable and conforming human types. And so I think society encourages these individuals. Following this line, I think that mass media, the spread of the ideal type, the American Dream as projected by television and books and so on, its wider spread, gives a more detailed and more easily available type to follow which the individual consciously and unconsciously imitates. And individualism in terms of deviation from this type becomes more and more unlikely.

[A twenty-seven-year-old Ph.D. candidate in art history at Harvard University.]

Because it seems that society dictates many of the things in our life, many of the functions. There's many more laws than there ever were before, and every type of our behavior is somewhere predetermined for us, even so far as all mores or folkways, or even your manner, or anything you do is either acceptable or not acceptable by society. When you enter the business world of any different field, society has set up different ways of determining your success. I guess where I stand, your monetary wealth or how fast you advance within your own company is kind of keeping score in relation to playing a game. And so we find ourself trying to play this game as best we can, the game that's already been put up by society, oftentimes rather than living life the way we might like to, or maybe not competing as much. I mean, to be an individual you have to decide—a true individual doesn't necessarily use the same goal or the same scoring system that society does. And so, because of all these laws, written and unwritten mores and folkways that we're constantly trying to adhere to, it's very difficult to be an individual.

[A twenty-three-year-old salesman of an auto parts manufacturing firm in Detroit and heir-apparent to this multimillion dollar industry of which his father is president— and his present employer.]

Individuality to me implies a certain amount of confidence in oneself. And to develop this kind of confidence in oneself, one has to be exposed to experiences where you have the opportunity to create. I know that loads of people say why spend time reinventing the wheel all over again. I think that this process is very important. I think that the process of self-discovery, the process of even though something has been discovered before the fact that an individual comes to it, to the end of it, by himself is very important. And this does a great deal in developing the whole concept of individuality in an individual. To know that you, yourself, have created something, that you've succeeded, that you've built something, is very important. I don't think schools offer enough opportunities for people to become involved in this. You're on this track or you've got to pass that regents', you've got to pass that test. And you tend to emphasize this whereas you should emphasize more the creative process.

[A forty-one-year-old black codirector of a community resource center in New York City.]

For one reason, there are so many more people. And the more people that you have, the more likely persons will have some degree to which they have likenesses. And the other factor is that the economies of our culture make it profitable to mass produce many things and they make it very unprofitable to tailor-make items, and consequently many people will find that not only do they find similarities from one home to another, they find it from one state to another, from one culture to another, and pretty soon it looks as if the whole world has so many great similarities. Another factor is that you have communication systems now that keep the world informed at all points so that almost simultaneously something that happens in one country is seen and heard in another. More than that, I think that we play around with the words a little bit on this. Many people who are concerned about their individuality and the fact that they can't be individualistic frequently are saying this when they really are acting more as if they

are alone, which is another dimension of being an individual. So you find extremely lonely people in these very, very densely crowded areas. And if you've toyed with the word it would mean that the person does feel as if he is sort of an individual and he's lost his relevance. So it's a funny kind of a mix here, it's like W. I. Thomas and some of the people saying that you have a drive both to be different and to be alike. This is a complex of a man.
[A fifty-four-year-old professor of educational curriculum at Teachers College, Columbia University.]

How does a man doing time in prison, living day after day or year after year with hundreds of other men, feel about the problem of being an individual? The guard admitted another blue-clad youth to the space near the cell block of the Soledad Correctional Facility where I interviewed for three days. Like the thirteen others I talked to, he looked like any ordinary citizen you might meet on the street, have working at the desk next to you, or see at a lecture or sports events. As he sat down before me, I thought, "There, but for the grace of God, sit I."

I think it's hard to be a real individual because there are so many people living under such crowded conditions. Everybody expects you to conform to their way of thinking. The society that you live in and, uh, many other things. Depending upon the individual, it doesn't have to be hard.

Struck by such a sane and balanced view of the relationship between the individual and society, I asked, "What kind of thinking brought you here?"

The type of thing that I think brought me here was I was young, I'd been in trouble before, and at the time I was in a rather bad situation where in order to get away from it, not actually to get away from it physically, but mentally, where I wouldn't have to see what was going on around me, I more or less relied on drugs and drinking quite a bit, too much, in fact. And I really didn't care at the time. I was under the influence so much that I was just a walking dead man.

"Would you have answered these questions as you did today if you had answered them forty-four months ago when you came in here?"

No, I wouldn't have.

"What has happened?"

I think the main thing that has happened to me in the forty-four months I've been here is that I've just grown up. I've learned that there is another life besides this one and it's a lot better on the outside than it is in here. This place just isn't worth it any more. It's like the new saying goes, it just isn't where it's at.

"You must have learned something here."

Yes, I definitely have learned something.

"What has helped you to grow up?"

I think learning about myself. I have two years of psychology now and a year of sociology. And I think while taking these courses I really felt for them. I enjoyed them because it would help me learn something about myself, learn something about the world around me, why, as I sit around here I think the way I do and act the way I do, and why other people act the way they do.

"What do you intend to do when you get out?"

IBM programming. I go back to board in January, and the way this last year has been I'm very confident I'll be getting out.

He was twenty-four and had a high school diploma. One might ask why he didn't get courses in the human sciences that would have led him to come to the self-understanding that would have helped him to cope with his earlier "bad situation" instead of having to spend almost all of his young adult life in the penitentiary to get them.

At the close of a fiery panel, during which four college student leaders of as many campus activist groups aired their views to an auditorium full of educators, I asked one of the panelists for an interview. On the question of individuality he had definite ideas.

A person is not an individual nowadays and those that profess to be individuals have only rejected the majority of our society. The reasons why we are not individuals, why we don't have any Washingtons or Jeffersons or Bolivars or Martis or Chavezes is the fact that people are basically part of this melting-pot concept, where from the minute you are born you are taught one ideology, one way of thinking. You go to school and the same principles are taught. The minute any professor or any teacher, either in grammar school or high school, says the wrong thing, he is automatically expelled. You have Dr. Smith in San Francisco State, which in a way has posed a threat to the power structure of Reagan and Rafferty and all these other people. They then become very easily vulnerable to the punishment of this myth that they have created and the only way to become an individual is to stick to whatever beliefs you do have and then fight for them. There are a few such people around, but we must always realize that the power structure, the system, will not allow such people to be around for long because they will kill 'em, they will kill the Kennedys, they will kill the Martin Luther Kings, and they will continue to do this because the people do not realize that human beings of this capacity are much more, are—are of much more value than a typical politician or a typical high school student or a college student that never dares to stick his neck out on anything, he never takes a position on anything. [A twenty-three-year-old Chicano (Mexican-American), a graduate student in foreign languages at Fresno State College in California.]

I think unless a man can, as an individual, take good stock of himself first, analyze himself from every possible angle, he then, if he cannot do this, he has a great deal of trouble in trying to make any change in society, in an educational system, or anything else. If he is able to break through the welter of constant bombardment from all sides about the things he should do in order to be a good citizen, in order to provide for his family, in order to become a material success, I would say that it's becoming increasingly difficult for a man to be an individual and with almost every system that we have, including the educational system, sort of geared to fitting man into the pattern which currently seems that, that it's necessary to be successful. I would look, hopefully, for more and more people following the practice of some of our young people at this point in history in trying to make a break, in holding up their hands and saying stop, let's reflect, let's see who I am, let's see what I can contribute, knowing that I can contribute very little about anything without a full knowledge of myself first. That's why we must continue to try to be individuals and it becomes exceedingly hard and harder all the time to achieve this individuality.
[A sixty-three-year-old retired businessman turned clergyman, in San Francisco.]

In spite of the fact that the vast majority of people of all ages and in all walks of life said that being an individual today is more difficult than ever before, what about the one out of ten who didn't agree? Here is a range of their responses:

Well, I don't agree in the first place that it's harder to be an individual now. I think that individuality develops with character. And character comes from contact with others and with learning and knowledge of the past. Any man, or woman, will have definite ideas, and they probably will be strengthened as they get older. And with definite ideas you form character and individuality. The world is full of indi-

viduals. The trouble with some governments is that they don't allow the individuals to express themselves. Individuality, however, is still there, although it may be latent, suppressed. In this country the individual has the opportunity to express himself. But I think the individuality is there all the time whether it is evident or not.
[An eighty-year-old financier and land developer in California.]

First of all, I really don't think it's any more difficult to be an individual now than it ever was before. I think one of the reasons that so many people are talking about being an individual is people have more leisure, they're better educated, and more people are thinking about it now. Fifty years ago, if you talked about individualism, they wouldn't know what you were talking about. People are more conscious that one can do things with one's life because there's so many different possibilities open to people now than once was the case. You can go to all sorts of areas, the arts, business, no matter what your backgrounds are.
[A twenty-six-year-old international business major at Columbia University.]

I don't agree with the basic premise. It seems to me the reason why we're concerned about being an individual is precisely because we have made such incredible progress in becoming an individual. To me the society which is most constraining where an individual has least opportunity to be an individual and doesn't even think that much about it is the preliterate undeveloped traditional society. These are societies in which one grows up in a set of circumstances in which the whole value system is given. One is socialized tightly into this and is not concerned essentially about individualism in the same way in which we are today. It seems to me, however, that as our population grows and the ecology of our living pattern is dominated by areas of high density, that we of necessity will find ourselves facing increasing need for limitation on the certain aspects of individual freedom.

[A forty-nine-year-old dean of student affairs at a large Eastern university.]

Well, I don't think it is so. I think if you had a good look at the Middle Ages, for example, you'd find very few people doing anything which looked like the behavior of an individual. The lord of the manor and a few artists that he might subsidize—but the ordinary man was living an extremely routinized life, I think. There is a greater variety today than ever before, but still not by any means enough. This, I think, is partly due to education which doesn't teach the kinds of things that permit an individual to express himself. But it's also the whole structure of society which still puts a premium on doing essentially what other people do.

[A sixty-four-year-old, internationally famous professor of psychology.]

Primarily, I disagree with that view that it's hard to be an individual. I think that man can be an individual just as much nowadays as he could ever, but the old stereotype of being an individual, a rugged frontiersman, is of course dead or obsolete. The technology nowadays causes such a dependence upon other people, such a need for teamwork, that this old style of self-reliance is gone, but I seriously doubt if that's the proper definition of individual.

[A twenty-two-year-old California student in zoology.]

Well, I don't find that trying to be an individual is any harder now than it ever was. Myself, in my individualism, it's just that I'm that way, but within a larger framework, and that is just being black. I don't care to be an individual when it comes to making gains for my people. I think that there needs to be a kind of unity, a sharing of all the potentials from the entire group. But I think there's adequate room for me, or anyone else, to display individualism, you know, within the larger framework.

[A thirty-five-year-old black college sophomore, one of a group who staged a takeover at the opening session of the 1969 National Conference of the Association for Supervision and Curriculum Development, in Chicago.]

I don't think it's so. I think that regardless of whatever restrictions you may think society's placing on you, I think you can always be your own person if you really want to. I don't think it's easier to be your own person if you're living alone by yourself in the woods or whether you're living in the middle of a big city. I think it's up to you, and your surroundings merely enhance your decisions. They don't determine them.

[A twenty-one-year-old University of North Carolina anthropology major.]

Trying to be an individual in these times is no different than in previous times. We still have to get along in a society, abide by the rules and regulations, in order that all may have the benefit of everything, not to deprive anyone. So as long as we just observe rules and regulations, we can still maintain our individuality.

[A fifty-five-year-old comptroller of a Detroit manufacturing plant.]

Trying to be an individual today is actually no harder than it has ever been. The problem perhaps today is that people do not see the individual in relationship to the society, the various societies, in which he lives. There is a tendency to view the individual as totally separated from these various societies such as the government society, the home, the church, the school, and so forth. As a result, we are heading toward a certain amount of chaos.

[A thirty-year-old white English teacher in a predominately black high school in Washington, D.C.]

Perhaps the dilemma of Western man has been summed up most cogently by the legendary movie producer, Samuel Goldwyn: "Include me out!" Many of our young are quietly dropping out; yet even as they do, they tend to live and move in groups just like those of us who have stayed in society. Man seems to have as strong a herd instinct as most other animals, but his dual role as an individual and as a member of society seems to cause him more trouble than lower animals experience in getting along in the herd. Perhaps somewhere, maybe in some combination of psychology, sociology, and religion, we can find more workable answers to the problem. John Gardner, in his book *Toward a Self-Renewing Society,* has said:

> We have spent enormous energy exhorting the individual to act responsibly and very little energy designing the kind of society in which he can act responsibly. . . . We must identify those features of modern organization that strengthen the individual, and those that diminish him. Given such an analysis, we can design institutions that would strengthen and nourish him.

In other words, as Jeremy Bentham put it in 1789: "What is the greatest happiness for the greatest number?"

CHAPTER 9

WHY SHOULD PEOPLE WORK?

"... precisely. Lots of work and little meaning, that's the prescription—or 'recipe' as we medicos write it!" The jinni settled into a self-satisfied smirk.

"That's what I meant," said the man, who often realized what he had meant when someone told him.

"Ah, two heads always better than one—even acid-heads, I suspect," said the jinni, who thought himself a jokester. "Anyway, we can work that out together. Three elements, actually: lots of work; no meaning; devastating consequences from not doing it faithfully. Hey, an inspiration!" He struck his hand at his superstructure. "Maybe we could even get the colleges to keep out all but the kids who did the most meaningless work most faithfully.

"And another," he added. "Maybe we could even get industry to reserve all the good places for college kids. And then give them meaningless rewards when they qualify—like swamps of gadgets, oodles of choices, a plethora of things that nobody really wants or needs. It's perfect nonsense from beginning to end. But deadly serious."

"O.K.," said the man, "we're great. I can see our brave new world a-coming."

"Yeah," said the jinni. "A-coming sure as tomorrow." [1]

You may have read this little drama for what it is: a piece of fiction. But do you realize that it is a larger-than-life parable of the way millions upon millions of high school and college youth feel about work and the schooling for work we are giving them today?

> I personally feel that it's a very bad stand to take that people should work. I think that people, if left alone to develop their own interests, their own drives, that they will eventually do something with those drives. I don't think it's natural for a man to just sit around and not work. But "supposed to work" is a different thing, or "should work" is a different thing. I don't think people should work unless they feel that they want to. You know, like if you're into a good thing, if you're into a thing that you can really enjoy, something that you can expand yourself with, then working's good. But this idea of having to get up in the morning, you should have a job—I don't agree with it.

So said a twenty-five-year-old longhair in the mountain country of the California coast, after four years in three colleges—the first two years of which he was a cadet midshipman at the U.S. Naval Academy in Annapolis. "Reb," as he wanted to be called, spoke for more and more of the young as they address themselves to life.

What has happened to the Puritan work ethic—the notion that nothing serves better than hard work to get you in God's good graces? For many, especially the older, the less educated, the rural, those who hold to "the old-time religion," it's still there. For increasing numbers, working to earn a living is becoming questionable, and work defined as "a nine-to-five activity" is out of the question. From a comparison of the responses to those of high school and college age with those "over thirty," and from my recent observations and experiences, there is little doubt that among an increasingly large number of the young the virtues of work "to make a living" are giving way to the attitude "my work must be interesting or I won't work." Conversely, to most children aged six to fourteen, and the average over thirty—especially those in blue-collar and routine white-collar clerical, supervisory, and managerial jobs—one works "to buy food and clothes," "to get money," "to take care of one's family," "to keep out of trouble," and so forth.

Typical of nearly one half (45.8 per cent) of the 1,000 responses to Question 5, "Why should people work?" are these:

People should work so they can have money to raise families and to have fun on vacations and to buy clothes and food.
[An eleven-year-old girl, black, in Washington, D.C.]

People should work, well, because if they're going to have anything they've got to work. If they don't, well, they're not going to have anything.
[A nineteen-year-old twelfth-grade boy in Cranks, Kentucky.]

Well, first we should work to better our station in life, make it more comfortable for the people we support, try to give our children the things we was deprived of.
[A forty-three-year-old union steam fitter in Pittsburgh, Pa.]

Of course I think that people should work to support themselves and support their families or their dependents. I've always been a worker all my life, and my family before me, and I hope my family after me. I'm not a believer in giveaway programs. I think that working is good for people, that it keeps them busy, not only physically, but mentally, and it keeps them out of meanness. If they're not working, they have time to sit around and do too many thoughts.
[A forty-four-year-old small-town banker in Arkansas.]

It is interesting to compare the responses of the people who "work to eat" with the responses of those who question the traditional work ethic. The former are shorter and have an "open and shutness," a finality of judgment, which relates work mainly to material gain. The skeptics, on the other hand, are exploratory in their definition. For them, one's work is almost synonymous with one's self; work is to be considered an expression of one's total being. Work should be seen as expanding the humanness of the individual, not constricting it. There was also greater variety in the responses of the anti-traditionalists to the question, "Why should people work?"

> It's not at all necessary that people work. The hippie movement has shown that if there is money enough there is really no need to work. It's a matter of personal priorities again, and that seen in a larger context, the fact that the world does need cleaning up, but the idea of work has a Calvinistic ring. You see Carlyle with a Puritanical ethos telling people to "work, work, work for the night cometh in which no man may work." Well, I think that perhaps we should get over this, the mentality that there is anything basically noble about work itself, in itself. Work directed for some purpose, whether altruistic or for the personal betterment, is what has to be judged here.
> [A twenty-five-year-old doctoral candidate at Harvard.]

> Perhaps some people shouldn't work. Perhaps that's one of the problems that we have, that our society with its work emphasis, the idea that the devil makes use of idle hands, this sort of thing, perhaps this is one of the problems. It's no longer necessary that people work as long. Perhaps more time could be spent in emphasizing the leisure hours which obviously are very much increasing, and learning better how to simply live one's life and enjoy it and enjoy the things which are really pleasant rather than trying to spend your time getting ahead, progressing, and being successful in the old terms of the definition.
> [A twenty-one-year-old college graduate, about to enter Columbia University Law School.]

I don't always think it's necessary that people work. I think that we could build a society in which machines would do most of the work if we just went about it right. I don't think that work, as such, is necessary for people, you know, just to do their souls good. I think it's—obviously there's much to be done in the fields of research and creativity, these things. This will naturally come about, but just work to make money, to do this, to do that—it's unnecessary. [An eighteen-year-old freshman coed at San Jose State College in California, planning to be an art teacher.]

In the past people needed to work because of general subsistence, because they needed to eat. Now many people really don't need to work. All could probably eat with less people working but, but it's part of the Protestant ethic that "work, work, the night is coming" sort of thing where everybody feels that people should work and—although probably 80 or 90 per cent of the people today need to work, fewer people in the future will need to work, and some sort of a basic change in philosophy is going to have to happen.
[A twenty-one-year-old economics major in a mid-California college.]

Breaking with the traditional work ethic is not confined to the young. This fifty-four-year-old San Francisco woman said:

I wish ideally that everybody didn't have to work. I've gotten farther and farther away from the idea of going to school just in order to earn money and to work, say, nine to five. I think there are many unhappy people that don't know why they're unhappy, but their lives are completely lacking in a creative sort of a life and I would like to—I would love to see the time come when people could be busy, but busy at a creative sort of an existence and yet able to eat and have the necessities that one has to have. I'm just not too sold on work for work's sake.

Interviewing the young advocates of "no work" or "no work unless it is interesting to me," I got two distinct impressions. One was that somehow these people had more insight than their elders into the potential of our electrotechtronic age to free man from drudgery in work and to provide the "good and creative life." The other was that they had lived such sheltered lives because of the long period in which we "educate," i.e., incubate, our young that their expectations were unreal. I ran into several such individuals in a quasi-underground group at Harvard through an interview with a black woman in Cambridge, who was doing graduate work at Harvard and teaching English at a nearby university. After our interview I asked if she could put me in touch with other mature students to interview.

"Yes, I'm sure my husband will be able to help you find a number of people in our student community. And he'll be glad to get the twenty-five dollars you mentioned. You can use one of the rooms in our apartment, too." She would arrange our meeting for the following day.

Across the lobby of the Commander Hotel facing Harvard Common came a white-faced, long-haired, drooping-mustachioed figure carrying a mulatto papoose on his back. "You are Dr. Parker?" he asked in surprisingly cultivated Harvard speech. After getting acquainted over coffee to the raised eyebrows of others in the staid old dining room, we taxied to his apartment. I followed him up three flights of creaking stairs, puffing with the load of my brief case and tape recorders. C——— opened the door to a dark, book-lined hallway leading to a room in such disarray I have seldom seen. Hanging askew on the walls were five huge curved knives and one battleax, alternating with psychedelic posters. On the floor the parts of a disembowled tape recorder mingled with the broken toys of the "papoose." "Why don't you put your tape recorder here?" he said and went into the next room to deposit the little papoose. I began pushing aside a half-eaten sandwich, three ash trays, a spray of pencils and pens, and the magazines and books that covered the desk. My host smiled as he reentered the room. I had done the routine thing. We were soon into our interview. To Question 5, "Why should people work?" the twenty-four-year-old Harvard graduate (with honors) answered:

> Basically in this country we have reached a plateau where, with a certain amount of income redistribution and a certain amount even more of rechanneling resources away from whatever the current success is to chrome tailfins, and, indeed, advertising—false economic activity, spurious, wasteful stuff—into genuine production, that it will not be necessary for people to work. I mean, there is—in thirty or forty years there will be a guaranteed annual wage.

A few phone calls later I began interviewing a range of young men and women aged eighteen through twenty-six, but mainly in their mid-twenties. The first, neat in blue jeans and a man's shirt, looked out of place in the rampant disorder and ugliness of the apartment. She was beautiful. Golden hair falling below her shoulders framed a patrician face. "This is Dr. Parker." She extended a hand graciously and beamed. "Hi!" C——— left the room and we settled down next to the tape recorder. Soon Question 5, "Why do people work?"

> Well, I don't think that people should work. I think some people have to work and some people want to work in terms of getting jobs and making money. The other people, the people who either don't have to have jobs in order to make money should, of course, have something else they want to do in terms of art or in terms of writing or in terms of something that gives them meaning in their lives and a kind of objective. I'm trying to look for a job, copy editor, and the publishing field is not eagerly receiving my applications, but I'm trying to hold on to the financial level as long as I can so I don't have to have a job that I don't want, like

selling—selling insurance or selling dresses or selling books. I've moved to Cambridge from New York, which is what I wanted to do. And I just spent most of my money going to New Mexico to visit one of my friends, which is what I wanted to do. The young white people can have anything they want, really. I can have anything I want literally. I can hold out for the job I want pretty much as long as my mother will give me money for that, and that's pretty much indefinitely, till she thinks I'm not looking for a job.

This kind of thinking is carried on by a twenty-five-year-old Ph.D. candidate in English whose mother is a waitress:

I don't think I can tell you why I think people should work, but perhaps I can approach the answer by saying why people should not work. Some people have argued that in a vast capitalistic society there cannot be revolution, because the working classes have been coopted in a sense, because most people today work for security, for material things. One's happiness in life is equated with what one has. In other words, emphasis on acquisition of things, materialism. I don't think people should work mainly to possess things. I don't think the measure of happiness, the measure of meaning, the relevance and meaning, the purpose of life, depends on how much he has or how much he owns. I think work should be a liberating force. It should liberate all the potentials of the individual, and there should be correlation between what the individual is and what he does. I think that in today's society there is little correlation between what the individual is and what he does. People fit into a system and I think there is a great amount of boredom, frustration, and apathy in the American way of life. And this can be clearly shown by the fact that many young people, for example the hippies, most student activists, reject the reasons why people work.

This twenty-four-year-old Harvard major in anthropology and social relations left college in February, took the money his grandmother gave him for education, and went into movie making. "Why should people work?"

I'm not sure they should. I think that what people should
—people should only do things that they want to do. I
really believe that. And I believe that people, especially if
you've had a creative education, if you're a creative person,
have lots of things you want to do. And that it's really sort
of one of the tragedies that people are not excited by
things, are not turned on, are not in touch with themselves
enough to know that there are things they want to do. I
think there's no—I mean America's rich enough, perhaps I
can only speak for America alone—a very underdeveloped
country has all kinds of other problems. But in America
there's no reason why people should do things they don't
want to do. I think that, for example, welfare mothers—
you know there's a lot of talk about welfare mothers, you
know, because they're not working, being cheaters. They're
living off the system. Well, for one thing, I think we've got
enough wealth in this system so that if there are lazy people
then we have to support them.

Furthermore, he seems convinced that one can have his
cake and eat it, too.

What am I trying to do in my life? What do I think really is
important? What kind of job do I want to do? What do I get
pleasure from? I think that jobs—obviously there should be
all kinds of, well, rewards and securities, perhaps. But I
think that there should be enough security so that what
people do is something that they really get interested in and
excited by.

One might ask: How many of the really creative inventions
and ideas we now enjoy would have been born if their crea-
tors had felt secure?

Does "thirty minus three" put an individual so near the
"thirty mark" that he is tainted with old-fashioned thinking?
This twenty-seven-year-old Ph.D. candidate in art history
seems to be walking the thin line.

I know that myself I still have a certain Puritan satisfaction
in doing a job, and I don't think this will ever disappear

from the make-up of human beings. I would say that prideful accomplishment is essential to human well-being. Not necessarily work, hard work in the accepted sense, not necessarily forty hours a week or anything like this, but certainly productive contribution to community, productive self-improvement is essential to human health.

But "not necessarily forty hours a week or anything like this. . . ." replied a twenty-six-year-old graduate student in architecture, also working as an architect's assistant, to "Why should people work?"

I'm tempted to say that no one should have to work as a lot of my friends at school used to say and a lot of my friends, especially the ones who are still in school, say now. But as someone who works, I suppose I have to justify myself, and I think work is something that has to be done at least for a while longer to support life. We in this country, we don't necessarily have to work to earn a living, and it's getting to be a time where, uh, there will be such a thing as make-work if people want to work.

"If I get a guaranteed annual wage of $3,000 a year, who's going to work to pay me that?"

Well, two answers. First of all, I don't really have an answer, but I think that's the issue. It's not how I get my job or how the next person gets his job. It's how the society's going to operate, you know. The whole system is really questionable. And to use make-work is the question. Are we going to do that, you know?

"If I get $3,000, someone is going to have to have earned that and give it to me."

Not necessarily. I'm not sure of the quantitative amounts, but there are still going to have to be people who go out and do certain things that just can't be automated. But, for instance, there are things like all the light bulbs in the United States are made by two men. But I'm not, I'm not going to propose that I have—I really don't know what the answer is. This is the problem.

"Do you think a lot of the young people talking about not working aren't out from under the parental handout yet so they don't know?"

That's largely true. Although I think some of the real hippies, they're on their own. Their parents kicked them out a long time ago.

While only about 4 per cent of the total sampling questioned the need for "work" as the term is generally accepted today, over one-third (39.7 per cent) departed from the narrow definition of work as a means of getting food, clothing, shelter, and perhaps a little fun. This encouraging percentage seeks the ideal blend of work that is "interesting" and "helpful to others." Of these, three out of four were concerned chiefly that their work be interesting. The remaining one out of four stated his strongest desire was work that would lead to the betterment of society, the improvement of the community, and so forth. The ages of this latter group, surprisingly, formed a curve with two humps—one at around age eighteen or nineteen, the other at about age forty-five. Could it be that the older men of the tribe are now agreeing with the younger? Or vice versa? Or has it always been this way? Where is the generation gap? But it is noteworthy that they had one thing in common: higher education—at least two years of college in the case of the young, considerable graduate work, and often doctorates for the older. Black people and other ethnic groups, incidentally, occurred in the sampling to a larger degree than their percentage in the general population.

A few adults have made a complete switch in their attitude toward work, as did this sixty-three-year-old Episcopalian vicar of San Francisco. Until five years before I interviewed him, he had devoted twenty-eight years to the military, followed by years in the Establishment in the fields of advertising and the stock market. Suddenly his whole idea of the nature of work changed. Oddly enough, though he turned to the church, he did not turn to the usual "religious" view of work.

I've always been of the opinion, and it's had to suffer some changes, I could say, in the last few years—I've always thought of work as such, any kind of work as being dignified regardless of the kind it might be, and that it was absolutely necessary to work. But I think that this was, in the usual connotation of business, starting with a company at such and such a place and progressing. I'm no longer quite so sure that our emphasis doesn't need to be shifted to what does man do with time, not necessarily in how it repays him financially and in what we term success materially, but how it expands him to become a better part of mankind again, not in his narrow sphere but on a world-wide family-of-man basis.

Let's sample more of this encouraging third who seek either interesting jobs or the opportunity to help others, or, hopefully, both rolled into one.

Well, I don't know about anybody else, but I'm going to work and strive for a goal because when I die I want to have something attributed to my name. I want to, well, know within myself that I've done something for somebody else and that I wasn't selfish and I feel that I can, if I can give of myself, that's one of the finest things that you can do. And I think that's what working is. There's pay involved, but I think it's the idea of giving of yourself and I think that's great.
[A fifteen-year-old Chicano (Mexican-American) girl in California.]

I guess people should work because—working, to me, is contributing something to society, and it's being—pleasure is, well, if you don't work, all you do is lay around all the

time. I guess it's to give something to society and do something for someone—that's what I think working is.
[A sixteen-year-old black high school senior girl in Washington, D.C.]

Everyone should work to improve the world. I don't believe that when you're born into the world, it owes you a living. And for one to really contribute to everyone else for the betterment of mankind, you should be educated. You should acquire certain skills so that instead of just doing what has been done before you, you can invent new things, make new discoveries, and make a better way of life.
[A nineteen-year-old University of Tennessee major in journalism and advertising.]

I'm not sure I'm answering your questions. You ask why should people work, and I'm inclined to answer why people do work. I think they would from varying motivations. Most people work simply because they have to, in order to earn a livelihood. Some people work because they enjoy working or because they feel that through their work they're contributing something to humanity, to mankind, to their fellow man. I think that would really be the best answer to why people should work. That is, as a means of contributing to society as a whole so that all of us can live fuller, better, richer lives.
[A prominent fifty-one-year-old attorney in Chicago, father of a mentally retarded son and a brilliant daughter attending college.]

People should work because it's part of the process of life in making one feel important and a contributing factor. I believe it's a basic need we all have to contribute to our humanistic way of living, and this is our way of contributing to the future through our own contributions, through our own assets. And this process is called work. And in our own culture, capitalism is enhanced by our own efforts. And since capitalism in a democratic setting appears to be the type of philosophy I want, this helps enhance not only

the individual, but other individuals helping each other through this process. Work should not be a process of drudgery, but one of accomplishments and one of a sense of contributing to the welfare of self and to others.
[A forty-four-year-old field representative for a large publishing firm in Florida.]

Why should people work? That's different. If you said why do people work, I would say probably just to live, perhaps. But, all right, why should people work? My interpretation of that is really it's motivation. I'm just going to give an idealistic answer because I think that, well, why should people work? People should work because they like what they're doing. That's all. And whatever it is, this could be gaining an education or working on a job. And I know what I'm talking about, I think, in regard to that because I was in business for twelve years and I hated it. And I switched over to education because I felt it was something I would like and would really get something out of. And this has been true, it's something that I do like. And I know what it means to hate what you do because I hated it for twelve years. And one day I said to myself, "What are you, a zombie or a robot? Let's change; let's get out of this." So it would seem to me that the best reason for working is to do something that really you enjoy. And I don't even want to be altruistic about this because I think that if you do something that benefits someone else, it still has to be something that you want.
[A forty-six-year-old woman teacher of developmental reading in an Oakland, California, high school.]

A forty-nine-year-old dean of students in a West Coast college offers some views on work which might not appeal to status-seeking parents who push their offspring into higher education not for self-development but to get them a leg up on the rat race. His views may also be a little disturbing to those who place the energetic pursuit of improving society high on their list.

I don't believe that it's a case that people should work. I think that as we look ahead we're going to find a whole new concept of man's survival in a society. It's not necessarily true that a man should work. Perhaps what is work for one man is pleasure for another. A man who is artistic by nature may enjoy the artistic pursuits and may, in a sense, work extremely hard at this. Another man who is not artistic but who is good at physical work outdoors may really enjoy this kind of work. So I would feel that man should be perhaps occupied to the extent to which his physical and mental and emotional demands make him feel that he should be occupied. But I don't feel that it's necessarily true that man should work, that man should produce, that man should be a productive member of society. I think it's true that man should not be a burden on society from the standpoint of his activities and actions which interfere with others. But if a man chooses not to work and chooses to go through his life experience in such a manner that he can exist and survive and this is satisfactory to him, then perhaps he isn't working. He may be contributing to society by just being a person who is not detracting from society, and he may be adding to society. I can't subscribe to the concept that man should somehow work unless he feels that that work is the thing that will achieve the ends that he's after. For example, if a man who desires to marry, to have children, to have a certain quality of food on the table, to have a certain quality of furnishings and a certain quality home and transportation and medical care, then he probably finds himself going to school to seek some kind of employment that will bring that level of achievement that he desires. This in a sense is work for his own gain. So, on the other hand, another man decides to get married and have the same size family, but decides on a—doesn't decide but for him a lesser quality of all these things would be in keeping with their happiness and this might require very little work on his part. I would say that the two people should be permitted to do just that, and that society shouldn't, or educators shouldn't indicate to the second one that he's a nonproductive member of society. I think that the concept that work means that you have now taken your rightful place in society cannot be the criteria that we should go by. We've got to find some other means of evaluating or valuating a person's existence in society other than work or a contribution to that society completely.

So, after all, it's not a question of "to work or not to work." Both the traditionalists and those of the newer persuasions agree that work is important. The real question is "Work for what?" which brings us back to our main concern: schooling for what? In view of the enormous range in the reasons given why people should work, isn't it amazing that we continue to teach school as though everybody was expected to go out and do the same thing with the same degree of motivation? Our schools are merely a series of sieves, screening out successive levels of intelligence. Starting at about the fifth grade, we send youngsters into the streets with a sense of failure and a desire to get back at a society which has rejected what it has spawned. Unable to make it in school and too young to get a job, they live by the law of the jungle: Survive at any cost. It is now we who are paying the cost in billions of dollars to deal with a dropout rate of 40 per cent—four out of ten children between the fifth and the twelfth grades, a rate that has only begun to lower in the sixties. Ignoring people's individual differences in our schools has been costly and remains so. The push-out rate is still approximately 30 per cent.

Ignoring individual differences in the workplace is proving equally costly. In the name of "work for work's sake" we have alienated our young—we are literally driving some of our best brains away from the workplace. In the name of "efficiency" we have created a satisfaction gap by separating the worker from the results of his work. Whereas the craftsman or small working group used to know the joys of honest workmanship and the satisfaction of seeing their work used and appreciated, the modern worker is seldom so fortunate. Instead, along with his fellow men, he has been robotized, and has become the victim of robotized thinking about the human race.

As a psychologist, I have worked with all kinds of people —children and grownups, the mentally retarded, average and the brainy—ranging from manual workers to the top idea men of corporations. The range of individual differences is beyond all imagination, but I have found them all alike in one thing. They cherish getting satisfaction from what they are doing while they are doing it, and they all like to have a sense of achievement in what they are doing, whether the result is a thing or an idea. The extent to which an individual is satisfied with his job is directly related to the results he is able to see or visualize. A person will often work for less money to get more job satisfaction—to more directly experience the results of his work. Twenty-two years ago, at the age of thirty-six, I kicked thirteen years of "company training" and seniority in the face and started from the bottom in work in which I could "see" some results. Today more people are doing the same and starting sooner. The young no longer are wasting years and years of their working life before they ask, "Is this work something in which I can be my best self, both as an individual and as a member of society?"

With all of our technology, all of our resources (still!), and all of our high-minded idealism, why can't we devise ways for individuals at all levels of intelligence, with all kinds of interests, to find satisfaction in their work? Instead of robotizing the individual in a massive, frenetic danse macabre with the machine, why not have smaller working groups, for one thing? Instead of having a hundred people all doing the same thing and another hundred doing another "same thing" and another . . . *ad nauseam,* why not break down the huge production lines and assemble only one or two or so of each kind of worker in a room or area, with each group completing whatever is being built? Think of the satisfaction of standing back and seeing the result of your work as it took shape. Contrast this with the usual picture of workers dropping their tools when the whistle blows, glad to get out of the work prison and back into life. Pride of workmanship and trust in one's fellow man, now fast disappearing from the American scene, might once more return under conditions in which the individual could see the results of his work and feel himself a responsible and trusted member of a group.

To the cries of "Dreamer!" "It won't work!" and "What about production costs?" I can only reply that big business and industry are now paying through the nose for massive job dissatisfaction. Could it be that the never-ending demands for higher and higher wages and more and more fringe benefits are powered mainly by revenge for the prostitution of the individual in the name of efficiency? The money spent reorganizing to give first priority to "being human" instead of "making like a machine" might be recouped in getting a better-quality, *less* expensively produced product. The same substitution of hard cash for job satisfaction may also be at the roots of America's galloping inflation. We are learning that "efficiency" over humanity is, in the long run, not very efficient at all.

The closer you are to the results of your work, the greater your satisfaction in your work—this is axiomatic. Yet not only do big business and industry deprive their blue-collar workers of this kind of satisfaction but increasingly white-collar workers as well. Why do you think some of our brighter young people are throwing aside their schooling? Because they feel it is only preparing them for meaningless work.

Hardly anyone would disagree that work should be interest-

ing, but most of us at some time during our lives—perhaps
most of our lives—have done work that was not interesting,
at times deadly dull, as a way to make a living. In jobs like
this we learn to wait until after work—evenings, weekends
—to do enough interesting things to make life worth while.
Will the young, seeking only "interesting work" only to find the
world of reality, prefer to live off the dole? How many free ri-
ders can our economy stand? How long will those who work
put up with those who won't work?

The picturesque hobo, content to live on society's back-
door handouts, was celebrated for his rarity. But then the
beatniks extended the cavalier attitude toward work, followed
by the hippie movement, which has spread the "why work?"
infection to lower and lower age groups across the nation. In
the Deep South and in rural areas generally the virus has yet
to strike. Nevertheless, the idea is now flourishing among the
young intellectuals who see work as evil, but not as a necessary evil. They count on technology to free man to bask forever in the Elysian fields.

But there are other and more realistic views among the
many thinking young who represent a growing backlash
against our often ugly, soul-destroying materialism. In the
past, those who earned less money have been looked down on
as incompetents, and often were. Now, however, more and
more people, especially among the young, have *chosen* to earn
less money and spend less. Their philosophy and living arrangements nourish the notion that "the best things in life are
free," as they have moved toward less expensive, nature-oriented life styles and pleasures and away from the more expensive, artificially contrived patterns of suburbia. The better educated and more intelligent and sensitive they are, the more
they are likely to break out of the Establishment mold and
seek a more natural and nature-oriented life style. The less

educated, being less "adaptable"—the very definition of intelligence—find security in traditional patterns, are line holders for the *status quo*. Why should the more adaptable and sensitive—those who seek more natural, diverse, and less frenetic life styles—be penalized by the Establishment attitude that unless an individual's goal is making and spending more money, he is unworthy of being a full member of society? Couple the earn-less, spend-less trend among increasing numbers of the young with their newly perceived need for halting the wanton consumption and despoiling of our natural resources, and business economics as we know it today may well vanish.

Instead of being caught in the nine-to-five vacuum, increasing numbers of young people are dropping out of the job scene to work with their hands to produce something they can see, feel, sense. They read books and teach themselves or learn from each other how to make jewelry, do leatherwork, design ceramics, and develop new crafts. They often live commune style, working only enough to "get some bread" and following a life style that defies the materialism of "the world out there." Although their experiments by most standards seem immature, could it be that they are looking ahead and seeing something that we—caught up in our wires and cables, mesmerized by whirring wheels and flashing lights, our senses deadened by air not fit to breathe, our ears assaulted by a fearsome din, our nerves hair-triggered by tension—don't see? Whatever it is they see, they are asking the question, "Work for what?"

CHAPTER 10

PROGRESS?

"Stop!" cried the terrified apprentice. But the broom only turned again toward the river to fetch yet another bucket of water to pour into the already flooded room. "Cease!" "Enough!" "Abracadabra!" . . . but try as he might, the distraught apprentice could not find the magic word his master —away for the day—used to command the magic broom to stop. The word to start the broom? Oh, yes, he had remembered that easily. How much easier it was going to be to have the broom to carry the water he needed to wash the floor. But now he was drowning! Fortunately, just as he was about to perish from his own folly, his master, the Sorcerer, returned, spoke the magic word, and saved him.

Like the Sorcerer's apprentice, we have turned progress on, but can we turn it off? If we can't, who will come and save us? In the name of progress we have filled our atmosphere with bone-rotting strontium 90, life- and property-destroying smogs; our rivers and lakes with industrial and human waste; our food with poisons like DDT. We have addicted ourselves to super-stimulation, driven our young to drugs, automated much of life out of living, caged 70 per cent of our people on the 10 per cent of the land called cities, built high-rise housing blocks with no toilets on the playground so that children have to urinate in the elevator; we have produced a hair-triggered stockpile of atomic explosives sufficient to blow every man, woman, and child on earth to bits; meanwhile, we are busily turning out enough people to double the population of the world in the next thirty years. By 2070 people pollution will have reached 25 billions, instead of the approximately 3.5 billion now depleting the planet.

Of the nation's 135,000 coal miners, an estimated three-quarters have "black lung," a form of pneumoconiosis, because today modern power-operated machinery churns up far more dust than old-fashioned picks and shovels. "It used to take a lifetime to get black lung," says one mine union official, "now you can get it in a few years. That's progress." According to official government figures, U.S. workers are exposed to no fewer than 182 "hazardous" agents. On-the-job accidents last year disabled 2,200,000 workers; each month 1,100 were killed outright. Recent technological advances have brought new hazards faster than old ones have been controlled. And we are told this is only the beginning.

Travel which, by the turn of the millennium, may rocket even the ordinary citizen halfway around the globe in an hour, could turn a planet of then 7 billion people into a seething can of worms. The computer may well see the dissolution of private life. By 1973, in the area of credit information alone, the network of local credit bureaus across the nation will have 160 million Americans computerized. Credit on a shopper in Buffalo, New York, will be instantly available to a storekeeper in Carmel, California. Under the guise of a social report to "measure the quality of American life" our feelings and social mores are soon to be fed to giant computers for study. By whom?

Biologists now assure us that genetic engineering may soon

enable us to produce people to order, even hundreds of identical people, through the process of "cloning." By combining an unfertilized human female egg with the body cell of another individual, the egg cytoplasm is "switched on" so that the egg nucleus starts dividing into the billions of cells required to produce the human body. The individual thus created will be an exact replica of the individual from whom the body cell was taken. If the body cell is from a male, the resulting individual will be a duplicate male. If the cell donor is female, the carbon copy would be female. If you want 50, 100, or 1,000 identical individuals, you simply take that number of body cells from a single individual, male or female, implant them in as many unfertilized eggs, and nine months later you have that number of individuals identical in every respect with each other and the body-cell donor. It began only a few years ago with carrots; it is already being done with frogs. From there, scientists assure us, it's only one short leap to man—and to a *Brave New World* complete with test-tube baby factories.

Control the sex of your offspring? "Soon," science assures us. Would you like him (or her) to be six feet tall? Seven feet? Five feet? Bright, dumb, or average? "Entirely possible," say the biologists. "How long would you like to live?" Playing God? Not at all, playing "science." Suddenly the human race has found itself like a five-year-old in a brand-new Cadillac —able to reach the accelerator but not the brake. To the conquest of nations we now plan to add the conquest of human nature. Our efforts in this new sphere of science could produce results analogous to those already achieved by the physical sciences—the ultimate pollution of what humanity still remains in human beings, even as we are about to achieve full pollution of the planet, the only one we have. For science has become engineering. It is studied not because it is worth knowing for itself, but for its application. The scientist has become the servant of society preoccupied with technology, and the "moral neutrality" of science requires that he not be a check on the whirlwinds of technology but simply an adjunct to it.

For some reason the word has gotten out that only science is careful, accurate, honest, and objective. Therefore what cannot be called science must be careless, inaccurate, dishonest, and biased. One of the chief characteristics of science is quantifying. "If you can't count it, it doesn't count." Now we are even trying to measure love by counting the number of increases in temperatures and pulse rate that are said to occur under its influence. "My love for you is 55.5." "Oh, John, I thought you loved me at least 60!"

The other day I heard one of my colleagues say, "The Greeks couldn't broadcast their great dramas, but they could write them." We can broadcast them (if we can find a sponsor), but could we write them? If not, perhaps it is because our preoccupation—even our misconception—of science has led us to ignore the perennial problems of humanity. Robert Hutchins has written:

> Science began as part of the search for understanding. Now it is part of the search for power. . . . Preoccupation with power, technology, and innovation has led to something new in the world—Big Science. The enormous costs associated with this phenomenon are met by persuading corporations and governments of the commercial and political value of science. Big science is therefore a propaganda machine for more Big Science. In the United States Big Science is carried on principally in the universities. They thus become the instruments of corporations and government; they seek to achieve the objects that those who put up the money have in view.[1]

R. J. Forbes, holder of the Leonardo da Vinci medal of the Society for the History of Technology, put it this way:

We have come to the time when it is proper to speak of a technological order, and already many people do so, often with fear and trepidation. Technology can no longer be viewed as only one of many threads that form the texture of our civilization; with a rush, in less than half a century, it has become the prime source of material change and so determines the pattern of the total social fabric.[2]

How did technological progress get so out of hand? The idea of "progress" has not always been with us. It has taken centuries for the idea of progress to grow from a speck in man's collective consciousness. Only with the birth of science and the invention of the machine did the idea of progress— the idea that man could control his own fate—become widespread. With the coming of the Industrial Revolution, the idea of progress achieved the respectability that only in our own time has begun to crumble. Marveling at an unprecedented rush of new inventions and techniques, nineteenth-century thinkers put science on a pedestal, seeing it as the key to the solution of all man's problems. The feeling of moral superiority generated by such optimism accounts for the smugness that we associate with the Victorian era. But with few exceptions these thinkers were blind to the fact that science and technology were being used by a handful of entrepreneurs to enslave entire populations—at home and abroad. What the triumph of technology really meant was that the individual weaver no longer could have his own "trademark" of a personal pattern. Instead, miles of the same cloth were turned out to enmesh hundreds and even thousands in conformity. No more was the shoemaker solely responsible for his craftsmanship, depending on his own integrity for his whole livelihood. Instead, he sat at an impersonal bench with many others, where one man fashioned the sole, another man the heel, another the upper, still another the quarter, and so on until the umpteenth stitched the pieces together so that everybody's responsibility was nobody's, and everybody's pride in workmanship became nobody's satisfaction.

True, more shoes were made, shoes became cheaper and more people had shoes. True, men had more money to buy a widening assortment of goods now pouring out of factories, instead of bartering shoes for coats or food or wine. But he was no longer his own man. Now, he was a chattel of the man who organized his work, told him what to do, and often controlled his whole life by forcing him to live in company housing and buy at company stores. No more could the average workman wake up on a sunny morning, sniff the air, and say, "What a fine day for a stroll along the river," and simply not open his shop that morning. Such privileges were only for those who now managed him.

For most people today the situation is little better. Progress has made rank-and-file workers even more specialized, their productive efforts more fragmented, more dully repetitive, and their satisfaction in work less. Bad enough, but this condition has been increasingly extended to the kind of people who require variety in their work, who must have some opportunity for decision making, who do care what their efforts add up to. More and more of these kinds of people—the life blood of a society—are being turned off, especially the young. We simply are losing their regenerative capacities, their potential forces for renewal.

No doubt some inner necessity has prompted man in this restless, often wanton craving for progress, which has resulted in a denial of his birthright—the opportunity to live as the splendid biological specimen he really is and was for nearly 2 million years till he began tasting the cup of "civilization." The question is, with so much of his environment and so much of his "self" already used up, is it too late for man to grow up, to reclaim his birthright? If it is not too late, what can he do?

He must not only turn off progress, he must also *reverse* it, reverse the process that brought it on. And when I say "man," I mean all the passengers of our spaceship Earth. But since the United States has been the world leader in progress, we Americans must set the lead in turning it around—switching its focus from *things* to *people*.

Do we then scrap technology? No, not even if we could. But we must slow it down and redirect it. Here are some considerations:

1. We must begin a variety of experiments to utilize technology for human good instead of letting it turn out a diarrhea of things which merely waste our resources to titillate the fancy of the few, while leaving the many without even the fundamentals of life support.
2. We need experiments in a variety of life styles to rework much of our thinking about where and how man should live, and the kinds of technology he will need—and not need—to live in new (or perhaps very old) ways.
3. We must redirect our schooling. Instead of schooling for *taking,* for freebooting exploitation of our resources, we must begin teaching for *giving back,* restoring, cooperating with nature in order to preserve the only resources we will ever have. In teaching our children the full meaning of *conservation,* we may also convince ourselves that we must stop killing our planet, and forcing ourselves to live a life for which we are biologically unsuited. And the teacher always learns more than the pupil. Ask any teacher.

Slowing down our galloping technology should also slow down the pace of life. How many people would not welcome the opportunity of doing things a little more slowly, and perhaps a little more thoroughly, and with more satisfaction? Putting our "thing progress" in low gear might shift some of our best minds from adding more deadly miles per hour to the already lethal instrument we call the automobile to designing new rapid-transit systems that would attract us to use them for comfort and speed, free our streets for walking and our highways for enjoyment of our open spaces in quiet, nonpolluting cars that will not go over fifty miles an hour! The electrical industry can produce a light bulb that will last for years; yet it would prefer to keep us changing light bulbs every few months—because they can make a profit, and because we keep on doing it. Why do we let the Establishment keep us doing so much busy work—and paying it for the privilege? There are hundreds of ways we could slow down our hectic pace and find more time for creative pursuits to nourish growth of the self as a human being instead of an extension of the machine.

The increasingly barren producer-consumer existence is bad enough for those consigned to it, but what about those not allowed to put even a foot in it? The United States is the richest nation in the world, yet look at this "it can't happen here" picture: One-sixth of our nation, according to the U.S. Public Health Service, is ill-fed. In 1966 the median income of the American white family was $7,170; that of the black family little more than half—$3,874. In the fall of 1969 a congressional study turned up the fact that it would require $27 billion to bring every needy family in the United States just even with the "poverty line"—an annual income of at least $2,400! What an admission for the most wealthy nation on earth. Yet Congress said that even to give each family this small amount could not be considered for another two years! All this in the

face of a burgeoning cybernation revolution by which more
and more goods are produced by less and less people.

Job holding has been the mechanism through which economic resources are distributed. But cybernation is taking
over more and more jobs, especially those of the less intelligent who formerly performed the less skilled and repetitive
operations now handled by machines. How, then, can we continue to operate on a "no job, no income" basis for distributing resources? We've either got to invent jobs, give away resources on an increasingly large scale, or experiment with
ways to do one or the other or a combination of the two. A
major economist and presidential advisor has said that because work is such an important thing for the growth and development of the individual, one ought to pay people who do
not hold jobs, because by not working they are performing a
social service! Brains bright enough to invent cybernation are
bright enough to devise ways to eliminate its evils, or, more
positively, to spread its benefits.

"But why not simply redistribute the wealth more equally?"
you ask. Because the redistribution of current wealth would
be meaningless and its effects fleeting unless we changed the
power structure and the human greed that maintains it, by
which wealth now goes disproportionately to the few. As a
psychologist and student of individual differences among
human beings, I feel there can be no doubt about the conclusion of the Durants, that the concentration of wealth is a natural result of the concentration of ability or "intelligence," if
you will. Knowing this, "the few" must find ways to be less
greedy, to be satisfied with less of the profits of an enterprise
flowing into their own pockets and more paid out to workers.
I am convinced that even in this welfare age the vast majority
of people want to work for what they get. I have found that

all but the most inured welfare "clients" actually long for the
challenge of work to do, and the self-respect and independence that go with a pay check earned. This forty-two-year-
old black mother of four in a Detroit vocational training center for adults said:

> I entered this school because I didn't want to accept
> welfare. I thought if I could go to school I could learn bet-
> ter and I wouldn't have to accept welfare help.

"Do you think there are many people like that?"

> Many of them, yes, most of them are younger people. So
> many of them that are on welfare don't want you to know
> they are. They feel low-graded on welfare.

Even the most confirmed "reliefers" stay on welfare more
to get back at society—"make 'em pay me"—than to avoid
work.

Our present evaluation of effectiveness on the job as a criterion for paying wages, or for hiring in the first place, may
have to give way to ingenious, complex, perhaps even expensive ways to make it possible for each person to have a job
suited to his capacities. The alternative is increasing welfare,
increasing flabbiness in a larger sector of society, and creeping
discontent as the electrotechtronic monster continues to gob-
ble up jobs once open to those of lesser abilities, or presently
handicapped by youth or by skin color.

If fear of failure is keeping us from experimenting with
ways to utilize technology for the greatest good for the greatest number instead of for the favored few, we can write that
reason off on two counts. First, we can't fail any more misera-
bly than we are; second, we don't have to fail all the way.
We can learn through pilot studies. We can afford to fail a
little here and a little there knowing that some experiments in

some places will work and provide guidelines for reworking the less successful as well as spread the good ideas discovered. Why not launch a number of experiments in different locations involving various segments of the population and see what happens? In a nation that worships science and spends billions on "research," why can't we think this way about people? And why can't we let those actually involved—the poor, the less able, the less fortunate—participate in or even design economic experiments? They might surprise us with the wholesome, life-giving simplicity of their ideas. Instead of coming up with the kind of superefficient thinking that cuts people out of their jobs, they might set up an "inefficient" economy in which everyone was busy producing less, but having more time to enjoy it!

Economics is only one area in which we need to throw out many of our ideas of progress and make room for more human thinking. What keeps us from experimentation in a variety of life styles—ways of living that seek to answer the question "What is the good life?"? For one thing, most of us seem to be looking for or advocating *the* way to live, as if there were only one way and we must all find and embrace this way and no other! Anyone who has traveled about the world a bit soon divests himself of this notion. What's one man's poison is often another man's meat. I recall the life style of the sampan people in Hong Kong's harbor. They have lived in what I would consider cramped quarters, inconvenience, and filth for generations, but they don't want to leave their watery environment. As recently as 1967 the Hong Kong government simply had to fill in a portion of the harbor and build high-rise apartments to keep the sampans and junks from becoming too numerous. In Venezuela the government offered high-rise facilities to thousands of families living in filthy huts sprawled over

182 SCHOOLING FOR WHAT?

the mountainsides around Caracas. When these "rancheros" found they couldn't keep their pigs and chickens on the twenty-first floor, many refused to move.

A diversity of life styles, side by side, is another thing we find hard to accept. But take Singapore. Within that tiny city-state of 2 million people, four different life styles flourish next door to each other: Indian, Chinese, Malaysian, and British. There are no walls. Each tends to flavor the other while retaining its identity. Each has its family life style, its ways of getting and spending, its sexual mores, its ways of looking at life and death. Singapore is a more exciting city because of this variety of life styles.

Yet Singapore is also a city of too many people. The city seems to be the focal point of man's troubles; it is also one of his newest social inventions. Man has rushed into urban life too fast, actually doing violence to his very nature—violence turned on his fellow man in the form of crime in the streets, violence to his health from an environment increasingly polluted by waste, noise, and hurry. Are we doing something innately wrong, something that actually goes against the grain of the kind of animal man really is?

In their book *Man the Hunter,* anthropologists Richard B. Lee and Irven DeVore report on the symposium of the same name held in Chicago in 1966. Here seventy-five scholars in the disciplines of social anthropology, human biology, archeology, demography, and ecology from around the world drew some interesting conclusions. For one thing, man has been a tribal hunter-gatherer for over 99 per cent of his 2 million years on earth. The closing remarks of Dr. Sol Tax epitomize the consensus of the meeting:

> . . . we should study the reason for the persistence of these peoples [the hunter-gatherers] all over the world in the light of all the conditions militating against their persistence. I think that

the case of the North American Indians is especially significant. They seem to be waiting for us to go away. I am certain that there is something for us peasant agriculturalists, or, if you like, industrialists, to learn from the values associated with tribal life and with the determination of these people to preserve this way of life at all costs.[3]

Desmond Morris, author of *The Naked Ape* and *The Human Zoo*, holds that all the evils we now fight are the result of man's ignoring the simple, honest, biological signals with which he is endowed as a result of hundreds of thousands of years of development as a hunter. "Unfortunately," says Morris in *The Human Zoo*, "we tend to forget that we are animals with certain specific weaknesses and certain specific strengths. We think of ourselves as blank sheets on which anything can be written. We are not. We come into this world with a set of basic instructions and we ignore or disobey them at our peril." As a hunter, man developed built-in behavioral sets for survival: cooperation, shared leadership, and tribal sharing of resources. His immense variety of exposures as he moved over ever-new territory in search of game and dealt with an endless variety of animals afforded him a range of stimuli that made him the most adaptable and creative of all animals on earth. Compare these hundreds of thousands of years of stimulating living with a mere 10,000 or so years of settling down to the relatively tame existence of farming. Man simply was not made for it. After only a few hundred years the excitement was not enough and men moved back toward the more stimulating "hunting" way of life. This time the prey was other men and the territory was the city. But because of sheer numbers of people and the consequent shrinking of space, freedom of movement had to be curtailed, and the new intermingling of tribes produced "strangers." Now doors and locks replaced sharing. Man, the hunter, began to feel uncom-

fortable. Instead of simply moving out into the open country
to again put on the veneer of the quiet family life, he sought
to take the territory of others—and made war. Now that the
atom bomb has made wars obsolete, where can the restless
hunter direct his energy?

Perhaps we can look for an answer in another point made
by Morris: Man's strong biological drive toward the tribal
identity, by which he survived for hundreds of thousands of
years, is stronger than the new nationalism, or what he calls
"super-tribe" identity, a development which began a mere six
or eight thousand years ago. I would like to postulate here
that if man were to move backward toward simply tribal identity in which he counted as a person, he might be taking a
giant step forward. It might be a step away from "the lonely
crowd," away from the empty feeling "what I think or do
doesn't count." A return to smaller, more intimate, more self-
sufficient living units would better serve man's two selves:
Man as an individual and man as a member of society. To accomplish such a move in the vast spiderweb that is today's
techniculture will require the greatest of social invention and a
completely new kind of schooling. Some will call it revolution; others will call it progress.

How do we begin? Again, by experimentation and by working in several small areas with a range of population types.
How to select these? Let them select themselves. Put the
whole thing on a do-it-yourself basis—back to the American
way. How many Americans, especially the young, would leap
at such a chance? First there might be seminars around the
nation to discuss the several forms which experiments in life
style might take. In such sessions, conducted over a period of
time, natural leadership would arise. He, or she, would attract
followers for one idea or another. Experimental formats
would be developed for implementation in rural, urban, or
suburban settings. Each of perhaps two dozen experimental

projects would be open to only a limited number—the number the experimenters felt most suited to their goals. Participation would be by volunteers attracted by the particular project. Initial financing would be largely by government, with financial independence at the end of a prescribed number of years one of the goals of the project. In Chapter 11 we shall have a look at some previous social innovations and their implications for today's social inventors.

As they look around them, the young are asking questions. What they see in their schooling is a negative answer. They feel we are giving them schooling for "progress"—excessive, wanton, prurient progress—instead of schooling for being human on a planet that may yet be saved for humans. *Fail Safe*—the push of the final atomic button by a drunken sergeant; *On the Beach*—the atomically devastated nightmare world greeting the returning submariners, the now common street-corner sign designating "bomb shelter," even the nightly TV newscast, all these now hang like the sword of Damocles over all our heads. "Anti-ballistic missile," "massive retaliation," and "overkill" are now a part of our everyday vocabulary. The young have never lived otherwise, yet they imagine, they dream, it could be otherwise. To move toward that dream, the young idealists often resort to the thing they deride: human violence. And their selection of immediate targets may be just as illogical. They storm military centers, burn draft cards, and curse the ROTC in a world not yet free to lay down arms and live by brotherly love alone. Hardly anyone could argue against the proposition that the first step to stop the fighting is for each combatant to put down his weapons—fists, knives, rifles, or bombs. "But when will this laying down of arms begin?" ask the young. "We will fight against anyone who tries to draft us to fight. We will fight against anyone who has anything to do with war. Universities that take contracts for the military and companies that provide the weapons are our enemies and evidence that we may even have to destroy the establishment to end war." But this is not the whole picture.

My continual visits to college campuses include walks through their student unions to look at bulletin boards, talk with "politicos" passing out literature, and sample the latest issues of the underground press. Recently something new has been added: ecology on the march. A huge sign over one of the student-manned booths in a traffic-filled corridor proclaimed the rising mood of the young: "Earth—love it or lose it. Nature always bats last and her demands are *not* negotiable. Join Ecology Action."

Our society's answer to the question "Schooling for what?" has resulted in our three major evils: overpopulation, overindustrialization, and overurbanization. In the name of progress, man has placed himself in an environment foreign to his biological make-up and strained his adaptive capacity to the breaking point. Instead of providing sex education to allow for the natural exercise of a biological nature unique to man while controlling the population, we avoid the subject, preferring, one would suppose, to carpet the planet with wall-to-wall people. Instead of teaching about the extent of our resources and their wise use, we teach "mining and manufacturing," identifying countries of the world by their products instead of by their people and how they think. Instead of teaching how we might live more widely distributed over the land —living and learning with nature—we seem chiefly concerned with how to stack more people on top of each other and how to train ourselves to exist in a human zoo when we could be learning how to create and live in a magnificent game park.

We have followed the technologists wherever their techniques have taken them. Are we going to continue on this mindless suicidal course? Our schools are the place to start turning it around.

CHAPTER 11

WHERE DO
WE START?

Actually, our school curriculum down through the years seems to have been based on the Seven Deadly Sins rather than the Seven Cardinal Virtues. Instead of conducting our schools in a manner that exemplifies and inculcates the qualities of justice, prudence, temperance, fortitude, faith, hope, and charity, we have more often provided a working model for the development of sloth, pride, envy, anger, covetousness, gluttony, and lust. Consider:

1. Because we largely ignore individual differences in the learning rates and capacities of students, we condition at least two-thirds of them to *sloth: disinclination to action or labor.* At best we teach only the middle one-third. The lower one-third, lacking the capacity and the speed to learn as much or as fast as others, begins to tire of continual failure and gives up, become lazy. The upper one-third, able to complete more work in less time, finds school a bore and lapses into idleness. Since neither laziness nor idleness is natural to them, young people opt out of a situation that so goes against the grain,

but not before they have adopted failure and boredom as a way of life. We see them on our streets and berate them for the indolence into which we have forced them.

2. Because we give "grades" we build *pride: inordinate self-esteem* among students who have naturally superior capacity and who have somehow learned to put up with an often meaningless curriculum. They receive good grades for doing what comes naturally. This makes for *vanity, overboldness, extravagance, and other forms of self-glorifying excess.* Unfortunately, because our schools are largely training institutions and allow little or no time for real education—the educing of thought, creativity, and self-generative knowledge—students have little opportunity to experience the feeling of pride in its more positive attribute: *a sense of delight or elation for some act or possession.*

3. We give bad grades to those who have a less-than-average degree of natural learning ability or to those of superior ability who can't find meaning and relevance in the curriculum. In both of these we build *envy: a painful awareness of the advantage of others and a desire to possess it.* These students take all they can of humiliation and self-debasement, then they drop out. Thus it is that *each year* we send over 4 million students out into our streets with *malice* in their hearts toward a society which *begrudges* them success. And we are chagrined when they take out their *spite* in hundreds of millions of dollars' worth of damage to schools, crime in the streets, and drug addiction.

4. We teach history as though man's *anger* were the only thing worth recording—the Peloponnesian Wars, the Napoleonic Wars, the War of 1812, the Civil War, the Spanish-Ameri-

can War, World War I, and so on—remember: Each is a story of man's *fury, indignation,* and *rage, usually implying a griev-ance* (real or imagined) *and a desire to revenge or punish.* We have taught our children a wide range of models for express-ing their *resentment.* We have aroused the *animosity* of the thinking young by saying one thing and doing another; we have *offended* their sense of honesty. They are expressing their *hurting feelings.* In addition to their *strong feelings of antagonism* over our unjust war in Vietnam, a polluted planet, adult attitudes toward sex, and a host of other things, they rightly accuse the Establishment of conducting schooling as though it held a *grudge* against those not equipped by nature to learn as well as others.

5. We have held up skill-drilling and fact-packing as the way to economic success, on the assumption that economic success is the goal that one must reach at the price of all else. From the very beginning of school we implant in each child *a deep desire to own wealth.* We teach him *covetousness.* Forcing our children to work for grades instead of the joy of learning has put materialism above all else in their minds. Fortunately, this teaching has begun to backfire as the thinking young see how it has led to a society steeped in *greed.* A visiting Martian watching our TV or flipping through our magazines or news-papers might well describe our civilization as *ravenous* or *ra-pacious.* Indeed, thanks to our materialistic schooling, we are engaged in raping our portion of the planet—and helping other "less developed" countries to rape theirs.

Our *insatiable grasping* has turned us into a "thing nation." Congress appropriates more money for education mainly be-cause economists have proven that more education makes more earning power which, in turn, produces more buying power, which turns the wheels of industry faster and faster—

for what? For decades our country has been run mainly by economists whose reputation rested on how much they could increase the annual GNP (Gross National Product). Recently a leading member of that fraternity conceded, "It is not enough just to grow—it's a question of growth for what." But even as he spoke we were introducing into our schools a new philosophy of "accountability" in which the teacher gets paid only if the pupil learns! Even more deadly, we have devised new schemes for polluting the joys of learning and making a mockery of education by rewarding "a learning bit" with a lollipop or a green stamp!

6. With only 6 per cent of the world's population, the United States consumes 40 per cent of the world's resources —even as nearly one-half of the world's population goes underfed. One TV commercial exhorts us in sight and song to partake of a king's feast of food and drink; the next one urges us to lop off our fat with this pill, that wiggly belt, or these polyunsaturated something-or-others. Putting on fat in the United States is big business. So is taking it off. *Gluttony*. We have gotten this way because generation after generation of schooling has emphasized the material—that if having something was good, having more was better. Our philosophy of schooling has enabled the "haves"—those who could learn what we wanted them to learn—to experience gluttony: *an excess in eating and drinking,* while the "have-nots" look on. For the first time the have-nots are able to see this *excessive indulgence* and are beginning to ask "where's mine?"?

7. The Janus-faced attitude of the typical adult toward sex —taboo it on the one hand, commercialize it on the other— has created a profound confusion in most of the young. The notion that "stolen fruit is always sweeter," reinforced by con-

stant "sex sell," has often turned a normal, healthy *sexual desire* into *desire as a ruling passion.* The young today are crying for psychological as well as biological understanding of their overpowering drives. They cannot understand why a thing so important as sex should not be a part of their regular schooling. Those who have sought to withhold sex education or to water it down to meaningless mush do not lessen the *intense need.* Instead, they drive the young away from what could be a new and beautiful concept of man-woman relationships and turn their natural *craving* into mere *lust.*

Our schools are hopelessly bogged down in the mud of tradition. Only occasionally does a tiny point of light appear. Take East High School in Rockford, Illinois. Under a new "open campus" policy students need be present only when they have a class scheduled. "We used to operate on the original sin concept," says Superintendent Thomas A. Shaheen. "That is, if you leave a student alone, he'll do something wrong." With open campus, Shaheen claims, problems of vandalism, fights, and smoking in the school building have disappeared.

We really don't know how much responsibility the young can take for their own learning. We've seldom given them a chance! Why not? Are we afraid that they might handle themselves better than we do? Or do we think that children are just naturally lazy? Is there really such a thing as a lazy child? I have never seen one. I have seen only disinterested pupils trying to stay alive in schools that kill interest. Have you ever seen a pupil who failed in school? During the past twenty years I have personally worked in over 900 classrooms in more than 150 schools in the United States and 12 other countries, and I have never seen a failing pupil. I have seen only failing schools. As large as life is, as multifaceted as man's activities are, and as individually different in interests and natural abilities as we are, why do schools have to be so dull and constricting and so heedless of our individual differences in learning rate and capacity?

Is it any wonder that only 10 per cent of the 512 high school and college students I interviewed across the nation express even mild satisfaction with their schools? The dissatisfaction increases as one goes up through the grades, as schools fasten their vise-like grip on the minds and feelings of children. Why did 3,157 middle school, high school, and college students in the United States and Canada write the *Educator's Guide to Media and Methods* to say that "school is a bore"? Why has suicide become the third biggest killer of college and university students? Why are physical attacks on teachers—to the point of cutting throats—increasing to the extent that in a mid-continent school system with 1,900 faculty members most of the teachers carry guns?

The other day as the jet I was on came in for a landing over a large city, I looked down and saw two buildings several blocks apart. Why, I asked myself, were two such large schools so close together? Then I looked again. Although both appeared very much alike, I saw yellow school buses begin streaming into one. It was a school. The other was a jail! Why do we take our kids out of the real world, put them in an education box, and lock the door?

Is this what we want? If it isn't, where do we start changing things? We start by turning away from the answer given by the sixty-four-year-old labor union leader in Pittsburgh:

> If for no other reason, to teach discipline. I think discipline and the habits that are formed in the child carry on through life.

Or the response of this fifty-four-year-old floor sweeper in an auto parts factory in Detroit:

We should have schools to educate the kids more of the way that us parents used to be taught in the olden days.

Or the deadly pronouncement of this forty-seven-year-old English teacher in a small Pennsylvania town:

To train and fit the citizen to the society he's going to be a part of.

Or the locked-in thinking of this brain-washed twenty-year-old small-town Minnesota girl in her junior year at the University of Denver:

I think we need schools simply because we live in a very highly civilized and technological, scientific society. . . . So right now we need schools to educate and even mold the people to function in the society that they have created.

The answer to the question "Schooling for what?" lies not in schooling for technological progress but schooling for human progress. We must now dedicate a major part of schooling to educing from the child, the pupil, the student the use of his total faculties in dealing with the questions of *what? why? when? where?* and *who?* instead of merely *how?* Our schooling today consists largely of the "how" training. We've got to turn the whole thing around: switch the emphasis as well as the proportion of time spent in the school day for mere *training,* or skill getting, and that for *educing,* or skill using. And we must enable the learner to move easily back and forth between training and educing as he, himself, perceives the need for more skills in the pursuit of his interests.

What about the curriculum? The curriculum is in the head of the learner. Following his own interests, he seeks out, tries out, and combines knowledge in ways new to him. In a word, he *creates.* He continually experiences the joy and the excitement as well as the tribulations and demands of creativity— even though what he creates may have been done a thousand times before. What matters is the process—the *feeling* of creativity.

What about man as a member of society? Working both as an individual and as a member of a group, he will be a student of *humanics,* a new area of learning I am proposing here. Humanics would replace fragmented, irrelevant courses with a program to help the student to pull together such disciplines as biology, psychology, anthropology, and sociology and relate them to man—and himself—both as an individual and as a member of society. Furthermore, humanics is concerned with ways in which we can utilize our scientific and technological know-how to create organizations devoted to serving man, instead of creating men to serve organizations.

This does not mean tossing aside new teaching machines, TV, and other gadgetry. We must make every worth-while aid to learning available to the learner—when he needs it—but without losing him in the flashers, wires, cables, and keyboards or leading him into a technological trap in which learning becomes so abstract, so divorced from life, that he comes up with a living model of 1984!

Doesn't this twenty-six-year-old senior at Oglethorpe University in Atlanta give a better answer to the question "Schooling for what?"

> We should have schools to help people learn—to learn how to live, to learn how to be a better person, to learn how to learn.

Or this twenty-one-year-old Indianapolis history major:

> We should have schools to assist man's quest for knowledge and to help people to learn to think for themselves.

I asked a black nineteen-year-old sociology major from Greensboro, North Carolina, where her mother is a maid in one of the city's schools. Her answer:

I think we should have schools to give everyone an equal opportunity for life, liberty, and the pursuit of happiness.

A twenty-four-old Columbia University English Ph.D. candidate, a leader of the Students for a Restructured University, said:

We need schools in order to develop responsible citizens capable of contributing to a culture that is worth living in.

Basic to this last notion is developing a culture worth living in, which means correcting what's wrong with the culture we have now. How can young people even begin to face the problems of today's world when a major portion of the school day all the way up through the grades is a variation on teaching the 3 R's, skills, with little time devoted to helping students relate them to life? When students ask "What is the use of this?" we tell them "Learn it because I said so," and press on to reach Chapter 7 by Easter. We treat knowledge in the same way, stuffing in the bits and pieces. Don't ask why. Don't ask that they be connected in some meaningful whole. You're not interested? We don't have time to worry about your interests. Relevance to life? Don't worry about it. Schooling for what? We'll tell you what's good for you.

Do we have some sadistic need to kill motivation in the young—denying them the opportunity to learn about things that interest them while force feeding them what they can see no use for? We all know, if we'll just think about some of the skills and knowledge we've developed in our businesses or our hobbies, that we learn *because* we are interested—and we will not even attempt to learn a thing that does not interest us. In addition, what we are motivated to learn because of interest we retain. Much of what we "learned" under coercion in school we have forgotten. Furthermore, we learn things in which we are intensely interested much faster than things in which we have little or no interest.

I barely passed algebra and flunked geometry in high school. I simply couldn't see any use for it—all those x's, y's, triangles, trapezoids, and other trivia. Some years later I began studying to become an airplane pilot. Cross-country navigation brought me face to face with an old enemy—the triangle. This time, instead of being turned off, I was turned on. Instead of lessons and weeks of senseless struggle, I learned about the major properties of the triangle in perhaps two hours. I passed Latin in the same way—by the skin of my teeth, hating every parsing and every conjugation. Many years later, through my work as a psychologist, I became interested in developing better learning systems for the teaching of reading and other communication skills. Before long I was studying Latin and Greek word origins to find clues to underlying commonalities in language that might make learning more efficient. The work led to the completion of my doctoral degree at Columbia University.

Examples of learning fired by interest are common, yet we continue to deny the privilege to our children in schools and colleges to the cries of "irrelevant, not meaningful, unreal!" What would happen if after, say, the age of twelve, a student could begin to study whatever he wished? Oh, he'd soon become lopsided, you say. He'd only want to learn all about airplanes, or cars, or butterflies, you say. Yes, that may be how he starts. But when he wants to build a more complex model airplane and is up against the problem of reading more difficult instructions, don't you think learning to read better is suddenly going to become mighty important—even interesting! Figuring the wing surface needed to lift his own version of air travel might bring on a frenzied rush for arithmetic— and more. Not too ironically, you may be one of the millions of adults now taking reading courses because you just discovered the need to read better!

Why can't we raise to major importance the *educing* (from Latin *educere, e* out + *ducere* to lead: hence to bring out, elicit) part of schooling to make our schooling relevant and release the true learning power within each individual boy and girl, all the way up through the grades, colleges, and university? This is not to cut out the training or skill-getting part of schooling. It is simply to make it available when the learner wants it and accomplish it more effectively through the use of newer technologies for learning. Most important, make it possible for the learner to move back and forth between activities that educe the use of his skills and further training to get more skills.

But suppose he wants to be a dentist; you'd let him study just anything? I didn't say that. Dentistry requires the possession of certain specific skills and knowledge. If in his self-selected pathway he comes upon dentistry as a way of doing his thing, we can be sure he will buckle down to the requirements of becoming a dentist, and spending the years needed to fulfill them. As we move further down the hierarchy of intellectual capacities toward those with average or below-average intelligence—people who will be technicians or skilled, semi-skilled, and unskilled workers—less and less "schooling" is needed. Why not let them move very early out of formal schooling to find a useful role in the workings of society— provided we make further schooling easily available, perhaps even as a part of their ongoing job, if and when their interest is sparked. We might then be able to break through the crust of the high school diploma and eliminate what one Harvard student thought about college:

> I think we've backed away from society, from important things, by going to college. I think it's a moratorium for four years. You can do your work, which may be meaningless to you, but you can go on, and so the carrot's in front

of the horse. After four years then you will be able to earn
$15 or $20 thousand a year and everything's going to work
out. That isn't necessarily true, and even if that is, I think
that's a horrible thought. All you have to do is put in your
time and then you can sort of live in peace in a narcotic
state, and not deal with some of the more important things
of life.

How much more exciting it might be never to know that
you'd completed some bit of learning but that you've got
enough for now and can come back for more when you want
it!

Having taught adult classes in the United States and in
Latin America, I can tell you that the desire to continue to
learn, the concept of learning as a lifetime pursuit, is not confined to the young or the brainy. I have worked with doctors,
lawyers, businessmen, and housewives in the improvement of
communication skills. I have worked with *campesinos* in
dark, dank basements of industrial buildings in Caracas, Venezuela, with some of the most eager learners I have ever experienced—men and women in their twenties, forties, fifties,
and even sixties—acquiring the skills of literacy and simple
trades. The *campesinos* came to their learning late in the day,
tired from eight or nine hours of work. The courses were provided by the government as one means of upgrading worker
productivity, earnings, and, hopefully, the economy. The
workers came for more money but stayed, in spite of extremely poor conditions, because they found learning exciting.

We have discussed how work for the vast majority of people in the United States has lost its excitement. One aspect of
this loss is the thrill of learning. Wouldn't it be ironic if we
found that the hue and cry for more wages stemmed more
from a need for excitement than a need for more money! Put

another way, we might be surprised to learn that because the worker doesn't feel he is growing on the job or in activities related to his job he takes out his frustration in demands for more money. Put still another way, because workers, especially those in large organizations, feel they are not appreciated or even known by their employer, such feelings as, "Well, he doesn't care about me, why should I care about him?" are becoming more and more widespread.

The best evidence that you care about someone—man or woman, young or old—is showing you are interested in his welfare, especially in his growth as a person. If an employer wants to demonstrate his interest in his employees as human beings, he will do something that, in effect, says, "I know that because of the nature of large organizations today it is becoming harder to have interesting work and to grow on the job. I know, too, that you are a human being, one capable of unlimited growth and creativity in so many more directions than a job is able to offer, therefore . . ."

If I were a businessman today, responsible for the efficient operation and employee morale of a large business or industry (and I was for thirteen years), I would announce the creation of a learning center—"a springboard for your adventuring mind right here in our own building." From the standpoint of my own and my company's selfish interest such a center might do more to show my employees I was really interested in each of them than continuing to add so-called fringe benefits while battling wage increases.

The center would literally be a "springboard for the adventuring mind." It would be a cafeteria of learning, where employees would find a large roomful of books, pamphlets, specialized magazines, and such modern learning aids as self-operating slide projectors, tape recorders, movie films, microfilms, teaching machines, and even computer terminals, each with a library of materials in wide-ranging fields of interest. Here each individual could start where he was and move ahead as fast and as far as his learning rate and capacity would allow in pursuing what interested him. There would be no teacher, only an attendant to show how the various learning aids work and to guide and consult on which steps the learner might take beyond the facilities of the center—the public library, a formal course in a nearby college, further individual study, or group efforts to form a camera club, model-racing association, little theater, or whatever. All employees from floor sweeper to vice president would have one hour off three, four, or five days a week *on company time* to use the center in any way he saw fit. Schedules would be staggered so as to interfere minimally with the ongoing work of the business. What little disturbance it did cause might serve to shake the business out of the lethargy accompanying years of the same routines. Very large businesses might need to set up centers in more than one location for maximum use and to prevent overcrowding of facilities.

The result of all this would be individuals continually expanding in their thinking, living more creative, thoughtful, and interesting lives, and becoming more interesting to live with. The explicit purpose of the learning center would not be to generate new ideas to improve the business. However, if there were some fallout of new ideas and ways of doing things better I'd want to make sure the contributors were rewarded in proper coin. And what would be *my* reward? In addition to the distinct possibility of having more efficient and thoughtful employees on the profit side of the ledger there would be the pleasure of running "a happy ship" as my old Navy skipper used to say—of walking down office hallways or past working groups and getting smiles of real appreciation as a person, instead of merely smiles of respect. Things might go so well that even the stockholders would finally understand. They might even make me chairman of the board!

Where would the money come from? Not from employees' wages or future apportionments of income to be spent for wages. No, it would come from company profits—reflecting my reassessment of the nature, purpose, and role of business in the United States of today. Business has not only the responsibility but a golden opportunity to make the individual's work—or identification with his work—more meaningful. Another approach to fulfilling this obligation has been discussed in the previous chapter. By adding richness to the lives of those in its own sphere of influence, business and industry could well directly attack the spiral of poor productivity and higher wages that fuel our deadly inflation. Perhaps if there were more real satisfaction in work, more favorable identification with it, the worker would be less likely to push more and more for the higher wages that drive inflation up and up, keeping us working harder and harder to make money to purchase things we often don't really want but only buy as status symbols. Instead, if business devoted more time and dollars to helping people follow their real interests and develop new and exciting ones, perhaps our whole value system would change. Instead of lifetimes spent in grim pursuit of the dollar, we might begin to learn how to pursue learning for living. For many the notion that "happiness is a warm blanket" might turn into the idea that "happiness is a hot interest." It is what the young are searching for—often in vain—as they painfully try to sort out the fragments of learning we throw at them daily in the name of schooling.

We must turn the school curriculum upside down, so that the major part of the student's time is occupied in educing the use of the skills and knowledge he has in pursuit of goals he himself sets, based on what his interests are, instead of the meaningless acquisition of skills and knowledge for which he has no use. Typically, today, around 90 per cent of the student's time is taken up with skill training and fact packing. If he is lucky, he gets the remaining 10 per cent to utilize his skills and knowledge in pursuit of something that interests him. What a waste of skills and knowledge! Yet the same businessmen who wouldn't think of keeping 90 per cent of their capital money idle in a checking account that does not earn interest sit on school boards and demand a curriculum that simply piles up skills and knowledge that can only deteriorate from disuse. Furthermore, our headlong rush of "progress" is making skills and knowledge learned today obsolete tomorrow. The industrialist would not think of laying in a supply of machinery to use when his present machines wear out. He knows there will be new and different machines—and he will have to get them to compete. Yet this same industrialist will demand that schools teach the same outworn skills and knowledge he himself learned years ago in school. Moreover, the successful businessman spends much of his time seeking ways to meet the increasingly diverse and individual demands of his customers, catering to their every whim. There was a time when the soapmaker offered a simple bar of soap, the function of which was to clean. Today soap comes in every imaginable form, size, shape, scent, and packaging, and is marketed more as a status symbol than for its basic function: to clean. Yet, the successful marketer will support a school system that forces each student to use the same book at the same time and expects the same amount and the same speed of learning from each, and, worse, he will expect the school to brand the student who is not able to keep up—or who refuses to be kept down—with a "grade."

Our course offerings from first grade right up through high school, college, and university are really not so bad in themselves, although the ways of exposing the learner to their content often leaves much to be desired. But the real problem of "relevance, meaningfulness, realness" comes from our insane desire to stuff heads with knowledge in the same way that one stuffs a turkey, forgetting that the dressing doesn't do the turkey much good. How do we justify our frenzied passion for speed in packing knowledge into our children? We seem to have a hang-up on knowledge and speed in administering it —perhaps some notion that the more knowledge one has the more wisdom. Of course we forget that some of the world's outstanding criminals and dictators have been brain boxes who absorbed knowledge like a sponge, but somehow escaped relating enough of it to life to use it for anything but the destruction of life! Why so much knowledge so fast? Why so much "required" knowledge when we are fully aware of two things: First, knowledge becomes obsolete, and second, knowledge when not used rots. With the knowledge explosion we can scarcely get new knowledge into a course of study before facts are changed by new findings. With more knowledge than one has the opportunity to deal with, it dries up, decays, finally vanishes like all dead matter.

How much knowledge, then, should we be giving our young as they move through schooling? Only as much as they can use. The rest of the time we should be teaching them how to seek out knowledge, to generate knowledge on their own, to learn how to learn. Knowledge is the lumber needed to build the house of life. If we are going to help the student learn how to use it we will have to furnish enough to give him sufficient practice in using it; we must help him lay in a reasonable supply of assorted pieces to draw on from time to time. But we can't give him a lifetime lumberyard; we might give him a lot of pieces of the wrong kind, the wrong size, or the wrong quality, which would simply lie and rot. So we don't try to fill his "warehouse" with a lifetime supply of knowledge—even if he had a big enough storage capacity for all of it and we had enough time to stack it in. Instead, we give him the tools of getting the knowledge he needs on his own *when he needs it*.

As we noted earlier, only a little over 200 years ago all the world's knowledge was said to be contained in the three volumes of the *Encyclopaedia Britannica*. Today its editors are quick to point out that its present twenty-three volumes merely touch on a range of man's knowledge, and by no means all of it. In olden days a scholar could claim to know almost all there was to know—and he could integrate all he knew in his own head. Today there is not only an impossible amount of knowledge to deal with, but we hurl it at the student in bits and pieces. How can a student hope to pull together such fragments as this thirty minutes of geography, that forty-five minutes of history, or the hurried hour of science? Do we ever stop to add it up? Only rarely, if at all. Instead, we rush on covering course after course, mile after mile of schooling terrain, without ever being able to see the scenery, much less being able to think and feel "what it means to me."

A college freshman recently said to me, "I signed up for a course in geology because it was all I could get at that hour, even though I knew I'd probably hate it. But you know it's about the best course I've ever had. This guy—this prof— doesn't seem to have a course we have to finish. He just brings out ideas and then says, 'Go out and see for yourself.' And I do, and I'm learning how to look at the land around here in a completely new way, even though I've lived here all my life, and to see what it all means to me." Why didn't this thrilling experience happen to this individual when he was in early grade school? I'll tell you. Because he wasn't lucky enough to find a teacher who would defy the system enough to slow down—to stop the race for page 153 by Christmas—to give only so much knowledge while encouraging the learner to use his own senses and to develop skills for generating more knowledge meaningful to him. Instead, his teachers had been hidebound by a school board that bought knowledge in books and were determined to stuff it into his head, fragment by fragment, with none of the glue of "what it means to me" to hold it together—and later to test it out of him in the same way.

This brings up the diabolical scheme called "National Assessment," designed to draw the noose on individuality even tighter and fasten the chains of lockstep even more firmly on learners clanking down the track of the coming "national curriculum." Our boys and girls are tested to death, with little result other than to use up reams of graph paper and more cups of coffee in conferences asking, "What shall we do now?" I did this for years and finally got sick of it. There's nothing wrong with evaluation of performance—provided the results are placed in the hands of the learner. With feedback, a knowledge of "how am I doing?" the learner can improve his performance. But we merely test and chart, or test and simply file and rob the boy or girl of his learning—while educational publishers make millions. The same can be said of basal readers, still a fixture in our schools, which not only do not provide a feedback of reading skills learned, but lockstep the millions of our boys and girls through learning to read as though each were an identical twin! This was true of "Dick and Jane"; it is true of the villain in new clothes, the "linguistic" reader. The picture improves very little short of the graduate school level. Since only about 2 per cent of the population ever gets to graduate school, this leaves 98 per cent whose impression of school is that of being driven through like a herd of cattle. Educational testing, like technology, has gotten out of hand. Basic textbooks continue to demand of the young machine-like thinking—except for the 30 per cent who won't take it, and drop out. We now claim that we are containing all but 29 per cent. How are we doing it? By spending today unnecessary billions of dollars to "adjust the curriculum to meet a wider range of needs" when we could have been doing it all along for mere millions—if we had not been gearing our schooling to an unrealistic and immoral blindness to individual differences. We're now paying for what we bought, but the bill is going to be much higher if we don't provide for a diversity of learning rates and capacities and switch our emphasis in schools from training a robot-like producer-consumer citizenry to educating a society that asks "produce and consume for what?"

In his *Two Worlds* C. P. Snow, the famous British scientist and author, poses the battle between the sciences and the humanities. He makes the point that the humanities are coming off second best—alarmingly so as the technology monster shapes man to its own needs rather than helping man to become more human, a being more in keeping with the biological creature he is. If we are to reverse this deadly trend, we must take the *humanics* approach; first, "unfragment" knowledge; second, integrate the sciences and the humanities. Humanics conceives of schooling not so much as "study" as a "learning experience," and this should apply at all grades and age levels. In humanics-oriented schooling there would be a time set aside at many points all through life when the individual, alone or with others, consciously adds up the bits and pieces of knowledge and skills he has learned and asks the ancient *quo vadis?*—whither goest thou? A school with humanics as its basic tenet would, on the one hand, provide for many points along the way at which the learner would spend time in meditation, in simply adding up his several studies to answer the question, "What does it all mean to me?" On the other hand, humanics would be the guide to his selection of areas of study, and reselection as his interests broadened, took on new intensity, or changed direction.

The experience of humanics is a time for considering and discussing the *what, why, when, where,* and *who* of things, temporarily freeing the self from the often stifling *how* and regenerating dreams of one's own humanity. Now technology (the *how*) can be put in perspective. Instead of being seen as battling opponents, the sciences and the humanities can be viewed in a dynamic relationship, each acting on and being acted upon by the other; yet man is firm in his search for ways to be true to his being instead of losing himself in a whir of wheels or polluting himself off of his planet.

Humanics is not a matter of people staring at their navels. To the contrary, it enables people to get into the main stream of life. Already there are straws in the wind to indicate that such a movement is under way and ready for joining.

The beatniks, followed by the hippies, were, of course, devoted to what I am calling humanics but with an informal and sometimes negative, even self-destructive, way of going about it. However, what they have been trying to stand for, often in quiet desperation, is now cropping up in more formal and positive settings like the experimental college, the "free university," and the Esalen Institute. Simulation, or role playing in life-like games, is another way of educing one's knowledge and skills in "playing out" a humanic approach to a problem.

What are some of the things that go on in these early attempts to revolutionize the learning experience?

Beginning in 1967 with two classes and twenty participants, the Experimental College of San Diego State University by the end of 1969 offered over fifty courses involving "well over 900 faculty members, students of all ages, and community people." The catalogue of courses ranges from the ordinary to

the exotic: Candlemaking, Creative Writing Merging with
Theory of Poetry, Humor Environment, Building a Counter
Culture, Witchcraft, Liberation: Male and Female, Filmmak-
ing, Communal Living, Black Power and Theology, Life Insurance: How to buy it, and many more. There is no paid faculty. Operating under the general aegis "If you know
something, teach, if you don't, learn," students who feel themselves qualified offer courses for volunteer, no-credit attendance. The college provides rooms in the student union building. Other free universities operate on campus or in somewhat
makeshift quarters with equally shaky financing.

One of the more exciting of the ninety-odd groups around
the nation moving in the direction of humanics is the Esalen
Institute, described as "a center to explore those trends in the
behavioral sciences, religion, and philosophy which emphasize
the potentialities of human existence." Michael Murphy, president and founder of the institute, says that Esalen was inspired by the concept that repressed, forgotten, untapped resources within each human being are practically limitless in
positive potential.

At the institute one may participate in one-day, three-day,
or longer seminars, workshops, and group experiences while
living with others in the mind-expanding setting of the Big Sur
mountain and sea country some 200 miles south of San Fran-
cisco. Among the dozens of offerings are:
Encounter
Sensory awakening
Creative awareness and education
Gestalt and movement
Craft workshops (ceramics, graphics, and so forth)
Aggression and peace revisited
Kinetic theater
Ecological awareness.

Founded in 1962, Esalen has attracted a number of nationally known figures in psychology, anthropology, sociology, and related human sciences, but it has seldom put them together with members of the "hard sciences," which I would call a true humanics approach. But the institute is not standing still.

When I asked Mike Murphy about schooling, he emphasized "the principle of the free learner," but added, "Even if we do follow the principle that learning should be based on true interests and needs, still there has to be some kind of apprenticeship and some kind of sustaining discipline to carry that line of learning through, whether it be arithmetic or writing or the kinds of things we're working on here at Esalen which have to do with altered states of consciousness, or personal relationships, or the exploration of your values."

Could he think of ways to make schooling better? Indeed he could. In addition to his free-learner principle, he would inject a large measure of emotion into the schooling process. He cited a Ford Foundation–Esalen experiment in applying psychodrama to the learning and appreciation of literature in classes of dropout and problem students. "And they even scored higher on objective tests of remembered facts," he added.

Enlarging the whole domain of creative, affective awareness in each individual is a major goal at Esalen. As to man's future, Mike is not only optimistic but enthusiastic. "My belief is that man is on an evolutionary voyage toward fantastic destinations. One of the main directions is the enrichment of consciousness. One reason to work—why I work—is to create a world in which this richer consciousness can grow and flourish." Murphy believes that we are in the greatest renaissance of all time. "The renaissances have been times of enormous ferment. Those were not peaceful times; they were exciting times and sometimes violent because the most important things that people live for were at stake. And when those things are at stake, people are going to shout, scream, and often storm the barricades."

Simulation holds great promise for giving humanics form and body. At a conference on simulation I attended we spent three days studying the theory and possible application of games and simulation, then broke up into groups of twenty or thirty men and women to take part in a simulation activity. I chose the "Crisis" group. My group was broken down into several nations, in which we became presidents, secretaries of state, cabinet members, and so on. Conducted by three instructors using such media as slide films, bulletins, and announcements, to project us rapidly into various situations, we lived through "months" of national emergency conferences, international intrigue, onrushing war, and a host of crises which, after three hours, left us breathless—and happy it was only simulation. There are immense possibilities for playing out the dynamics between a decision based on mere technological feasibility and one based on real human need. It is emotion that moves the intellect to action, not the reverse. Simulation provides a chance for emotions to run a collision course—even smash into each other—yet it allows the participants to walk away from the wreckage and consider ways of avoiding a violent result next time. The simulation concept works with children and grownups alike.

In this chapter we have examined the need for changing the emphasis in our schooling from technological progress to human progress. We have seen that to do this will require a complete turnaround in the way we run our schools, giving first priority to *educing* instead of *training*. We have become aware that we need to face directly the problem of science versus the humanities—machine versus man. We have discussed humanics as a new experience to be introduced into our schools and our continuing education as adults, as a means of integrating fragmented knowledge and connecting it with life. In the next chapter we shall consider new patterns of life style as an approach to making human instead of technologically feasible decisions.

CHAPTER 12

SCHOOLING FOR LIVING

The millions we have spent and the billions we intend to spend on "improving schools" have produced and will produce little more than improved gadgetry and mere administrative tinkering to indoctrinate our youngsters into maintaining the *status quo*. Dr. Donald W. Stotler, a nationally known science educator and one of the twelve-man National Science Foundation Advisory Committee on Education, has put our plight this way:

> Certainly our bureau-centered plan of education has become as elaborate as Ptolemy's earth-centered plan of the solar system [the notion that the sun revolved around the earth] had become 600 years ago. Regretfully, it is being protected in much the same way. Each time a new weakness was found in the Ptolemaic system, great energy was expended to correct the weakness by inventing a new epicycle rather than by permitting the basic theory to be challenged. We have been responding in a similar fashion. When the discovery of a weakness in our educative maze is isolated, great energy is expended to correct the weakness by inventing a new "epicycle" rather than by challenging the basic theory. We now have so many epicycles [textbooks, grade levels, departments, groups, etc.] that it is no wonder many people feel that we are at best making only circular progress.[1]

Schooling has been wrong on two counts: First, it does not reflect the needs of society today. Second, it seeks to maintain society as it is. Instead, schooling should not only fill the needs of the society in which it exists, but should also be the vehicle for continuous social evolution. The other alternative is to brace for full-scale revolution.

No matter how much we work at changing our schools in their present setting we need a completely fresh approach. The major purpose of schooling must be for students to learn new ways of living together both as individuals and as members of society. To put it simply, we need schooling for living.

Despite all the pretty pictures we see of new school buildings, fancy gadgetry, and mini-skirted teachers, our schooling today remains much the same as it was in 1647 when Massachusetts passed the first state school law, the "Old Deluder Satan Act." The goal of schooling was then and remains now to prepare the young to fit into society. We have been turning out "products" to fit into the economic machine. As a high school principal in Atlanta put it: "Lots of times we say education doesn't count for much, but when you look at the unfinished product and then come over and look at the finished product, you see a lot of difference." But now these "products" are talking back, calling the machinery into serious question. As one young man told me, "We are beginning to feel like so much sausage meat being fed into a meat grinder to come out in a string and all alike." Then, parodying a famous line of Dylan Thomas, he said, "And believe me, we do not go gentle into that meat grinder."

The prerequisite for starting over in anything is either to get rid of what you've already got or completely to ignore it. Since we probably won't burn down our schoolhouses (although some are bound to go unless we make many changes in what goes on in them—and quickly), we have the alternative. But since not everyone, fortunately, will want to ignore tradition, we have another alternative: Let those who would like to start over, do so. Give those who envision a new kind of living, hence a new kind of schooling, the opportunity to try out their notions and to live with them long enough to experience the consequences.

If we want to change schools, we must first change society. Schooling must become a *learning laboratory for living*. Real learning requires experimentation, trying things out. All else is merely theory. To envision a school, one must first envision a society.

In speaking of society, the thinking young often get down to the nub of things in a hurry: They talk about *life style*. After obtaining a splendid interview with him, I invited a twenty-four-year-old leader of a radical action group and his wife to my home in California for a long weekend. He came from an affluent and well-educated Connecticut family, and his speech and manner said as much, although his clothes and those of his wife were typically hippie. He declined the invitation with the words, "Well, thank you very much but I'm afraid your life style and mine—the things we are trying to do here in this group—would not mix."

They have rejected us, and we are busily rejecting them. We show them in every possible way that we believe their ideas in schooling, work, love and sex, and living in general are not only distasteful but simply won't work. How do we know? Have we ever tried them? Have we ever tried any new life style? We are the most experimental nation in the world when it comes to physical things. We actually set aside billions each year for research and experimentation to change the shape, size, color, or performance of "things" because we are not satisfied with them, because we want to make them better. Yet we do not spend one penny to enable people to experiment with changes in life style—even as we cry to the heavens to know why the human situation is not better here on earth! Oh, we formulate, legislate, and stimulate—but do we simply dedicate even some of our resources to a direct approach to discovering a better life style, perhaps *many* better life styles?

In the early days of our nation we gave away land without a qualm but for the selfish reason that homesteaders would make the land more productive. Is it, then, so out of order to think about giving away money, perhaps land, too, which could end up making our country a more worth-while place in which to live? Why not give the counter culture a real chance to try out their ideas; they might come up with something.

"But," you may say, "we can't give everyone money and land to go off and live the way they want to." And you're right. But not everyone has a desire to initiate change in his life. Most people prefer to follow the norm or simply to stay where they are. However, we are blessed with fresh young thinkers who rank with Columbus and the astronauts in their pioneering spirit. Only this time these are social pioneers who refuse to turn back. They have expressed leadership in various ways. Some have sought to wreak revolutionary destruction on the society they seek to change, but others have chosen constructive ways to improve the quality of life. Because there is no room—either psychological or physical—to work within the Establishment, many of them have left comfortable, middle-class suburbs to live in communes. With few funds and a sincere desire to return to fundamentals and do with little more than the bare essentials of food, clothing, and shelter, some have found old homes in rundown parts of the city, doing their own carpentry and painting to make them livable. Others have sought the outdoors, building shelter from odd pieces of wood, highway signs, and even automobile bodies.

For their life-style models these young social explorers have reached way back beyond the scores of Utopias tried and failed. Often they have taken a primitive model, and they refer to their group as "our family." In so-called "primitive cultures" the family might consist of thirty, forty, or a hundred or more people of all ages living and sharing the means of life together. Even without benefit of the pill, sex was shared and so were the children. And in these benevolent cultures there were no unwanted children. They were wanted because they were needed. The attrition of war and the hazards of primitive living kept the population pretty much in balance. Today birth control can be substituted for war and disease.

On a lecture tour in Southeast Asia I talked with both leaders and tribesmen in New Guinea and Fiji who had one foot in the old tribal culture and the other in the white man's "civilization." "We used to share everything," one New Guinean told me. "If I caught twenty fish today, I would give you one, perhaps two to someone else, and so on, according to their need, and I'd keep one or two for myself."

"Why would you do it?" I asked. The question stopped him. I could see his mind wandering back over other days. Had he stayed with his tribe, he told me, he would have been a ranking chief by virtue of his birth. Now, having gotten an "education" (quotes mine) he had one wife and a highly responsible job as a civil administrator in the fledgling Australian-sponsored government of the Territory of Papua–New Guinea.

"I would have given the fish because it was the thing to do. And tomorrow I'd expect you to give me a fish or two. It's the way things are in a tribe. We shared. What's mine is yours and what's yours is mine. But out here it's all different. Now I work for myself and my own family. And I work for money. My friends and relatives find it hard to understand this. They still think I should give them some of what I have, what I work for. But they can't give me much in return, and I need the money to get things I need for the way I live now."

"Which is better, the way you live now or the way you used to live?" I asked.

"I don't think I really know—yet," he answered.

Nor do the young know yet. They know only that they don't like the life style in which they have been brought up. As a guide to evolving a more satisfying way of living, the young communers have taken the basic tenet of Marxism: from each according to his abilities, to each according to his needs. They are quick to point out, however, that they dislike the so-called communism practiced in Russia as strongly as they do capitalism. But their emphasis on cooperation rejects certain basic ideas of our social system—the importance of private property, private enterprise, and family child rearing.

The idea of direct community sharing in food, shelter, and the necessities of living is anything but new. Prehistoric men cooperated to club to death an animal from which each tore a piece of flesh to satisfy his hunger, and they huddled in caves for mutual protection and warmth. With increasing intelligence man became more capable of organizing his energies—and more subject to being organized—all the way up to today's "organization man," or, more accurately, man *over*organized. But the graph of man's groping up through twenty-five, fifty, or, as some say, seventy-five million years has not been a straight line. There have been steep climbs upward toward freedom and declines into oppression, but the whole way has been pockmarked by violence. At first the trends were of long duration, occurring in widely separated places involving only small numbers. Increasingly, there has been less and less time between cycles; wider areas and greater numbers have been involved. Simply to compare the scope of World War I with that of World War II, then to imagine the scope of an impending

World War III, is to realize that our gyrating graph line is about to go off the top of the chart.

But through it all there have been optimists—people who have believed that there can be a sensible plan for men to live together—learning to communicate rather than exterminate. An early expression of this was Plato's *Republic,* written over twenty-two centuries ago. Three centuries later Jesus Christ lived out the idea of the perfectibility of man. With the collapse of the Roman Empire, the night of the Dark Ages closed in on these dreams, and it wasn't until medieval institutions began to break down that a new economic individualism appeared. As he came out from under the tyranny of feudal lords, Western man began to dream of living in equality, with no man as master. In 1516 Sir Thomas More published his *Utopia,* literally about "no where" (from the Greek "not" [*ou*] and "place" [*topos*]). More envisioned a dream community on an island "south of the equator" based on an optimistic faith in human nature, a returning to lost innocence and integrity, and, in the words of E. H. Harbison, an "exaggerated uniformitarianism, from clothes to equal apportionment of children among families." More's ideas, sparked by the Protestant Reformation and the opening up of the New World, had enormous influence after him. For example, in June, 1794, poet Samuel Taylor Coleridge met Robert Southey at Oxford, and the two worked at the idea of a "pantisocracy" —a term invented by young Coleridge, twenty-two years old at the time. It was to be a Utopian settlement in America, an ideal community where twelve young men and twelve wives would conduct "an experiment in human perfectibility." Although the poet's scheme never got off the ground, a number of Utopia-like communities were launched in America beginning in the early 1700s, reaching a numerical and developmental peak in the middle of the nineteenth century. An examination of this little-known but widespread phenomenon shows that today's youthful experimenters are working within a unique and powerful American tradition.

In 1732 Ephrata was founded in Pennsylvania by Johann Conrad Bissel, a pious German Mennonite who had fled religious persecution in his homeland. The colony had no written constitution, no ritual, and ministry. There were two classes of members: cloistered celibates living in almost complete seclusion, who dressed in white robes and worshiped four times a day; and the "outdoor" married membership living nearby and sharing the work of running a paper mill, flour mill, tannery, and bakeshop. After Bissel died in 1786, the colony went into a slow decline and was legally dissolved in 1905.

A "Community of Equality" called Harmony was founded in 1803 by George Rapp and his son near the mouth of the Wabash River in Indiana. The Rappites renounced marriage, and all persons lived in celibacy. In 1831 a troublemaker calling himself Count de Leon came along and began advocating marriage and the enjoyment of luxury. He persuaded 200 members to secede and take away their share of the common fund. By 1886 the 250 surviving members controlled a property whose value was estimated as high as $20,000,000. In 1905 the affairs of the community were wound up on the authority of the Supreme Court of the United States.

The largest of all the religious groups that can be called "communist" in the purest sense was the Shakers. Calling themselves prophets, they believed that through "the agitation of the body" they received the gift of prophecy. In England their more extreme form of behavior became ritualized into a rhythmic dance, and the group became known as the Shaking Quakers or Shakers. In 1774 "Mother" Ann Lee came to America with eight disciples. Within a few years several thousand had flocked to the movement, and by 1826 there were eighteen Shaker villages in eight states. The sect was organized as a family, presided over by a dual rule of elders and eldresses. The Shaker villages did not seek to be self-sufficient economically but purchased from the "world's people" what they needed, making specialized products that could be sold outside. In the history of American arts and crafts the Shakers left a distinctive heritage. Shaker furniture is prized for its distinctive simplicity, and Shaker ingenuity developed the buzzsaw, rotary harrow, threshing machine, and the common clothespin as well as uniquely woven woolens. The Shaker dance has passed into the repertory of modern choreography. The Shaker impulse reached its height during the 1840s, when about 6,000 members were enrolled in the church, but by 1874 the society was advertising in newspapers for members, emphasizing physical comfort above spiritual values.

In 1841 John Humphrey Noyes, having "studied the mistakes of others," established in Putney, Vermont, a "Society of Inquiry." The society soon turned into a socialized community ". . . because a spirit of love led naturally to a community of goods," said Noyes. Taking the idea to its ultimate, the leader proclaimed the practice of complex marriage wherein each woman in the group was the wife of every man in the group, and every man the husband of each woman. Within six years the idea of complex marriage and Noyes' proclamation that the spirit of Christ had returned to earth and had entered into the Putney group became intolerable to the surrounding community. Noyes pulled up stakes and founded a new community at Oneida, New York.

In its early years the commune of some 200 persons earned a precarious existence by farming and logging. Then a new member gave the community a steel trap that he had invented. Manufacture and sale of Oneida Steel Traps, soon considered the best in the land, became the basis of a thriving set of industrial enterprises producing such things as silverware, embroidered silks, and canned fruit. Forty-eight departments supervised by twenty-one committees carried on the various activities. Women worked alongside men, often wearing trousers and cutting their hair short. Although marriage was "complex," the perfectionists denied the charge of "free love." Sexual relations were strictly regulated, and the propagation of children was controlled through a process they called stirpiculture. Children remained with their mothers until they could walk, after which they were placed in a common nursery. To keep members in line, "Father" Noyes presided over "cures" or "shaming sessions," therapeutic techniques no doubt similar to those we are now discovering in encounter groups, sensitivity training, and psychodrama. The group thrived for thirty years, but the mounting hostility of nearby communities to the practice of complex marriage led Noyes, in 1879, to recommend to the group that the practice be abandoned. Noyes and a few adherents went to Canada; those remaining set up Oneida Community, Ltd., which has become a highly successful commercial enterprise producing among other things the famous Oneida silverplate.

Many other experiments in life styles were based on the idea that through religious and ethical practices, hard work, and education and discussion, each member could achieve his potential abilities. In almost every instance these dream communities were started by a single powerful personality. Many of the colonies flourished during the lifetime of the leader, then declined slowly after his death. In spite of the fact that not one of these Utopias exists today, at least in anything like its original form, many of the groups developed ideas, art forms, products, and even enterprises that persist in our culture. Certainly the idea of human perfectibility as a requirement of learning to live together received new impetus.

A contemporary model of commune living that has attracted much attention is the Israeli *kibbutz*. Begun in the late nineteenth century by Jewish migrants fleeing persecution in Europe, the *kibbutzim*—rural cooperative settlements—have flourished increasingly. From 60 to 2,000 members may live in a single *kibbutz*. They work without pay and are supplied with individual housing, clothing, medical care, and other personal needs. Dining rooms and kitchens are shared, as well as child-care facilities. Until recent years boys and girls slept in the same room and used the same toilet facilities together until age eighteen. Now they move to separate facilities at the end of grammar school. As one young *kibbutznik* put it: "How can you marry someone you sat next to on the potty?"

Increasingly the *kibbutzim* have established enterprises other than farming. With greater wealth there has been a change in life style toward more privacy for member families, larger allowances for spending money, and private ownership of clothing and furniture. But even as the *kibbutz* concept developed there were those who from the outset envisioned cooperation only in the area of work, giving rise to the *moshav ovdim,* an association of villagers purely for the joint cultivation of land. This life style afforded more privacy and individualism than the *kibbutz*. Another arrangement called *moshav shitufi* combined some of the features of the other two for those who preferred a middle ground between complete commune living and mere cooperative ownership of the means of livelihood.

A rare eyewitness account of the major commune experiments in the United States is a book published in 1875 by Charles Nordhoff, literally a human movie camera in the precinematic age who recorded for us the sights and sounds of these pioneers in life styles. Titling his book *The Communistic Societies of the United States,* Nordhoff, a seasoned journalist

and Washington correspondent for *The New York Times,* not
only gives us a vivid picture of each community, but also sets
forth his findings and conclusions. Among other things, he
was curious to know how it was that so many of these societies, while "composed for the most part of men originally
farmers or mechanics—people of very limited means and
education—have yet succeeded in accumulating considerable
wealth." He wanted to know what the successful "communists" had made of their lives and what the effect was of communal living on the character of the individual man and
woman. He compared the life style of the communal societies
with that of "an ordinary farmer or mechanic even in our
country, and more especially with the lives of the workingmen
and their families in our great cities." His conclusion: "I must
confess that the communist life is so much freer from care and
risk, so much easier, so much better in many ways, and in all
material aspects, that I sincerely wish it might have a further
development in the United States."

Before his investigation Nordhoff had become deeply concerned by the slothfulness of rank-and-file union tradesmen
and laborers who, he alleged, "determined to remain hirelings
for life, and only demanding better conditions of their masters." Did he find less laziness, discontent, and grumbling
among similar people living communally? On this score, he
says: "The lazy men, who are the bugbears of speculative
communists, are not, so far as I have heard, to be found in the
existing communes." He concludes by noting that his observations "forced me to take some views on the nature and capacities of the average man which I had not had before."

Some of the societies Nordhoff studies had existed twenty-
five, fifty, and even eighty years prior to the publication of his
book. Others had failed. Success or failure aside, these were
years of experiment, of being involved with one's whole life in

a learning laboratory for living. While each member probably brought to the group some skills and social awareness, the necessities of simply wresting a living in often quite crude circumstances and getting along with others at the same time produced a range of skills and qualities most had not been called upon to develop before. In his final chapter, "Comparative View," Nordhoff gives a point-by-point summary of what he learned from the commune life style:

> Diversity of employments . . . broadens men's facilities. Ingenuity and mechanical dexterity are developed to a surprising degree in a commune, as well as business skill. The constant necessity of living in intimate association with others, and taking into consideration their prejudices and weaknesses, makes the communist somewhat a man of the world; teaches him self-restraint; gives him a liberal and tolerant spirit; makes him an amiable being. Why are *all* communists remarkably clean? I imagine because filth or carelessness would be unendurable in so large a family.

But had the eighteenth- and nineteenth-century commune reached the peak of possible perfection? Had it brought about learning in the higher reaches of man as *man* instead of simply a producing and consuming animal? Had the concerns of the communers reached, for example, into the realm of aesthetics? Did commune life involve its members in a consideration of the beautiful as distinguished from the merely pleasing, the moral, and especially the useful and utilitarian? Nordhoff says "no."

> In the beginning, a commune must live with great economy, and deny itself many things desirable and proper. . . . But I cannot see why a prosperous community should not own the best books; why it should not have music; why it should not hear the most eloquent lecturers; why it should not have pleasant plea-

sure-grounds, and devote some means to the highest form of
material art—fine architecture.

What is the result of this lack? He continues:

I believe this inattention to the higher and intellectual wants of
men to be the main reason of their generally failing numbers.
They keep their lives on a plane of the common farmer's life
out of which most of the older members were gathered—and
their young people leave them, just as the farmers of our country complain that their boys run off to the city.

Nordhoff also felt that another point of failure was the lack
of communication between the various communities, whereby
an interchange of ideas and learnings which could have been
valuable in the development of all was lost.

Although the early commune was an excellent learning laboratory for living, commune living, at least for the present, is
probably not for everyone. "No one can play at communism,"
says Nordhoff. "It is earnest work, and requires perseverance,
patience, and all manly qualities." What kinds of people are
drawn to communal living and make a go of it? A deeply religious man himself, Nordhoff readily admitted:

. . . success depends—together with a general agreement in religious faith, and a real and spiritual religion leavening the mass,
upon another sentiment—upon a feeling of the unbearableness
of the circumstances in which they find themselves . . . communism is a mutiny against society. . . . A commune could not
long continue whose members had not, in the first place, by ad-
verse circumstances, oppression, or wrong, been made to feel
very keenly the need of something better. Hence it is that the
German peasant weaver makes so good a communist; hence,
too, the numerous failures of communistic experiments in this
country, begun by people of culture and means, with a sincere
desire to live the "better life."

Perhaps, paradoxically, sharing is easier when you don't have much to share?

What life style is most conducive toward man's age-old dream of human perfectibility? Might there not be many? How can we discover them? The same way we have discovered everything else: testing new ideas and in a laboratory situation, learning from our successes and mistakes, and moving on to higher levels of testing. We should no more expect ourselves at this point to have produced the best possible life style than we would have expected the Wright brothers to produce the supersonic jet in 1903. Why shouldn't we invite those who wish to experiment in a different life style to do so and even finance their ventures to a reasonable extent? Why not set aside land and money so that groups of thirty or forty or more young can give fair trial, over a period of, say, up to ten or more years, to a life style they visualize and may already be practicing under cover? Why not finance it openly? Whether we know it or not, we are actually footing the bill as it is.

Even as you read this book, many young people, in a mutiny against society, are experimenting in a learning laboratory for living in what is loosely called "a hippie commune." The nascent nature of the movement makes it hard to get a fix on its true shape. Often a group starts by accident: Several young people, finding themselves all in the same boat of sex and drug experimentation or simply copping out, perhaps far from home, pool their meager resources merely to stay alive and stick together. After a time a leadership may arise, pointing out new goals beyond immediate gratification of the senses, and the group is maintained for communal living, growing naturally out of shared feelings. There have been some failures, but the movement is burgeoning. In a *Time* magazine poll of 130 freshmen entering fourteen representative universities across the country taken in the fall of 1969, approxi-

mately 30 per cent of the students said they'd like to try commune living.

Money from home supposedly going for college and a
"decent" dormitory life often finds its way into a hippie commune. Some parents give their offspring substantial monthly
payments just to "stay away from home until you grow up."
College dropouts often take a job just long enough to qualify
for welfare benefits, then join a commune. Others panhandle
in the streets, while still others simply steal. Young squatters
take over land or old buildings, which may require expensive
and time-consuming action to eject them. Motivating them in
getting resources by these devious means may be emotions
ranging from the Robin Hood syndrome—steal from the rich
to help the poor—to simply the grand gesture of thumbing
their noses at the Establishment. So one way or another we're
already paying for experiments in life style, often conducted
quite crudely because of meager resources. Why not give sincere and experimentally minded young people a chance to
start living out their ideas? Why not enable groups in several
locations to start at once? Why not spend money for positive
social action instead of paying billions for mopping up crime
in the streets, rehabilitating those driven to drugs, and bending
youthful energies to the continuance of decaying institutions?

We have seen how commune living begets, *demands,* new
learnings. Are not those skills and understandings required in
a commune life style the very ones whose loss we increasingly
lament in main-stream society today? And if they are, and
they seem to be easily acquirable by ordinary people who
enter communal living open-mindedly, then might not the new
skills and understandings generated find their way back into
the main stream of the population?

An experience in communal living would quickly bring the
participants face to face with the hard realities of what it takes

to provide the necessities of life and how much more it takes to garner some of the luxuries. As the communers reached out into "the world" to obtain goods they couldn't produce themselves and to sell what they could to get money to buy them, they would better understand how the generation presently in power thinks, and would see how it got that way. Conversely, the generation in power might learn some new ways of thinking by dealing with the often surprisingly sane ideas the young come up with for cutting through some of the needless complexities we have built up around us. At times it seems we of the Establishment generation are no longer capable of thinking in a fundamental, straightforward manner. Someone has said that if the safety pin had been invented today instead of long ago, it probably would have eight moving parts and three transistors and require a service checkup twice a year.

A fully self-contained commune would be physically and psychologically apart from the main stream. It would be self-sustaining to a maximum degree, buying "world's goods" only when necessary and with money generated through selling its products to the world. It could be located in rough, undeveloped countryside, or, conceivably, in the heart of a big-city ghetto, although financing of the former would be less expensive. Funding would be over a period of no less than ten years, progressively reduced during that time as the community became more self-sustaining. A learning laboratory for living would be financed when spontaneous leadership arose to create a vision and a plan of action acceptable to the consensus of the participants and to the funding agency. Criteria for acceptance or rejection of plans would be simple and straightforward, and recall of an experiment would be made only in circumstances of extreme emergency. One thing to be learned would be the extent to which a human group can be self-directing and the circumstances under which this happens.

We think nothing of 55,000 people killed, 150,000 people totally crippled, and a staggering 4,500,000 others injured on our highways in a single year—and we do little to learn from the experience. A laboratory for learning that degenerated into a *Lord of the Flies* or a *Pitcairn Island* would at least be more humane. Discontinuance of the experiment should be easy for individuals or the entire group if and when the idea no longer provides motivation to continue.

A basic premise of the experiments in new life style is that there should be no schools until the need arises. Another basic premise is that when people who are engaged in experimenting with a new life style are free to learn what interests them they will choose to learn about things that are not only of interest to them but are also important to the success of their community. At the outset, an experimental group might receive basic materials from which to produce food, shelter, and clothing. They would also receive a roomful of books and access to other learning aids as the needs of a developing culture become apparent.

We seem to be afraid that if we let high school and college students choose what they want to study, instead of what *we* want them to study, there will not be enough engagement in the "productive" studies to provide cogs for our machine. And we are increasingly right! More and more students are choosing psychology, sociology, political science, and the humanities instead of the "hard" sciences, engineering, and so forth. Often these wanted studies are pursued in spite of loss of degree credit and extending the time and expense of remaining in school.

The rise of the "free university" is concrete evidence that the vast majority of the young are not lazy, not irresponsible, not anti-school. They simply want to study the things they feel are important, urgent, relevant to them. There are said to be

between 300 and 400 of these "underground" centers for the
new learning around the United States. Some operate as an
extension of student union activities and are largely student
operated. At the experimental college of San Diego State, for
example, all courses and teaching are voluntary. There is no
formal credit. Any student or professor may offer a course.
Those who teach and those who learn all do it for the joy of
sharing knowledge and their personal growth as human
beings. In a very real sense the "E.C.," as it is known at San
Diego, is a "learning commune" and lists its nuclear membership as "brothers and sisters of the communal living family."

Another variation of the free university is the living *and*
learning commune. The Midpeninsula Free University, located near Palo Alto, California, is more or less typical of the
movement. Its paid staff numbers only seven, each of whom
gets between $200 and $300 a month. All other staff give
their services free under the general aegis "if you know, teach;
if you don't, learn." Its fall, 1969, catalogue listed ninety-
seven courses meeting at least once a week, usually in the evening and on weekends. Payment of a ten dollar membership
fee entitles one to sign up for as many courses as he wishes.
Offerings are listed in seven "departments": Arts and Crafts,
Encounter, Education and Philosophy, Inner Paths, Play, Politics, and Whole Earth Studies. Community Projects lists opportunities to participate in activities to acquaint the surrounding communities with the nature and purpose of the
university. Special Projects offers opportunity for service to
the university—without pay. Besides the modest membership
fee, the university derives income from publishing a monthly
magazine, *The Free You,* with subscribers in fifty states, and
operates a job-printing shop.

The university itself is really a group of young people
choosing the communal way to combine living and learning.

Most members hold quite ordinary jobs outside of the community, but what brings them together is a common feeling
that ". . . education which has no consequences for social action or personal growth is empty." They believe that "the present educational system . . . defends the *status quo,* perpetuat-
ing its evils and perils. The system has become rigid; it is no
longer receptive to meaningful change. A revolution in American education is required to meet today's needs and a new
type of education—a free university—must provide the impetus for change."

Course-offering titles give some idea of the learnings these
young people seek in developing themselves as individuals and
as members of the kind of society they are reaching for: Uni-
fied Modes of Understanding; The Art of Giving Away Bread
(in which bread is actually baked); Quilting Bee (quilts are
really made); Gardening with Flowers and Herbs; Wine Making; Earth, Sky, Wind, and Water; Creative Movement for Children; Greek Dance; Art Now; Improving Communication in
Marriage; Entry to Encounter; Coupledynamics Workshop;
Change and Grow, and scores more of titles found seldom if
ever in the usual university catalogue. In its own words the
Midpeninsula Free University "is a high-flying vision, a modern translation of the Renaissance, a community, a family, a
tribe in search of itself."

Recall Nordhoff's observation that the success of a commune depended largely on the fact that people were drawn together by a common need. Synanon, a unique experiment in
communal living, has grown out of the needs of drug and alcohol addicts to work out their own salvation. While Alcoholics Anonymous seeks to bring fellow sufferers together periodically for therapeutic encounter, Synanon carries the idea to
its ultimate conclusion: To really help each other, people must
live together, must establish a satisfying way of life together.

Furthermore, it is entirely possible that people who become alcoholics and drug addicts are special kinds of people whose basic needs require a basically different life style than that which has become the accepted standard of the Western world. Controversy has dogged Synanon for most of its eleven years, but it now has plans to expand the operation on the California coast, just over the Golden Gate Bridge from San Francisco, into a city. Says its founder, Charles Dederich, fifty-seven, "The philosophy that will guide the creation and development of Synanon City will challenge the validity of some basic Western notions of home and family." He describes a communal society where, ideally, husbands and wives live apart in small cubicles without locks and where children are raised by everyone. People will retreat to their cubicles (to be called "caves") when they need to "sleep, bathe, make love, study, or watch the tube," Dederich said. Otherwise everything will be done with everybody else. Half of the thousand acres of the city will be devoted to greenery and open space to allow people to play and stroll. "We'll be getting people to fit themselves more comfortably into the planet earth, making much better use of room, air, and everything else," observed Dederich.

In the industrial society through which we have just passed the goal of schooling individuals to fit the requirements of the machine may have been valid. But in today's post-industrial, electrotechtronic age this goal is at least questionable. And the rising tide of young voices may make it impractical if not impossible. "You boast that you invented machines to save labor and therefore time," they're telling us, "yet instead of using the time saved to improve the quality of life, you use it to produce more and more goods." They know that the schooling we give them is mainly *training* to turn them into better and better producers and consumers, rather than *education* to *educe* their creativity and to help them become better human beings. They suspect the whole thing is masterminded by a few at the top—the Real Establishment. Most of us adults—often referred to as "the Establishment"—are really only handmaidens of the Real Establishment; we have been brainwashed by so many years of producer-consumer life style that we are not even aware of, much less able to escape from, the tyranny at the top. The young say they can escape. They do not intend to become slaves of the machines, devouring more and more goods to pile up more and more profits. "Profits for what?" They want to know. And many of the young are making life-style choices to back up their words. They have decided on getting less of the world's material goods in return for having more of the human experience.

At one point in my life I made a similar decision. As advertising manager for one of the units of a large department-store chain I had become obsessed with the notion that my work consisted mainly in enticing people—often against their wills and better judgment—to buy things they didn't need and couldn't afford. One night I was working late and so was the store manager, a man in his mid-thirties whom I greatly admired. We happened to meet in a dimly lit aisle near the shoe department. We were both tired and sat down. The Great Depression, barely past midpoint, was still demanding, and jobs were scarce. To quit a job, especially a good job like this one, was unthinkable. But suddenly I could no longer hold back the feelings that had been building up inside of me, and I cried. I was twenty-seven, but sobbed like a baby as I told "Mr. Mac" how I felt—my work seemed phony, things seemed all wrong, the road seemed to dead end. He could easily have said, "Well, if that's the way you feel, you'd better quit your job," but he didn't. Instead, he said softly, "Yes, I know." Then, after a healing silence, "I guess that's the way things are." I loved him in that moment. Fifteen years later I heard he had died—still in his prime—of a heart attack, having burned himself out in the rat race to purvey more goods to more people—for what?

Beginning that night the sense of creativity that had sustained me in long hours of work began to dull. I looked around at other jobs, but they all seemed the same. Looking back on it now, I know I was naïve, too much a part of the great American producer-consumer tradition even to think about doing anything drastic to change my humdrum life. For the next several years I was promoted up the ladder and from store to store, almost in spite of myself.

But World War II and life in the U.S. Navy turned me around. For the first time in my life I had time to think, to look inside myself, and to have experiences as a person instead of a corporation robot. At the end of the war there was a decision to make: to return to the corporation and take the next step up to a five-figure managerial job, or to kick the corporate monster in the teeth and blast off into the outer space of humanity, to become a psychologist and explore further my own inner terrain and the inner workings of society. I made up my mind: I began college and a life style of near-poverty that lasted for eleven years as I moved from starting out as a freshman in a junior college all the way through the doctorate at Columbia. On the way my interests shifted from pure to applied psychology in education, and by good fortune the learning systems I had designed caught on, bringing me unexpected monetary reward. My point is simply that I can deeply empathize with the disenchanted young today, but it took a world war to wake me up.

If full communal living is not most people's dish of tea, and if we admit that there is little or no learning except by doing, then how can "most people" begin to learn the understandings and the living skills that grow out of communal living—actually learning by doing? Is there not some way for people who desire social experimentation on a less-than-grand scale to "get into the act" on a level more suited to them? Is there not some way for these, too, to experience a living laboratory for learning toward a change of life style in keeping with their private visions of man and his reason for being? I believe there is.

Commune living, at least in its beginnings, may be only for the young. Not only are the young more able to withstand the rigors of less-than-average creature comforts, to do without a warm house, a good chair to sit in, a good bed at night, but, less cynical and less fixed in their ways by years of repetition, they are more adaptable. However, no thinking person should rule out the possibility that older groups or even mixed young-old groups might find the idea of living in a laboratory for learning new life styles attractive. And there are those who are not quite ready to leap into full commune living but would like to try a one-foot-in, one-foot-out approach. We have mentioned the "levels" of tryout involved in the Israeli *kibbutzim* (full communal living), *moshav shitufi* (communal ownership of the means of production), and *moshav ovdim* (an association for joint cultivation of the land). The free university and Synanon City are examples of the infinite number of variations possible between full and partial commune living. I consider them all serious efforts to return to the tribe as the fundamental living unit that served man so well for hundreds of thousands of years.

Regardless of the degree of communal participation elected by a group, there are two principles I believe will prove fundamental to success: (1) the principle of *multilevel learning,* and (2) the principle of *social evolution.*

The principle of multilevel learning draws on three behavioral sciences: differential psychology, developmental psychology, and the psychology of learning. Simply stated, the multi-level principle recognizes that individuals are different in how much they can learn and in how fast they develop, and that there is indeed a science of learning. It holds that each individual, regardless of his age or station in life, should have the privilege of entering a learning situation by starting where he is and moving ahead as fast and as far as his learning rate and capacity will let him, both as an individual and as a member of society.

The validity of the multilevel principle can be seen by observing those around you and your own behavior. We readily refer to differences in learning capacity among people by such terms as "very intelligent" or "not so smart," or something in between. We can see differences in the rate at which our individual children or our employees develop. "Well, he was slow for awhile but he's beginning to catch up now." Or, "She's a late bloomer." And as you go about your own work or hobbies, you've found that certain approaches produce more learning, others less. Learning systems based on the multilevel principle, even in the context of our out-of-date schools, have already proven that they can free the individual to learn as much as he can, at his own rate, using scientific learning methodology during at least a portion of the school day. The work has been mainly in the area of reading instruction, and, in just under two decades, its use has grown from thirty-five students in my experimental classroom to over 35,000,000 students of all ages in forty-nine countries around the world.*

The principle of social evolution assumes that a social group—a club, a village, a city, a nation—is always evolving from one condition to another. It is either growing or it is

---

* For a fuller elaboration of the philosophy of multilevel learning, see Don H. Parker, *Schooling for Individual Excellence* (New York: Thomas Nelson & Sons, 1963).

dying. Furthermore, at some point the direction of development will have gone as far as some members of the group wish to see it go. At such a point these individuals will split off to form a new group which in turn begins to evolve in a new direction.

The principle of social evolution is easily observed at work in the early American experiments in commune living, in the current Promethean communal efforts of the contemporary Israeli *kibbutz,* and the swings of capitalistic countries toward "communism" or at least "socialism," while some Communist countries swing toward capitalism.

In each of the experiments in commune living I discussed earlier there was a movement from communism toward capitalism. The same thing has happened in the Israeli *kibbutz* over the last sixty years. This left to right movement can be roughly schematized as follows:

Communes began with	*Communes moved toward*
little contact with the outside world	more contact with outside world to sell their products and obtain money to buy "world's goods"
group ownership, maximum sharing	more individually owned possessions, less sharing
physical proximity in living arrangements	more separate accommodations for families
maximum conformity	less conformity in thought and action
frugality	more individual and community wealth

But while some societies are moving away from communism toward capitalism, others may be traveling in an opposite direction. Britain and Sweden, for example, once ruggedly

capitalistic, have moved left continually, imposing national
ownership on a considerable portion of industry and expanding welfare activities to reduce the spread between the haves
and the have-nots. During the Great Depression of the 1930s
the United States moved in a similar direction, but the years
since have seen a resurgence of capitalism that has evolved a
behemoth society organized to the breaking point. Will we now
swing toward socialism and away from the private-profit motive? The Bolshevik revolution of 1917 toppled Russia's rule
by a privileged few and sought to establish a community of
man in which there would be "from each according to his
ability; to each according to his need," an attempt to establish
the ideal communistic society. Instead, what evolved was another overorganized behemoth that now looks to the injection
of capitalism's private-profit motive to get the machine un-
stuck.

And so it goes: like two trains starting from opposite ends
of the line, capitalism and communism pass each other coming and going. "Why," you may ask, "can't these two meet in
the middle, stop, exchange ideas to the benefit of both, and
cease this senseless running back and forth?" But perhaps
that's the secret. Man must move, he must evolve—and be
continually re-evolving. When his opportunity to move, to
evolve, is blocked, he turns from thoughts of the slower process of evolution to the possibilities of revolution—simply
turning the whole thing over and starting afresh with a whole
new thing. If, on the other hand, he can have the opportunity
for moving in a newly perceived direction and away from
frustrating roadblocks, he may well be willing to forego a revolution in favor of re-evolution.

The examples of early commune living I have cited are re-
markably alike in that they were in continuous motion during

their three- to five-generation existence from communism toward capitalism. Changes in the handling of their economy produced changes in life style. And perhaps this is the way social progress should be seen.

After a few generations, or even decades, a commune may become so big, or so industrialized, so "capitalized," that it no longer affords the commune life style for which it was established. At such a point a new group of adventurers, longing to return to lost ideals, may break away to seek a mental and physical environment in which their visions can be recaptured. Why not accept this evolvement from communism and smallness into capitalism and bigness, with periodic spin-off of disenchanted fundamentalists to begin a re-evolvement, as a necessary cycle in man's unceasing development as a human being, instead of regarding it as a tragedy? Each cycle or reevolution might then be seen as a part of an upward, everwidening spiral by which man travels toward ultimate perfection. Each cycle takes him a little higher toward his ideals—his own and "his" collectively as a member of society. And each cycle, spreading outward as well as upward, gives him a widening view, a larger perspective.

A living laboratory for learning can be an exciting experience. Everything is new. The physical environment is new. One's relationships to people are new. Almost every act is a conscious one, has to be thought out, is an act of learning. Old, automatic behavior, habits, and reactions may be inappropriate, may fail to give a satisfying feeling, or may even bring disapproval of one's fellows. One becomes more sensitive to others. To become sensitive is to learn. To learn and remain sensitive is often heroic, especially if one is young. Jerry Rubin, the brilliant young newspaper reporter turned yippie, says:

> Young kids want to be heroes. They have an incredible energy and they want to live creative, exciting lives. That's what America tells you to do, you know. The history you learn is hero-oriented: Columbus, George Washington, Paul Revere, the pioneers, the cowboys. America's promise has been "live a heroic life." But then when it comes time to make good on its promise, it can't. It turns around and says, "Oh, you can get good grades, then get a job in a corporation, and buy a ranch house and be a good consumer." But kids aren't satisfied with that. They want to be heroes. And if America denies them an opportunity for heroism they're going to create their own.[2]

To foster experiments in change of life style through communal living would remove considerable pressure on the Establishment from forces that are literally pulling it apart. We are threatened by a counter culture from within and a paraculture from without. The counter culture is composed of young whites driven up the wall by our headlong flight into the materialism of an electrotechtronic, tranquilized society. The counter culture wants to break down our life style, but, as much as anything else, it wants excitement. We, on the other hand, are afraid that it may break down the life style that has brought us a radio in every room and one in our shirt pocket, TV on the hoof, two- and three-car garages, and so much food that our restaurant garbage cans bulge with half-eaten dinners while one-sixth of the nation and one-half of the world go hungry. The counter culture wants no part of the dull, empty Establishment pie.

The paraculture is composed of blacks and, increasingly, browns and other ethnic groups—especially the young. They want the opposite of the counter culture: They want a piece of the Establishment pie—and we're afraid they'll take it. They are tired unto death of Whitey's tokenism—his hollow words without deeds. They do not seek fewer material things, but more! They do not seek to work less; they want to work more.

But they also want to work more productively. Enough young blacks now have had sufficient education to reject the whole idea of "nigger jobs." They not only want better jobs, more in line with their individual capacities, but they want a piece of the action. And they now know that action starts with capital. In spite of talk of "reparations" by some blacks, the paraculture as a whole simply wants the same privilege as Whitey to borrow capital. Actually, the brothers want to move from the status of paraculture, standing outside looking in, to joining the culture, being a part of the main stream while maintaining their identity.

The paraculture's project to experiment with a new life style might be the very opposite of the counter culture's. Blacks would be concerned with building an economy that would give each community member a chance to earn more and more material goods, while the white experiment would tend to deemphasize material possessions. I found, after my first year in the U.S. Navy, that everything I needed, outside of food and shelter, I was carrying around in a duffel bag thrown over my shoulder. I lived this way for two years and don't recall any sense of deprivation. To the contrary, I look back on those years as perhaps the freest in my life.

To the question "schooling for what?" the counter culture and the paraculture would give almost entirely different answers. For the counter culture, the goal would be to change society; the goal of the paraculture would be to join it. The counter-culture community might start with no formal schooling at all. As needs become apparent, various opportunities for learning skills would be developed by communal members themselves. The paraculture community, on the other hand, would likely choose to begin with a modern school plant, technically equipped for the most efficient learning of the skills and knowledge needed for producing the various components of material wealth, ranging from simple handwork to the administration of buying raw materials and selling finished goods to the outside world. But both "cultures" would have one thing in common: the excitement of creating an experiment in schooling for living.

If you were a member of a counter-culture experiment in new life styles, your group might begin at the extreme of community ownership and sharing—from the clothes on your back, to all living facilities, to sex partners. As individual differences in intelligence, work capacity, and temperament surfaced, the group might simply choose to tolerate the less intelligent, the lazy, or the rugged individualist, or it might move toward more private ownership of goods and living arrangements and less "share and share alike." On the other hand, if you participated in a life-style experiment devoted to paraculture goals, you might start with some minimum of living accouterments that you owned and controlled rather than shared, and seek, through the acquisition of skills, knowledge, and hard work, to gain more goods and more control with all possible speed.

In the paraculture's jet ride into materialism its members may quickly find they have created a kind of uptight world they can no longer endure, and seek to move back toward a more shared economy, a more relaxed way of life—socialism or even commune-ism. In the counter culture's slowdown some may find too little challenge and seek out private enterprise as a way to express their individualism. "But suppose each should actually end up where the other started?" you ask. "They've only been spinning their wheels." But haven't they done much more? Haven't they actually engaged in a constructive life process by which their energies were directed toward positive goals rather than violence? And along the way might they not have given us a chance to see ourselves as others see us as well as some ideas and models for change? And aren't ways to change what we are seeking—and must find?

Still, a learning laboratory for living must not be a goldfish bowl. We should not visit unless invited. Similarly, we should not require they "report" unless they desire to do so. But we should keep all communication lines open and invite them to tell us what they are learning, so that we do not have to wait five, eight, or ten years to begin applying some of their learnings to life outside the laboratories. Recalling that one drawback of early experimental societies in America was their isolation and lack of learning from each other, we would encourage communication among the various living groups. With the full realization that learning comes both from successes and mistakes, we would be prepared for a modicum of failures. But the criteria of success and of failure would be those of the experimenters.

We, the Establishment, of ourselves cannot change. We must call on help from outside. We need teachers. Our young both of the counter culture and the paraculture are now ready to teach us. Is it possible that one and a half centuries after William Wordsworth said: "The child is father of the man," we are finally ready to learn? The alternative, as we have said earlier —and it cannot be repeated enough—is to brace for full-scale revolution.

CHAPTER 13

DIVERSITY

Shall I ask the brave soldier,
   who fights by my side
In the cause of mankind
   if our creeds agree?

Shall I give up the friend
   I have valued and tried
If he kneel not
   before the same altar with me?

—Thomas Moore,
"Come Send Round the Wine,"
from *Irish Melodies*

Because of our billions of possible genetic combinations, the human race is literally "programmed" for diversity. Yet we fight it. Instead of rejoicing in the fact of the existence of individual differences and enjoying the uniqueness of one another, we are most apt to wish others were more like us—or at least more alike—and we run our schools accordingly. But individual differences bother the young less and less, and more and more of them are simply dropping out of schools that ignore them. Perhaps we shouldn't be discouraged. As school buildings become vacant, we can use them for low-cost housing for the poor. Of course with student unrest often directed at the object of their disaffection, some school buildings won't be available. They will be rubble, even as more major insurance companies refuse to provide coverage. And as if enough hasn't already been done to alienate the young by stifling individual differences and diversity of learning styles in our schooling, the Establishment is now bringing in "accountability."

Accountability for what? For the training—skill learning —or the educing part of schooling? In late 1969 Texarkana, Arkansas, made a contract with Dorsett Educational Systems of Norman, Oklahoma, to raise the reading and mathematics skills levels of backward students by one grade level in eighty hours, at a cost of one dollar per student. If the company succeeded in less than eighty hours, it would get a bonus, but for each student that failed to progress, payment to the company would be reduced. In early 1970 San Diego school officials made a similar contract with Science Research Associates, a subsidiary of IBM, and with Educational Development Laboratories, a McGraw-Hill subsidiary, for similar programs at figures of $779,000 and $1.4 million respectively. Fine as far as it goes. The training—the learning of skills—can be measured by standardized tests. But will big business stop there? Not if we know big business. With this foot in the door, it is only one small step to applying similar procedures to the educing or skill-using part of schooling. When this happens, the very soul of learning will be destroyed; diversity will be dead.

The essence of the educing part of schooling is creatively using skills acquired in order to generate knowledge to meet the needs of the learner—as an individual and as a member of society. The true criterion of learning, then, is the individual's needs, not some externally applied body of knowledge, force-fed simply because it can be measured. Accountability in social studies, for example, means we would continue to teach history by dates and other meaningless and irrelevant ploys simply because we could measure how many dates or meaningless facts students have memorized, only to forget when the exam is over. But how are you going to use a standardized test—or any test, short of a lifetime—to determine how much a student knows about why we are ankle deep in garbage, and soon will be waist deep? These are the kinds of learnings the young are really seeking.

Accountability to whom? To the learner? No, he is only a product, subject to the mass-production methods of the Establishment. Purporting to "help the taxpayer to see what he is getting for his tax dollar," accountability is just one more effort—conscious or unconscious—by the Establishment to "teach them all alike," to provide more cogs to keep the industrial wheels turning. Accountability and its counterpart, National Assessment, contrary to the strenuous objections of its promotors, simply are paving the way for a "National Curriculum" and more lockstepped schooling. The young have been provoked enough already to fire a revolt in the schools. We should not be surprised if accountability, taken to its ultimate, brings anarchy.

The real power behind such insidious moves still further to destroy diversity is the Real Establishment (the other Mafia) that hires Establishment executives as corporation heads at six-figure salaries to carry out its wishes. Its wishes: "Keep those wheels turning. Develop a technology that will turn them even faster." At each turn of the wheel, as each dollar passes through the machine, a dime drops into the coffers of the super-rich. In his book *The Rich and the Super-Rich* Ferdinand Lundberg documents the process and concludes:

First, the present concentration of wealth confers self-arrogated and defaulted political policy-making power at home and abroad in a grossly disproportionate degree on a small and not especially qualified mainly hereditary group; secondly, this group allocates vast economic resources in narrow, self-serving directions, both at home and abroad, rather than in socially and humanly needed public directions.

When, through its agents, it cannot enlist government support of its various plans at home and abroad it can, and does, frustrate the government in various proceedings that have full public endorsement. . . . It doesn't do any of this maliciously, to be sure, any more than an elephant feels malice when it rubs against a sapling and breaks it in two. An elephant must behave like an elephant, beyond any moral stricture. And power of any kind must exert itself. Historically it has invariably exerted itself in its own self-visualized interests.[1]

Thus, one-tenth of 1 per cent of the biggest industrial corporations, the 500 at the top, do about 33 per cent of all business in the corporate field. And the profits of the top ten are equal to about half of the remaining 490. Control of 150 of the top 500 rests in the hands of single individuals or the members of single families. The remaining 350 are controlled by small numbers of owners (as distinct from nonowning managers and many small stockholders). Only 200,000 households control 22 per cent of the nation's wealth and most of this wealth is inherited, put together by the nineteenth-century "robber barons"—men of pioneer stock, who could take care of themselves and saw natural resources—including people —as something to be turned into dollars. These accumulations of wealth are still being maintained and added to by the same tactics and philosophy. Although Lundberg generously imputes no malice to their actions, the facts remain that we are allowing these few to plunder our planet of irreplaceable resources, and they are permitted to stifle our diversity so that we will conform more closely to the electrotechtronic age they have thrust upon us in the name of "progress." To the Real Establishment, our true function is to keep their money machine turning faster and faster.

Perhaps, as writers such as Robert Heilbroner suggest, oligarchical monopolistic capitalism, by its very reliance on science and technology, contains the seeds of its own destruction. The young are getting closer and closer to the workings of the machine. Their protests, often breaking into violence, so far have been directed at campus-based research facilities that exist mainly to pump dollar-producing ideas into the Establishment money machine. While producing some visible changes, such as MIT's cutting off direct university connections with certain R & D activities, student protests have gotten little more response from the real sources of power than a fly bite on an elephant's hide.

Perhaps as some of the young enter the employ of the behemoths they can influence Establishment management in turn to influence their Real Establishment keepers. After our formal interview I talked with a seventeen-year-old computer genius at Harvard about ways of making big business shift away from its "profit now" orientation toward a longer-range social consciousness, if for no other reason than its own enlightened self-interest. I asked him what he himself might do along these lines. "I intend," he said, "to find a good corporate totem pole to climb. And when I get up near the top, I'm going to give it a good shake." I believe he will. Others I have talked with don't intend to wait that long. It may take actual physical disruption at the sources of production to get the Real Establishment to listen to demands that they spend more than token amounts to stop pollution, to create jobs to replace those destroyed by their technology, and to correct the many other social ills brought on by their single-minded philosophy: make that dollar. After all, they don't have to live in the mess they've made. They can take off in their private jets to the clean air of the Himalayas and escape nerve-racking freeways. Secure in penthouses guarded by armed men, they don't have to see the filth and the suffering of the inner city.

But for all their money there is much evidence that the rich and the super-rich are no happier than the rest of us. What a blow to the American dream that holds up money and material things as the goal of life—and schooling as the way to get there! Indeed, with each turn of its money machine, oligarchical monopolistic capitalism may be undermining its own structure as more and more of the young refuse to be stuffed into the corporate sausage grinder.

Two attitude surveys conducted in the Chicago area in 1965 revealed that women see their mates first as "breadwinners," only then as "father and husband." They see themselves not as "persons," but as mother, wife, and homemaker. About one-third of the women not only put their own role as mothers first, but considered their husbands as essentially outside the basic family unit of themselves and their children. Is it any wonder the young look at this bleak, soulless picture and say, "No, thank you"?

If the materialistic values put forward by the success cult make people into functionaries instead of persons, and if these values underlie our school curriculum, and our school curriculum is turning off more and more of the young, then what are we to teach? Schooling for what?

If we can stop pouring ourselves into the money machine long enough to listen to the young, we will find them eager to talk, and we will learn the answer to our burning question. We also will find that a surprising number of them understand how we have come by our unlovely Faustian image. They realize that the generation now in power passed through the soul-searing Depression of the thirties and that we experienced a world war such as man had never seen. They also know that part of the fallout from that war, besides the determination never to be caught militarily off guard again, was a technological urge that blinded us to human need—even the need for love—as we pursued money in order that "my child shall never have to do without things like I did." Many of the young express deep, insightful sympathy for those of us who simply got caught on the treadmill of the money machine. They understand how in the beginning of our nation it was natural and necessary for us to set out with our wagons and axes to conquer the land, cut down our forests, and later to bulldoze our mountains, and erect vast industries to take advantage of every resource offered open-handedly by a generous nature. What they can't understand is why we keep on this way. Looking at our skies, rivers, lakes, and now our oceans, they ask, "When are you going to begin to spend as much of your energy and your money cooperating with nature as you spend in destroying it? What irresistible force is it that drives you to continue this blind destruction?"

And while we have been keeping our feet on the treadmill and eyes straight ahead, they have been looking around, studying cause and effect. They're asking, "Why have you let technology, once your slave, become your master?"

Looking at our grimy cities and our suburban sprawl they ask, "What evil magnet have you contrived that has drawn people to live in monstrous seething cans of worms, when there are thousands, millions of square miles of country with enough elbow room for people to experience diversity and the healing realities of nature? With all your vast magic of technology—communication, travel, life-support systems— why can't these atrocities be demagnetized and people be invited to experiment with new life styles in communities small enough to permit a person to feel as though he counted as a human being? Why do you continue to support dehumanizing bigness?"

"But even if you reapportioned land to the present population," some have told me, "we would soon be overrun with people, because you will not deal responsibly with the population explosion. You treat birth control as though it were something dirty to be discussed only in back rooms. But by withholding it from the young you are not lessening sexual experimentation; you are only making the consequences worse. We can't understand a philosophy that won't include birth control in sex education but will provide special classes and even special schools for pregnant girls!"

Still others can't understand why we don't at once make it a public offense for a couple to have more than two children. Even with this limitation, they point out, population will still grow as medical care reduces infant mortality and increases the life span generally. They can't understand a philosophy that puts mere *quantity* of life ahead of *quality* of life, which is already declining as we run out of life space and are reduced to a deadening conformity in our attempts to exist side by side.

The young are mystified by our crass, undifferentiating attitudes toward drug use, by which we lump all drugs together as bad. They are further confused in the cries of "wolf! wolf!" by people—often their own parents—whose medicine cabinets are cluttered with drugs for "up" and drugs for "down." They are more than alarmed by the prospect of being made into drugged robots by the new wonder pills that improve learning and memory. "If drugs are here," they are reasoning, "and if education is the answer to all things including the wise use of sex, why not have drug education? Let's get the whole matter of drugs out in the open. How can we trust an adult society that plans to manipulate us with an arsenal of drugs while making it illegal for us to experiment—even with harmless marijuana?"

The generation gap has served to expose our treatment of black people, Spanish-speaking people, Indians, and other minorities. The more the young of all races mingle, the more they are asking, "How can you do this to people? While we find our diversities interesting and exciting, you find them confusing and threatening. Why?"

Our high-tension, Faustian society, which sells its soul by destroying nature and denying humanity, has turned off more and more of the young. A most dramatic example of this is the continuing practice of old men sending off young men to be killed in wars. I realize that if all of our young men refused to enter military service, we would soon fall prey to the military forces of other nations—and the young realize this, too. But I expect any day to see young leadership arise in this country who will take the message to young men everywhere in the world that it is time to turn on their elders and say, "I will not go to war. History has shown that wars only beget wars. Instead, we will look for another way to get along together on our shrinking planet." Such a campaign could well begin by mailing to the head of each nation, his cabinet members, his generals, ambassadors, and his leading industrialists, a ninety-eight-cent jackknife inscribed with the words, "If you want a war, use this."

Think how much humanity could have benefited if the 300,000 young Americans who have been killed and wounded in the senseless Vietnam war had, instead, spent a year of conscripted service in hospitals, schools, reforestation projects, and other conservation work as a part of the schooling we offer them. We would be hearing much less about meaningless and irrelevant curriculum.

The Kent State and the Jackson State massacres, killing six students and wounding more, mobilized youth power as even the Chicago Eight failed to do. When in history has a nation's youth risen up and closed down the universities *en masse;* refusing to study, or even discuss anything except ways to end a war? Today the nation confronts a university population of eight million, roughly half the size of organized labor—by any standard a potent force. As this power sweeps down into the high schools, will the nation seek to contain it—or to help it find constructive expression?

The sixties have been a time of breakdown. The seventies can be a time of breakthrough. There are many and diverse philosophies of "how things ought to be" abroad in the land; as Alfred North Whitehead has said, "The clash of doctrines is not a disaster—it is an opportunity." To make sure that the seventies aren't just a continuation of the sixties, we've got to "hang loose." This applies to students as well as school and college boards, teachers, professors, administrators, and those of us who foot the bills. We must go into the seventies in an experimental mood, not uptight. Schooling at all levels should be the arena where confrontations among philosophies, ideas, and life styles are played out. The alternative: shooting it out in the streets.

First of all, we should encourage a diversity of school types, ranging from a continuation of our present egg-crate variety, through ultra-permissive Summerhill types, to non-schools where there are no buildings, only information centers to be used by students as needed. Support for such diversity should come from local, state, and Federal government as well as from the Establishment. An example of big-business participation may be seen in the "street academies" sponsored by such firms as McGraw-Hill, Union Carbide, and others. To their credit, these enlightened few have sought mainly to support efforts by inner-city people to conduct the kind of schooling they know is needed to give "unteachable" dropouts a chance to learn things important to their way of life. In substance, they are a cross between a Summerhill and a nonschool.

Second, schools should be tailored to the diversity of our population. There should be all-white schools, all-black schools, all-Spanish-speaking people's schools, all-Indian schools, and all-anything schools, as well as mixed schools in mixed communities. I can see nothing but a waste of transportation expense and children's learning time in busing pupils out of their neighborhoods so that some children can sit in a better school than their neighborhood affords while others sit in worse. Think what even the $500,000 a year San Francisco spends to swap its children around could do to improve black schools on the spot! Black people themselves are beginning to want it this way. It will be salutary indeed when black people gain real control of their own schools and prove to the world that they have as much intelligence and innate learning ability as the white race, the unfortunate article by Harvard's Dr. Arthur Jensen notwithstanding. One such all-black school movement has been launched—the Parkway Program—in West Philadelphia. An encouraging feature of this attempt to break down the dichotomy between living and learning is, instead of continuing to crowd 4,000 children into a building designed in 1924 to serve 2,400, to take over a series of old three-story houses, each accommodating some 200 students. As a school type, the result will be a mixture of "the old school" and the nonschool, with a liberal dash of Summerhill.

Since the beginning of real desegregation with the Civil Rights Act of 1964, some 100,000 white children south of the Mason-Dixon line have been put into private schools. While in many ways this is regrettable, such diversity in the schooling effort should be encouraged. The "private school" with some measure of public support might well be the wave of the future. Its success, however, will depend—whatever type of schooling is employed—on allowing much greater diversity among the students than the public schools have allowed. Chances are that the private schools will fail in this, because the sponsoring groups seek to inculcate special values and to exact conformity from their young, rather than promote individuality, creativity, and diversity.

Whatever kind of schooling the pupil gets, he should have the use of any learning materials and technology that will individualize his learning opportunity in skill training—typically the 3 R's and related skills. With more efficient skill *getting,* both student and teacher will have more time for the now-neglected skill *using* or educing part of schooling. Here the teacher will do only three things:

1. open up a broad area of knowledge
2. act as a resource consultant to the student
3. act as an evaluation-of-learning consultant to the student.

One of the reasons for the breakdown of schooling in the sixties was the deadly chain of lock step fastened on each child by such concepts as the basal reader, the basic math book (even the new math!), the same dull homework for everyone, the required course, and other devices used to make the child conform. To survive, schools must reverse this trend and make diversity their watchword. I would like to propose a multi-level philosophy as a guide for establishing any new school or converting any old school in the seventies. A schooling situation should be provided whereby each individual may start where he is and move ahead as fast and as far as his learning rate and capacity allow him—to acquire skills and generate knowledge to meet his needs as (1) an individual, and (2) a member of society. This multilevel philosophy would set the stage for the development and application of humanics, which we discussed in Chapter 11. Humanics was defined as a concern with the "what? why? when? where? and who?" of things, freeing the self temporarily from the often-stifling "how?" and regenerating dreams of one's own humanity. Humanics is also concerned with the potential for the unity rather than the conflict of science and the humanities.

Humanics should not only be a way of thinking about schooling, but an actual period of time set aside regularly, when the individual, alone or with others, makes a conscious effort to add up the bits and pieces of information and experience he has had and relate them to the image he has of himself and the image of what he hopes to become. He concerns himself not only with the apparently conflicting worlds of the sciences and the humanities, but also with the problem of being both an individual and a member of society. During the time a person devotes to humanics by himself, he may write or simply meditate, preferably both. With others, he may participate in one or more of the currently evolving models— sensitivity training, encounter groups, exploration of awareness, marathon labs, human relations training, and so on. Based on the field-theory concept of the great social psychologist Kurt Lewin in the 1920s and the later work of Alfred Moreno in psychodrama, and combined with elements of group therapy, the first "T-groups" (training groups in human relations) were begun at Bethel, Maine, over two decades ago. Although participation has been largely by adults so far, such opportunities to see ourselves as others see us, to learn the dynamics of give and take, and to play a number of roles both as individual and member of society should be available for the young of all ages beginning with their first school experiences.

In giving free play to a variety of philosophies about how life should be lived we will find much of value in the notion of "simulation." Through gaming we can live out, in miniature, many real-life situations, playing them only to a point, but far enough to experience genuine feelings in ourselves and others and see how these feelings influence decision making. Because games are a "kind of caricature of social life," they allow both participants and observers to discover principles underlying real-life situations. "The Family Game," "The Banking Game," "The Crisis Game," "Revolution," and "International Game" give some idea of the wide range of experiences now being made available through simulation.

To many of us the sixties was a time in which the country was like a gigantic flywheel spinning with increasing speed and centrifugal force. Bits and pieces were beginning to fly off in all directions. The young dropped out of society and thoughtful adults began predicting doom. National unity became national polarity. Individual freedom was threatened by a growing police state. The seventies can turn from a breakdown into a breakthrough toward solving man's ancient problem of person as an individual and as a member of society. Although destined never to "solve" the problem, unless he makes periodic breakthroughs toward it, man cannot survive. He must work at more ways of achieving unity with his fellow man while at the same time retaining his individuality. We must literally find our unity in our diversity. What better application of our technology? Instead of permitting technology to make us into robotized conformists, why not use it to expand diversity? I don't know what a certain manufacturer of television sets had in mind when he placed a recent advertisement in a weekly news magazine, but he illustrated this very idea.

In a photograph captioned "Peace on Earth," a family of nine—children, parents, and grandparents—are shown watching seven different miniature TV sets of varying design, each listening on ear plugs so as not to disturb the others. Each individual, enraptured by his own screen (except for two who chose to share), was drawing a diverse experience from the national television environment. Think how much more interesting their dinner-table conversation must have been than if they all had seen the same program, several of them perhaps grudgingly?

Achieving individuality through diversity in fun is easy, you say, but what about in work? West Germany's biggest aviation and rocket research center, Messerschmitt-Bolkow-Blohm, found out when it simply tried to solve the rush-hour traffic problem for its 3,000 employees. While everyone, from managers to maintenance men, must work forty-three hours and forty minutes a week, they may check in and out at varying times. They can even take time off or pile up overtime one month to work less in the next. An impossible timekeeping job for management? Not at all. Computer technology is called into play to record arrivals, departures, and time worked. Not only has the imaginative use of technology solved the rush-hour problem, but people are beginning to feel more like self-respecting, self-operating individuals. Secretaries no longer stop typing in the middle of a letter to the clang of a quitting bell. Supervisors and managers are beginning to think of their employees less as machines and more as human beings. Over 100 firms are said to be studying the system for possible adoption. This is what I would call harnessing technology to humanize.

To my Question 5, "Why should people work?" I got such dull answers as "to eat," "to make a living," "to support a family," coming not only from those in less well-paid and more repetitive jobs but also from those in supervisory and managerial positions. Why should professional people, only a relatively small percentage of the population, be the ones privileged to answer the question with "to express one's creativity," "to contribute to society," "to continue to learn and grow"? With all of our technology, all of our remaining natural resources, and all our high-sounding ideals, why can't we devise ways to lift the level of work expectation and actual experience from negative drudgery to positive identification with work as an expression of self? Why can't we let machines do the repetitive work machines can do best, liberating human energy for things only humans can do? We may actually have to invent creative jobs for humans, or decide that things will take a little longer, but the whole process and product will be more humanized.

Take form letters that handle complaints, for example. How much better we would feel as human beings, and how much better disposed we would be to the company whose letter was warm and human, even if its English were not the "best." More and more of the young are demanding these feelings for themselves and are willing to buck the Establishment to have them. If the Real Establishment begins to see the light, becomes less afraid of diversity, and gives the Establishment the go sign to facilitate instead of inhibit diversity, it can save its crumbling empires. Otherwise, it can expect increased attrition and perhaps an explosive end to its fortunes. Or perhaps Establishment management itself will have to field the diversity ball before the game degenerates beyond the call of rules and umpires, merely to save its own skin. But I have found those among the management group who still retain enough of the divine spark to see the promotion of diversity as not only a major enterprise but also their contribution to humanity. They are beginning to visualize the excitement of involvement versus the kind of board-room boredom that comes from dealing in the abstract through the eyes, ears, and feelings of others.

The view that human nature is essentially bad has given rise to man's control of man. The result has been pressure to con-

form to a growing list of "thou shalt nots" in a time when
more people have more education, see more options, and visualize more diversity of thought and action. For most people
these newly visualized options are not bad, only different.
They are only "bad" in the eyes of those who are devoted to
the *status quo*. The few who rob and kill seldom do it to
achieve variety in their living pattern but rather to get back at
a society that has kept them out, most often through our
major instrument of rejection—the public school. Here our
heavy-handed demands for conformity only build up the resistance necessary to keep the young ego from shattering. This
resistance to school is generalized into a resistance to society.
The expression of this resistance is called "bad." As more people become disenchanted with society, the crime rate rises,
shouts for law and order go up, and whatever goodness remaining in the resisting individual is now literally killed—
often in the streets. We've got to give goodness a chance. The
decade of the seventies may be our last opportunity. Instead
of pushing people out of society, out of our "approval," we've
got to invite them in on their own terms, letting them play out
models of diverse styles of living and working instead of rejecting them out of hand.

In his book *Looking Backward* Edward Bellamy wrote in
1887 as though he were living in the year 2000. Extrapolat-
ing, he reflected on man's transition from ". . . the barbaric industrial and social system . . . those cruel and insensate days"
to ". . . that new world, blessed with plenty, purified by justice, and sweetened by brotherly kindness. . . ." He explained
how man's expectation of man changed from "bad" to
"good":

> It was the sincere belief of even the best of men at that epoch
> that the only stable elements in human nature, on which a social
> system could be safely founded, were its worst propensities. They

had been taught and believed that greed and self-seeking were all that held mankind together, and that all human associations would fall to pieces if anything were done to blunt the edge of these motives or curb their operation. In a word, they believed —even those who longed to believe otherwise—the exact reverse of what seems to us self-evident; they believed, that is, that the anti-social qualities of men, and not their social qualities, were what furnished the cohesive force of society.

Someone has said that "what man can dream, man can do." The new diversity in religion may be a significant force in moving toward Bellamy's expression of man's old dream. The old-time proselytizing Establishment religion also is being disturbed by the noise of revolution. A highly visible example is the breakdown of several Roman Catholic institutions which have, in the past, given papal authority virtual control of life and death over its adherents. Take the questions of marriage of priests and birth control. As a result of resisting the changing precepts of man as he gets more knowledge, the Church has lost many of its most valuable priests, and support for its religion-oriented schools is seriously diminishing. Similar conditions exist in Protestantism, but because that church is more fragmented, they are less visible. The conflict is but one more episode in the eternal battle between those who have become more enlightened and seek to use their new knowledge and those of established authority fighting to maintain the *status quo* and the false security of their own positions.

More and more enlightened ministry is turning social action —to the idea of co-creating with God a more humane society. Some actively enlist the help of the Establishment to get loans for community housing and other projects. Others set up store-front churches to rally ghetto people, to inspire the poor to see the riches within themselves, and to lead them in self-help neighborhood renewals. But for all those good works, the problem of the poor and the black, often one and the same, is barely touched. Hopefully, the new ministry will move more "haves" to compassion and personal action in behalf of the "have-nots" instead of waiting for a James Forman to walk into Riverside Church in New York to demand half a billion dollars in "reparations."

In another direction, the new theologian recognizes that the young, for all their seeming irreligiousness, are really seeking an even deeper religious experience. And they are doing it with a diversity that often shocks and startles the more conventionally "faithful." Tired of a liturgy unrelated to our life and times, disenchanted individuals are forming groups to experiment with new forms of religious experience, while many of the new ministry, abandoning organ music, stained glass, and candles, are turning to rock music, dance, and light shows to reach the young in their own idiom. My visit to Glide Memorial Methodist Church in San Francisco, for example, was at first jarring, then exciting, then a deeply satisfying human relationship with some 700 others—aged from a few months to many decades—all packed standing room only on a bright Sunday morning. If religion is not first a satisfying human experience, what else should it be? Another variety of religious experience is the religion-centered commune where all income is shared and the search for the best ways of living together amounts to a practicing religion. Out of such diverse experiments new sects are often formed.

If churches wish to keep their followings, they will have to learn to tolerate small sects within denominations. The recent ecumenical wave may well be halted as various sects and denominations begin to nurture their distinctive characteristics all over again. But religion's new exploratory thrust may promote even more communication among them—a new unity in diversity.

The people of the United States of America have so much more than any other nation on earth to be thankful for. We are like a man carrying huge bags of groceries out of the super- market who trips over a curbstone, or even his own feet, and spills everything on the ground. He has worked hard for the money to buy the groceries, he has selected them carefully, he has carried them with aching arms, in the anticipation of good things to taste and to nourish his body. But now there they lay, all over the ground. "Why didn't somebody tell me that I was walking off the curb? Why did I try to carry such a big load all at once anyway?" Perhaps we haven't got quite that far in this great country of ours, but no one can deny we are trying to carry too much. We may have to learn to think in terms of smaller, more manageable packages. Not only is the load too heavy for the carrier, but clutched in the package so tightly, the many diverse objects inside are becoming crushed, misshapen, pushed into one indistinct mass—instead of re- taining the diversity with which they were created. Smaller bags would be carried more easily and with more regard for what is in them.

Instead of our present Brobdingnagian body politic, we need regions drawn up naturally by terrain and custom. Even the U.S. Census Bureau recognizes the value of this concept, and much data in the *Statistical Abstract of the United States* are separated by regions. Many corporations plan their prod- ucts and deploy their sales forces regionally, not only to avoid bigness but also to exploit the factor of regional differences in what the people want. States seem to fall naturally together into groups because they share common characteristics, which are distinct from other groups of states. "It's fine for you fel- lows up North, but it won't sell in the South (or East, or West, and so on)" is typical of national sales-planning conference talk.

The United States is, if anything, a study in diversity. To anyone who has traveled about the world a bit, diversities of terrain, people, and customs seem greater among our various regions than among, say, four or five of the large Latin-American nations. Yet we continue to try to govern as though the people of the United States were a homogeneous whole.

I have lived in all five regions of the United States for a period of several years each. They *are* different. What one does and thinks in one may fit poorly in another—yet both may be "right." Why not let these diversities flourish instead of trying to crush them all together? Instead of voting for the President and a Congress of one wonderful but wholly unwieldy United States and hoping they can somehow understand problems peculiar to where you live, suppose you could vote for a premier and a Congress of your own North Atlantica, or South Atlantica, or New South, or Centralia, or Westlandia, or Pacifica? And wouldn't the over-all Presidency itself and the concept of a nation become more meaningful, more workable, more "government by the people"?

Couldn't we retain our allegiance to a national ideal and to some degree of national leadership, and yet seek our identity in a more closely felt, more responsive governing body? Such a move might spark further decentralizing which would give some of our sagging institutions new vitality, eliminate others, and create still others. Voting might become more meaningful as issues came closer to home. The electoral college would drop out of sight without creating a ripple. Kinds of schooling not yet dreamed of might arise in response to new freedom from a central authority which must, for its existence, insist on a high degree of conformity.

Even if we didn't go through with it, a feasibility study over a period of years could focus on our tremendous and exciting diversity and recommend institutions not to stifle but to preserve and enlarge these differences through experimentation with new political forms, new economics, new life styles, new ways of thinking about living together. Who's to say that in New South, for example, after ten, fifteen, twenty years of freedom from "desegregation" whites and blacks might not be living together or coexisting separately in far greater harmony and with greater mutual economic benefit than they have achieved so far or can ever achieve under forced integration?

As rudely awakened as Rip van Winkle from his hundred years' sleep, we have found ourselves in Marshall McLuhan's global village. Between TV and travel "you are there," and "there" is right here. Planet earth, says McLuhan, is like a finely tuned violin, one great resonating whole. When even one string is touched, ever so lightly, the vibrations are felt throughout the length and breadth of the instrument. With all of us doing different things at the same time, how can there be any sort of harmony—how can there be diversity? This is certainly "where it's at." Because in the past we have had so much life space on the planet and have made such free use of its resources, diversity has come relatively easy. Now, when even more room for more diversity is needed, we have less room for it. Now increasing individual options for thinking and doing must become a global enterprise. But unless we cut our population growth at once, and help the rest of the world to cut theirs, we will not have to bother about thinking up ways to promote diversity. The first requirement of diversity is sufficient life space in which one may do his own thing without bumping into someone else.

If we stop population growth now, there is still enough land on which to distribute people so that each may feel the reality of nature and commune with his own beginnings. Otherwise, one's thinking becomes so abstract, so devoid of cause-and-effect reality, that he loses his bearings. I recall how disoriented

I became during eight years in which I lived in the heart of New York City and Chicago, having come from the green countrysides near university towns. I now live in a village of 200 souls in the mountain and sea country of California, but my work takes me to the major cities of this and other countries several times a year. They are two distinct worlds. Each time I go to the city, I ask myself, "How did you ever live in this uproar, tension, dirt, and lack of identity?" When I return to the country, I can't believe the tranquility, the cleanness, and the warmth of human contact. Because most of our city planners live in cities, the city of tomorrow envisions people incarcerated in ever more concrete prisons piled still higher in the air and deeper underground as though there were no more space left on earth! We can be proud of the hippies and other young folk who have turned their backs on this childish play with building blocks and taken to the woods. Must we keep huddling people closer together just because we have the technology to do it? As Desmond Morris puts it in *The Human Zoo,* "The modern human animal is no longer living in conditions natural for his species. Trapped, not by a zoo collector, but by his own brainy brilliance, he has set himself up in a huge, restless menagerie where he is in constant danger of cracking under the strain."

Population control is only one side of the ecological coin. The other is simply "the good earth." We now know that we live in a closed system exactly the same as the astronauts in their space capsule, only magnitudes larger. Their entire life-support system, including the air they breathe and their body wastes, must be processed, recycled, and reused. In his Pulitzer Prize-winning book, *So Human an Animal,* Dr. René Dubos tells us that we must learn to do the same with our Spaceship Earth. We can no longer, for example, use our atmosphere as a sewer lest we choke to death, kill our forests, and melt the polar caps to flood our coast lines.

Man is coming to realize that almost his every act has upset some balance of nature and that he is on the brink of destroying the planet. From now on the nations of the world must work together to discover the multitudes of subtle ecosystems nature has designed and find ways to cooperate with them. Such an undertaking would provide a diversity of thought and action such as we've never before envisioned—in the United States and throughout the world. The study of ecology—now almost nonexistent in our schools—could be one of the answers to our question "schooling for what"?

Since so much of what we need to know—about ourselves, our planet, and beyond—is still unknown to us, perhaps the best answer to our title question is "schooling for whatever." I hope that some of the ideas that have been raised here will spark your own and introduce you to the excitement of seeking out, trying out, and combining our diversities in new ways, thereby discovering and creating our unity.

NOTES

CHAPTER 2

1 Will and Ariel Durant, *The Lessons of History*, New York: Simon & Schuster, Inc., 1968, p. 55. © 1968 by Will and Ariel Durant. Reprinted by permission of Simon & Schuster, Inc.

CHAPTER 4

1 *Monterey Peninsula Herald*, November 30, 1968, p. 23. Copyright © 1968. The Hall Syndicate.
2 Grace and Fred M. Hechinger, "In the time it takes you to read these lines, the American teen-ager will have spent $2,378.22," *Esquire*, July, 1965.
3 Anthony Storr, *Human Aggression*, New York: Atheneum Publishers, 1968, p. 33.
4 Harry S. Ashmore, "Introduction," *Britannica Perspectives*, Chicago: Encyclopaedia Britannica, Inc., 1968, Vol I, p. vii.

CHAPTER 7

1 Winter Park (Fla.) *Sun-Herald*, January 7, 1970, p. 1.
2 Frederic C. Wood, Jr., *Sex and the New Morality*, New York: Association Press, 1968, p. 46.

CHAPTER 8

1 Sarvepalli Radakrishnam, *Indian Philosophy*, New York: Macmillan, 1931, p. 236.

CHAPTER 9

1 John R. Seeley, "The Breakdown Machine," *The Center Magazine,*
September, 1968, p. 45. Reprinted, by permission, from the September, 1968, issue of *The Center Magazine,* a publication of the Center for the Study of Democratic Institutions in Santa Barbara, California.

CHAPTER 10

1 Robert Hutchins, "Doing What Comes Scientifically, *"The Center
Magazine,* January, 1969, pp. 56, 57. Reprinted, by permission, from
the January, 1969, issue of *The Center Magazine,* a publication of
the Center for the Study of Democratic Institutions in Santa Barbara, California.
2 R. J. Forbes, "The Technological Order: The Conquest of Nature
and Its Consequences," in *Britannica Perspectives,* Chicago: Encyclopaedia Britannica, Inc., 1968, Vol. I, p. 339.
3 Richard B. Lee and Irven DeVore, *Man the Hunter,* Chicago: Al-
dine Publishing Co, 1968, pp. 345–346.

CHAPTER 12

1 Address to the National Science Teachers Association national con-
vention, Chicago, March, 1962.
2 Quoted in Garry Wills, "The Making of the Yippie Culture,"
Esquire, November, 1969, pp. 126, 240. Reprinted by permission of
Esquire Magazine. ©1969 by Esquire, Inc.

CHAPTER 13

1 Ferdinand Lundberg, *The Rich and the Super-Rich,* New York: Ban-
tam, 1969, p. 29.

ABOUT THE AUTHOR

After working thirteen years with Sears, Roebuck & Co., and military service in World War II, Don H. Parker entered the field of educational psychology and testing while earning bachelor's and master's degrees at the University of Florida. He has been a reading and curriculum consultant to all grade levels and has served on the staffs of six universities, including Columbia, where he got his doctorate in 1957. He is the inventor and author of a widely used series of multilevel reading laboratory systems published by Science Research Associates, and heads the Institute for Multilevel Learning International, which he founded in 1964. He has lectured on four continents and has written numerous articles and one previous book, *Schooling for Individual Excellence* (1963). He lives in Big Sur, California.